£2

THE STRANGE LIFE OF LADY BLESSINGTON

BOOKS BY

MICHAEL SADLEIR

BULWER: A PANORAMA, PART I:

Edward and Rosina, 1803-1836

The Strange Life of Lady Blessington

LADY BLESSINGTON
(about 1820)
After the painting by Lawrence in the Wallace Collection, London

MICHAEL SADLEIR

The Strange Life of
LADY BLESSINGTON

WITH ILLUSTRATIONS

LITTLE, BROWN, AND COMPANY

BOSTON 1933

Published November, 1933

PRINTED IN THE UNITED STATES OF AMERICA

"There are so few before whom one would condescend to appear otherwise than happy."

— LADY BLESSINGTON
in a letter to Bulwer-Lytton

CONTENTS

BOOK ONE: MOUNTING MELODY

BOOK TWO: FANFARE

BOOK THREE: FALSE RELATION

BOOK FOUR: THE PAGEANT CRUMBLES

ILLUSTRATIONS

GENEALOGIES

I THE POWER FAMILY

II THE GARDINER (BLESSINGTON) FAMILY

THE POWER FAMILY

Edmond Power = Ellen Sheehy
b. 1767; *d.* 1837
(" Beau Power ")

- Anne (*d.* in infancy)
- Michael
- Maurice St. Leger Farmer, *m.* 1804; *d.* 1817 (no issue) = MARGARET, *b.* 1789; *d.* 1849 (COUNTESS OF BLESSINGTON) (no issue) = CHARLES JOHN GARDINER, EARL OF BLESSINGTON, *m.* 1818; *d.* 1829
- John Home Purves, *m.* ?; *d.* 1827 = ELLEN, *b.* 1791; *d.* 1845 (LADY CANTERBURY) = Rt. Hon. Charles Manners Sutton, *m.* 1828; *d.* 1845. Speaker of the House of Commons. Created Viscount Canterbury, 1835
  - (by John Home Purves):
    - Louisa, *d.* 1843 = John Fairlie
      - Isabella, *d.* in childhood, 1843 (" the beautiful mute ")
      - other children.
    - Mary
    - Margaret
    - John
    - Ellen
  - (by Charles Manners Sutton): one d.
- Robert
  - Margaret
  - Ellen
  - (" the Misses Power ")
- MARY ANN (no issue) = Count Saint Marsault, *m.* 1831

THE GARDINER (BLESSINGTON) FAMILY

Elizabeth Montgomery = Rt. Hon. Luke Gardiner, P.C., M.P. = Margaret Wallis
m. 1773; *d.* 1783

Rt. Hon. Luke Gardiner, P.C., M.P.
b. 1745; *d.* 1798.
Created Baron Mountjoy 1789.
Created Viscount Mountjoy 1795

Margaret Wallis
m. 1793. *d.* ?.
(DOWAGER LADY MOUNTJOY)

one d. (*d.* 1825)

Florinda
b. 1774;
d. 1786

Louisa
b. 1775;
d. 1848

Harriet
b. 1776;
d. 1849
(MISS HARRIET GARDINER)

Caroline
b. ?;
d. 1782

Emily
b. ?;
d. 1788

Luke
b. ?;
d. in infancy

Mary (Campbell) Browne = CHARLES JOHN = MARGARET (POWER) FARMER
m. July 11, 1812;
d. Sept. 19, 1814
1781

CHARLES JOHN
b. July 19, 1782;
d. May 25, 1829
Viscount Mountjoy, 1798. Created EARL OF BLESSINGTON, 1816

MARGARET (POWER) FARMER
m. Feb. 16, 1818;
d. 1849
(COUNTESS OF BLESSINGTON)
(no issue)

Elizabeth
b. 1783;
d. 1791

Charles John
b. 1810,
illegitimate
(CHARLES GARDINER)

Emily Rosalie = Charles Whyte
b. 1811,
illegitimate
(LADY MARY GARDINER)

COUNT ALFRED D'ORSAY = HARRIET ANNE = Hon. Charles Spencer Cowper

COUNT ALFRED D'ORSAY
m. 1827; *d.* 1852
(no issue)

HARRIET ANNE
b. Aug. 5, 1812,
legitimate
d. Dec. 17, 1869
(LADY HARRIET GARDINER)
(no issue)

Hon. Charles Spencer Cowper
m. 1852

Luke Wellington
b. Sept. 11, 1813,
legitimate
d. Mar. 26, 1823
(VISCOUNT MOUNTJOY)

BOOK ONE

MOUNTING MELODY

CHAPTER I

Sally Power

1

Sally was the ugly duckling of the Power family. Michael, her senior; Ellen, Robert and Mary Ann, her juniors — were beautiful, boisterous, ordinary children whose natural high spirits took them into mischief and out again, whose only periods of self-communion were forced upon them by the sudden rages of a savage-tempered father. But Sally (whose christening name was Margaret) was ill-thriven, dreamy, and in her parents' eyes a discredit to the brood. Born on September 1, 1789, in the village of Knockbrit, two miles from Cashel in the Irish county of Tipperary, she struggled through an ailing babyhood, and as a little girl soon found herself solitary in a tempestuous home, too frail to join her fellows in their games, too plain and peaked to tempt the easy geniality of adult visitors. In consequence she turned in upon her small and lonely self and her white-faced insignificance caught the sympathy of a good-hearted neighbour. Anne Dwyer, a spinster in young middle age, looked with natural disapproval on the rowdy materialism of the Power household; pitied the unattractive little girl who was odd-child-out in all the family amusements and, partly perhaps for mothering's sake, mainly from genuine kindliness, set out to win Sally's confidence and to teach her the consolation of reading.

During the few years of her influence over the solitary child, Miss Dwyer performed much the same service that another kindly spinster, Mary Greene, performed for another untutored and friendless Irish girl — Rosina Wheeler, afterward Mrs.

Edward Bulwer.[1] She countered parental neglect and gave her charge at least an opportunity of growing up with resources of comfort and stability within herself. Such an opportunity was to prove no less valuable to Sally than to Rosina; but whereas the latter let it slip, the former seized and made good use of it.

2

Sally's father, Edmund, was more typical of his kind than was healthy, either for himself or others. Handsome, intemperate, stupid, snobbish and cruel, he first mistook the noisy adulation of a few neighbouring squireens for evidence of his own ruthless strength, and shortly afterward the sham civility of a titled politician for a tribute to his growing social importance. In 1797 he had moved his family a few miles southward to the town of Clonmel, where he had joined a firm of corn-chandlers and seemed likely (on the entertainment side of the business, at any rate) to lead a congenial and even a slightly useful life. But in an evil hour his obtuse and swaggering personality attracted the notice of Lord Donoughmore, chief local representative of the Castle party and at that time on the look-out for some suitable dupe to do authority's dirty work in hunting Irish rebels. "Beau Power", as he was called, seemed precisely the type of local bully to combine servility toward rank with brutal assiduity in persecution. Donoughmore showed sudden amiability; matched Power at a drinking bout; hinted at sinecures to come and even a title if he served the Castle well; then offered him a magistracy. The offer was accepted; and the new magistrate, with a troop of dragoons and much smooth flattery from his noble friend but not a penny of stipend or any guarantee of reward, embarked on a campaign of terrorism among the miserable but desperate malcontents of Tipperary and Waterford. To any one less besotted with vanity and greed, the outcome of this surrender would have been obvious from the first. The peace and prosperity of the Power household began

[1] *Cf.* "Edward and Rosina", pp. 73 *seq. et. passim.*

forthwith to deteriorate. Clonmel was the centre of a district where disaffection and hatred of Castle rule were more than ordinarily bitter. Beau Power himself had until 1798 been known for a staunch Catholic and a man whose sympathy with the rebels was, if not very active, at least more or less avowed. Now, and almost overnight, he had turned his coat and rode the countryside from dusk to dawn, capturing and beating the men who used to be his friends. In revenge his grain stores were burnt, his cattle maimed, his plantations destroyed, and he personally was shunned by all the neighbours save those who, like himself, were of the Castle retinue. The officers of the local garrison were naturally the most numerous and important representatives of English rule; and Power soon found himself driven to their company, if he were to have company at all. His house became a rendezvous for the most unpopular men in the district; and there he and his officer friends would drink themselves daily into riotous contempt for all their enemies. When evening came the officers sought sobriety in the safety of their barracks; but Power sallied forth to work off his liquor and his collective hatred of his fellow men by hunting nameless fugitives over the desolate countryside.

This sort of life continued for several years. It had its ups and downs, Power's prospects and popularity fluctuating with the intensity or otherwise of rebel activity. He was still a member of the firm of grain merchants, who had offices and warehouses in Waterford also and from whose business a certain if variable profit was derived. At intervals he visited Dublin, and was received with skilful cordiality at the Viceregal Court, which preferred to pay its bravoes with easy hospitality rather than with cash. Meantime his family, now six in number, were growing up; and to the once ill-favoured Sally had come a beauty all the more extraordinary for its delayed development.

The move from Knockbrit had taken the eight-year-old child from the care of her friend, Miss Dwyer. Unhappy at the separation from the only being who had ever been kind to her, broken-hearted at leaving the lanes and fields which under Miss Dwyer's influence she had come to love, Sally stood miserably among her excited brothers and sisters, to whom any change of scene (and in particular a change from country solitude to the bustle of a town) was cause for jubilation. Her snivelling aroused the anger of the harassed mother. During the drive to Clonmel she was alternately pinched, scolded and slapped. Still snivelling, she hung awkwardly in the doorway of the new home. Her pocket bulged and one of her brothers drew malicious attention to it. The coat was snatched from her and a withered bunch of wild flowers roughly dragged to light. While Mrs. Power tossed the crumpled things out of the window, the children formed a mocking ring around their now weeping sister and jeered at her. The last link with Knockbrit was broken, the first plate was forged in that armour of smiling self-sufficiency — that shell of glittering suavity and gracious kindliness — which was so impenetrably to cover the dreams, the ambitions, the melancholy and the indifferent cynicism of the most gorgeous Lady Blessington.

CHAPTER II

Margaret Farmer

1

Physiology can doubtless describe in scientific terms the successive blossoming of loveliness and the miscarriage of feminine sensibility which marked the period immediately following Sally Power's arrival at the age of puberty. That beauty flowered is generally admitted; that the capacity to relate emotion and physical sensation was terrified out of existence before the girl reached the age of sixteen, has never before been suggested. As the story of her life progresses, as her personality is pieced together from her own spoken and written words, from her reaction to varying circumstances and from the impression she made on those with whom she came in intimate contact, it will become not only tempting but indeed almost compulsory to conclude that Sally Power in maturity was not all of a woman. Capable of affection, she was incapable of love; able by her physical beauty to provoke (and, if unavoidable, to submit to) desire, she lacked the power to reciprocate and was therefore unable to satisfy it. On no other basis than this can her life and character be convincingly interpreted; this granted, however, the apparent incongruity of her career and personality fades into mist and then, as in a changing film, they instantly take shape again, focussed into a new coherence.

2

Already at fourteen years of age Sally, with Ellen her younger sister, was making regular appearances at the half-and-half dance evenings which diverted the youth of Clonmel and its neighbourhood. The Powers' house was small, uncomfortably dominated by its violent master and the scene of persistent, extravagant and often unseemly revelry. So mother and daughters alike were glad of excuses to spend at least the evening hours under some other roof. Mrs. Powers was a negative, rather stupid woman whose spirit had been crushed into a state of apprehensive torpor by her husband's bullying. She descended, at some distance, from the Earls of Desmond, and more immediately from the well-known Catholic family of Sheehy, several members of which had, during the eighteenth century, suffered the last penalty on charges never even approximately proved. Probably Ellen Sheehy's Desmond connection had allured Beau Power during his courting days; certainly her near relationship to condemned rebels became a useful element in marital discipline, once Beau Power had become a bulwark of the pro-English and anti-Catholic aristocracy, and had decided to regard his wife as an incompetent but necessary bearer of domestic burdens. It is easy to understand that the unfortunate woman would readily permit her daughters to drive and dance about the neighbourhood while still little more than children, preferring to encourage them in a spurious maturity rather than to condemn them to the grossness and discomfort of a home which more resembled a noisy tavern than a private house.

Before very long, however, the father realised the attractions of his growing daughters; and being above all eager to surround himself with jovial companions from among the officers stationed in Clonmel, he began to force the young girls forward at his own table, using them as a lure to bring the soldiers more regularly to his house. Most assiduous among the visitors thus encouraged were two captains of the 47th Regiment of Foot, James Murray and Maurice St. Leger Farmer. Both of these men had made acquaintance with their host's daughters at the local assemblies, and both, having frequented the Powers' home for several weeks, began to pay marked attention to the now fifteen-year-old Sally.

For the former of her two suitors the child showed an innocent preference natural to her years; and he — a kindly, unassuming man of moderate means — would have been content to allow her very juvenile liking an opportunity to deepen gradually into something more worth having. But his rival, Farmer, was of a different, more ruthless type. Also he was rich. Sally was now well-formed and of dazzling complexion; her father was a drunken sot whose affairs were known to be embarrassed and whose social position was of the most precarious. What simpler, thought Farmer, than to buy the girl out of hand, enjoy the purchase till it palled, and then leave her *plantée* in whatsoever garrison town at home or abroad the chances of his profession might have made his temporary home? The bargain was struck; and on March 7, 1804, Sally Power, at the age of fifteen, was sold by her father into marriage and became Mrs. Margaret Farmer.

For three months she lived with her compulsory husband. Her sufferings during that time were never known in detail, but can perhaps be imagined. Even in ordinary circumstances the girl, pitifully young as she was, would probably have been first bewildered and then revolted by the whole business. But the circumstances were not ordinary. Farmer was a sadistic brute; and it is certain that only definite maltreatment could, at the end of three months, have given a helpless child courage to stand up to the man and refuse point-blank to live with him any longer. Yet this is what she did. Farmer, ordered to the Curragh and with no time to waste over disciplinary measures, beat her once more — this time in real fury — and let her go. She crept back to her parents' house; and from that moment, although she grew in loveliness, she never provoked real passion or sought to provoke it, because her sexual sensibility was dead. She was not yet sixteen.

Details of the life led by the brutalised and unhappy child during the next three years have not survived. It is known that she was harshly received by her father when she escaped from the three months' hell of marriage to which his greed had cruelly condemned her. It is known also that during this time Beau Power's affairs (and with them his temper) went rapidly from bad to worse. His evil genius, Lord Donoughmore, hastened the ruin of Power's private fortune by inveigling him into the launching of a newspaper, vowed to propaganda in the Castle interest. In this paper was published a serious libel, written in fact by Donoughmore himself, for which the ostensible proprietor was prosecuted. The plaintiffs won their case and Power was left to foot the bill. The treacherous patron denied all responsibility for the disaster, and for the first time Power realised that he was less the darling of the Viceregal Court than the dupe of his own headstrong vanity.

The house in Clonmel now degenerated into a pandemonium of drunken raving, debts and squalor. For a while — throughout 1805 and the early months of 1806 — officers would continue to frequent the place, and among them Lieutenant Colonel Lord Mountjoy of the Tyrone Militia made an occasional appearance. But before long Power's unsavoury reputation and lack of self-control kept even the visiting soldiery away, until only those individuals who inclined to love-making with one or other of the girls thought it worth while to come at all. Margaret Farmer seems more or less intermittently to have endured the miseries of home until the year 1807. She was deeply attached to her sister Ellen, and some say she held out steadily against her father for this sister's sake. Others declare that the two young women sought refuge from time to time with friendly neighbours at Caher and Fethard. Wherever they were spent, the months of 1806 and early 1807 produced one new intimacy for Mrs. Farmer — an intimacy with Captain Thomas Jenkins, of the 11th Light Dragoons, an easy-going, pleasant-mannered Englishman, with an estate in Hampshire and considerable (though as matters turned out illusory) expectations from an aunt. Beau Power made something of a set at Captain

Jenkins, who, with the indolent civility of his kind, responded pleasantly enough and was soon almost the only regular guest at the once crowded dinner table. There is no reason to think that Jenkins made formal love either to Margaret Farmer or to her sister Ellen; but likely enough he enjoyed their company more than their father's, and he certainly did what he could to mitigate the unhappiness of their home.

That the need for mitigation became suddenly of an extreme urgency was due to the crowning disaster in the life of Edmund Power, which took place early in 1807. The most reliable story of that disaster is briefly as follows. On one of his night expeditions in pursuit of a rebel peasantry, Power and his dragoons gave chase to an innocent lad who was taking some milk home from a farm to the cabin in which his mother lived. Power afterward maintained that he merely wanted to ask the lad for news of some fugitives of whom the soldiers were in search; that the boy made as if to fly; was threatened by the magistrate's pistol in order to make him stand still and answer questions, and that the pistol was inadvertently let off. Whatever the motive or the means, the affair ended in Power shooting the boy down and bringing him in a dying condition to the gaol in Clonmel. This shocking incident gave an opportunity to Power's many enemies which they were quick to take. He was tried for murder; and although acquitted, was declared unfit for magistrate's office and expunged from the roll.

The whole fabric of his ambition thus crumbled overnight. He had forfeited his religion, his neighbours' respect and much of his actual livelihood for the will-o'-the-wisp of Castle favour. Now that danced finally out of reach, leaving him ruined and alone among embittered enemies. The suave Lord Donoughmore, for some while on the lookout for an excuse to rid himself once and for all of a now discredited agent, showed clearly that he had no use for a magistrate who could not conduct himself without scandal; and Power's appeals for help in his extremity and for the long overdue reward for zealous service in the past were insultingly rejected. The wretched man turned in savage disappointment on his wife and family and particularly on the pseudo-widow of his old friend, Maurice Farmer. He looked back with angry regret to the days when Farmer was in Clonmel and this final horror of loneliness had not descended on him. Obscurely he felt that Margaret was responsible, not only for Farmer's absence but also for the passing of the good times when all was cheerful fellowship and aristocratic favour; that, in so far as she had hated Farmer and deserted him, she had played a part in bringing her own father to the sorry straits in which he now found himself. His violence toward her became so menacing that in real terror for her life she listened to Jenkins, who urged her to come away with him to safety. It was also reported that Farmer himself (who had drawn his sword on a superior officer quite shortly after his separation from Margaret, had been forced to sell his commission and had gone to India in the service of the Company) was on his way home from the East and intended to assert his rights over his wife.

This settled it. Flight from home had become imperative; and Jenkins, no doubt mildly stimulated at the thought of possessing this lovely girl, but mainly from the casual kind-heartedness which was his most definite characteristic, took her under his protection. Where they first settled will never be definitely known. There is evidence of a kind that from 1807 to 1809 they lived in Dublin; there are statements, which hardly claim even to be evidence, that they went forthwith to England; it is even probable that they visited Paris. But this much is fairly clear — that by the autumn of 1809 Margaret Farmer, just twenty years of age, was happily, if equivocally, established at Jenkins' house in Hampshire.

3

For five tranquil years the young woman lived in this sylvan solitude, absorbed in her books, asking for nothing better than a complete retirement which should conceal her from those she feared and give her time to forget her cruel initiation into adult life. She herself never spoke afterward of these shadowy years save once to her friend, R. R. Madden, and then she pictured herself as carefully withdrawn from public observation, treated with the utmost kindness by Captain Jenkins' relatives, and with lavish consideration by Jenkins himself. Inevitably, however, the domestic arrangements provoked curiosity and gossip; and Margaret was to find, the very moment that she appeared in London as Countess of Blessington, how widespread had been the knowledge of her Hampshire sojourn, how thoroughly the metropolis had made up its mind over the goings-on in Jenkins' country home.

It was accepted, not unnaturally, that she had been her protector's mistress. But rumour went further. It told of orgies to which the host invited parties of brother officers, at which the lovely Mrs. Farmer danced naked on the dinner table for the amusement of the company. Possibly she did. She was hardly in a position to refuse anything which Jenkins asked of her. But so lurid a general conception of their life together is too much at variance with what we know of their characters to be taken very seriously; and moments of compulsory wantonness do not make a wanton. Nevertheless, that such things were rumoured (or known) to have happened made all the mischief necessary. Ill-natured exaggerations of her conduct during this period of retirement became current gossip and later served conveniently to cloak the jealousies of her rivals under pretence of moral indignation. Many whose own petticoats were none too impregnable contrived to draw them in whenever her name was mentioned, thus ostentatiously emphasising their own virtue and, temporarily, securing it.

The actual relations between Mrs. Farmer and Captain Jenkins must be adjudged by what is known of later developments and can be reconstructed only on the assumption that the horrible experience of her few weeks with Farmer had permanently diverted her sexual impulses into another channel. No doubt

Jenkins, when he rescued the unfortunate young woman from the dangers of her wretched home life, took it for granted that he had acquired a mistress. No doubt Margaret herself, out of gratitude for her salvation, did her best to repay him for his timely help. But it may be assumed that the physical element in their prolonged cohabitation was neither important nor long-lived; Jenkins would soon become conscious of the "something wanting" and, being a person of tepid and volatile inclinations, would be content to find his amusement in the wit, sympathy and charm of his companion and to let sensual enjoyment go by the board. The renunciation was the easier, because Margaret proved herself better company with every month that passed. The womanly responsiveness, driven by Farmer's brutality out of its natural course, flowed by a sort of miracle into the stream of her native intelligence. Instead of stagnating and gradually contaminating her whole character, it mingled freshly with her instinctive tendency to read the minds of others and to live in spiritual harmony with her companions. As a result, she gradually developed a brilliance and charm of conversation, a power of putting others at their ease and inviting their confidence, which remained her outstanding characteristic and was the secret of her success as hostess and as ruler of a salon.

Probability is all on the side of this interpretation of her long intimacy with Jenkins and destructive of the theory that she was a willing plaything of debauchery. She left Ireland a comparatively uneducated person, though naturally reflective and disposed to reading books. She emerged from her Hampshire solitude one of the most widely read and, in artistic matters, best-informed women in London society. Self-education so thorough would require time, concentration and serenity of atmosphere. Are we to believe that Margaret acquired the suavity, the cultivation and the background of knowledge and intellectual appreciation which for nearly thirty years were to make her the valued friend of some of the most intelligent men of the time, in the intervals of bawdy revelling? Is it conceivable that Jenkins, if he had been the sort of man to organise his home on the lines of a disorderly house, would have tolerated a mistress who spent hours of her day in study of art and literature, and was liable gravely to discompose an expectant week-end party by devoting a whole evening to a discussion of Raphael's cartoons?

Nor are these the only demands made on our credulity by those who insist that Margaret Farmer was a harlot-de-luxe. Jenkins, rather late in life, married the sister of a once well-known figure in London society whose nickname was "Golden Ball Hughes."[1] This lady, by the acquisition of some property abroad, secured the title in her own right of Baroness de Calabrella, under which name she wrote and edited several books of fashionable, if transient, repute. She was on such friendly terms with Lady Blessington during the last years of her life that there was even talk, after Lady Blessington's death, of her providing a home for the latter's two nieces. One can imagine that two women of a cosmopolitan and unprejudiced mind might, even in the forties, find a basis of intimacy in having decorously partnered the same man at different times, but that the Baroness de Calabrella should have sought the acquaintance of any frankly orgiastic relic of her husband's past is incredible.

No less strongly does the next development of Margaret Farmer's life bear out the theory that her relationship with Jenkins was a liaison of convenience. Late in 1814 there came to Hampshire on a visit of some weeks that Viscount Mountjoy who had dined in her company years earlier in Ireland. He was now introduced to her in the house of his friend Jenkins as a stranger, whose Irish origin and Irish memories would likely ease the wheels of conversation.

Lord Mountjoy was in his early thirties, had an income of thirty thousand pounds a year, and can hardly be blamed for regarding life as an admirable succession of opportunities for

[1] *Cf.* "Edward and Rosina", p. 104 and *note.*

having a good time. In character he was a greatly exaggerated Jenkins — volatile almost to foolishness; a dabbler in every sort of dilettantism but without the talent or the application to excel in any one; eager to see all around him as happy as he was himself; casual; restless; and full of a delighted energy none the less attractive for being utterly futile. His father — the Right Honourable Luke Gardiner, who had been created Viscount Mountjoy in 1795 — had died in 1798 and had been succeeded by his second son Charles John, then a boy of sixteen at Eton. The young peer had passed from Eton to Christchurch, and from the very moment of coming into his vast fortune had embarked on a career of wild but harmless extravagance. He was never known to quarrel with any one, partly because his own good nature was extreme to the point of weakmindedness, partly because he could pay his way with smiling submission out of any menace of unpleasantness. He drew a little, wrote a little, hunted a little; but his real passion was for the theatre and it seems that as an amateur actor he had himself a definite proficiency.

Sometime during the early eighteen hundreds he had become intimate with a brother officer called Browne, who had a charming wife. After a time Major Browne was ordered to distant duty and cheerfully confided his wife to their rich and amiable friend. The years passed and no news was received from the absent man. Mrs. Browne had in the meantime borne two children to her genial guardian, and in one of the rare moments of seriousness which interrupted his life of useless bustle and unceasing laughter, she ventured the rather obvious remark that illegitimacy might handicap the infants' future. Mountjoy became as concerned to make instant reparation as formerly he had been unconscious of a need for it. Major Browne had not written to his wife for years. Therefore Major Browne was dead and Mrs. Browne could become Lady Mountjoy without more delay. The mother's change of name would not greatly benefit the prospects of the two existing children, but it would show good

LORD BLESSINGTON
(probably between 1810 and 1820)
After the painting by Holmes in the National Portrait Gallery, London

will on the father's part and would at any rate ensure him against moments of self-reproach in the future. The ceremony was performed; but a few weeks later Major Browne walked into the house and greeted them both with the contented affability of one who had been for too long away from home. The situation was embarrassing. Mountjoy, who hated anything disagreeable in social relations, put the matter frankly to the untimely husband and, one suspects, in four or five figures. Browne took a sympathetic view of his friend's quandary, told him to carry on, and departed. But the victorious Mountjoy was not spiritually at peace. He felt something ought to be done to emphasise the first and no longer convincing marriage between himself and the mother of his children. The ceremony was therefore repeated. But coincidence had still another trick to play. Very soon after the second wedding, news — and reliable news — was received of Major Browne's death. This time there was no doubt. Mrs. Browne was indeed and impeccably a widow. In the year 1812, and with a sigh of genuine relief, Mountjoy went with her to the altar for the third time. He bought a large house in Seamore Place and prepared to launch his wife in the most expensive society in the world. But the poor man was only to enjoy the conventional sweets of matrimony for two and a half years. The lady bore him two more children (of an unchallengeable legitimacy which delighted the father's heart) and in September, 1814, died at Worthing.

Mountjoy was plunged into a grief as facile and as extreme in self-expression as had always been his joys. The dead woman should have a funeral worthy of a queen; and so at the cost of nearly four thousand pounds she had. The body was conveyed with every pomp from England to Ireland, where the real ceremonies had been prepared. Dubliners talked for years afterward of the lying-in-state in a room specially hung with rich black cloth; of the pall specially embroidered in France of gold and silver thread; of the six professional female mourners who grouped themselves about the catafalque in attitudes of exquisite melancholy; of the master of the ceremonies from London, who conducted each caller round the bier and, bowing a lugubrious farewell, expressed a hope that the arrangements were to the visitor's personal satisfaction; of the splendour of the cortège which accompanied the coffin itself on its last journey to the family vault under the church of St. Thomas. Mountjoy, in his enthusiasm for the organisation and achievement of so grand a show, forgot his grief over the cause of it. By the time that he arrived at Jenkins' house in Hampshire, he was looking at the world with his usual excited and irrelevant curiosity, was all agog for whatsoever new diversion chance might put in his way.

That he forthwith recognised in his friend's beautiful companion the next and the greatest enthusiasm of his life is doubtful. The chronology of his doings remains for another two or three years very obscure. But his first visit to Jenkins was soon followed by others; in 1816, both Jenkins and Mrs. Farmer were his guests at Mountjoy Forest; and it may be hazarded that at each reëncounter he found the appearance and manners of the lovely young woman more thoroughly congenial.

In 1816 he was created Earl of Blessington,[2] for reasons so little obvious that they must have been financial. He celebrated his promotion by making a formal proposal to Jenkins of a very curious kind. Young Mrs. Farmer seemed an ideal person to become Countess of Blessington, but so long as her husband was neither dead nor divorced, the transformation was impossible. Blessington therefore suggested that he install the lady in a house of her own in London, while steps were being taken to set her free from the embarrassments of her past. In compensation for what he had spent on her during the years she had lived in his house, Jenkins was offered the sum of ten thousand pounds. On these terms the matter was settled, the Earl securing an ef-

[2] Sometimes spelt "Blesinton." It is not known whether the title was a deliberate revival of one bestowed on August 23, 1675, on Murrock Boyle, son of Michael Boyle, the Archbishop of Armagh, who is said to have "built the town of Blessington" in the mid-seventeenth century.

fective option on his future Countess, and Jenkins receiving adequate payment for what can only be termed his storage charges.[3]

So for a second time Margaret was sold by one man to another. But whereas her father had sold her body to one who only wanted to abuse it, Jenkins, in return for his out-of-pocket expenses, surrendered her social talents, in the perfecting of which he had played an important, if mainly passive, part.

In this extraordinary transaction is implicit evidence, stronger than any hitherto quoted, of the sexual nullity of Margaret Farmer. Jenkins parted from her with the amiable indifference of one anxious to do his best for an agreeable ward and glad to have found her a satisfactory establishment. Blessington took her in charge with friendly competence and showed himself sensible and considerate in his plans. He acted toward her with perfect correctness from the moment of her removal from Hampshire and her installation in Manchester Square. He never visited her alone; he always treated her with the attentive courtesy of an accepted but not very impatient suitor. Is it not obvious that he had heard from Jenkins how matters stood; that he had decided this girl would make an ideal ornament to his house and exactly the right sort of companion for the life of pleasure to which he looked forward? Is it not a fair assumption (particularly in view of later events) that he was no longer greatly interested in normal love-making; but looked to the taste, good temper and wit of a beautiful young woman to enhance the excitements of society and travel?

Investigations as to the possibility of securing a divorce from Farmer were set on foot as soon as the move had been made from

[3] In Appendix I will be found a statement by Walter Savage Landor about Lady Blessington's early life. This statement implies that something occurred during her years with Jenkins which is nowhere else recorded; also elaborates the version here given of the beginnings of her intimacy with Lord Blessington. The incident cannot be ignored; Landor would not have written so definitely without a knowledge of the facts, which were doubtless given him by Blessington himself. It is, however, printed as an Appendix, rather than in the course of this narrative, because its interpretation can only be a matter of guesswork.

Hampshire to London. But they had not progressed very far, when a fortunate accident made their prosecution unnecessary. Farmer, who had degenerated during recent years into a seedy and intemperate adventurer, got himself more drunk than usual one evening, fell from a high window in the King's Bench, where he was carousing with some debtor friends, and was killed on the spot. Lord Blessington experienced once again the delight of knowing that the woman of his choice was genuinely a widow. On February 16, 1818, at the church in Bryanston Square, a splendid marriage ceremony changed both of Margaret Farmer's names and set a coronet upon her lovely head. She was henceforward Marguerite, Countess of Blessington.

CHAPTER III

MARGUERITE, COUNTESS OF BLESSINGTON

THE Blessington honeymoon was spent in Ireland. The Earl had bought Number 11 St. James's Square for his bride's permanent occupation and wished, during the weeks still required for its final embellishment, to introduce her with all the éclat possible to his friends in Dublin and his tenants at Mountjoy. He had kept the fact of his wedding as private as his own passion for magnificence would allow and now took a characteristically naïve delight in staging a luxurious début for the new Countess in the Irish capital. Without explaining the purpose of the work, he had his house in Henrietta Street, Dublin, decorated from attic to cellar, and the tall room, in which a few years previously the body of Lady Mountjoy had lain in costly state, kindled to a blaze of gold and colour. Invitations were then sent out for what was ostensibly an ordinary evening party. When the company were assembled, the doors of the drawing-room were flung open and Blessington entered impressively, with his lovely wife in full bridal costume on his arm. Astonishment, congratulations, a buzz of excited comment. The Earl was enchanted. He had achieved a fine entrance, produced the desired sensation, and now made an end of ceremony for the rest of the evening. His ready, rather vacant laughter echoed through the house, as he ran from group to group, forestalling compliments by a chatter of delighted self-applause.

What the young Countess thought of it all was gallantly concealed. For her the very theatricality sharpened the ordeal. Even on her own account she could hardly have come back to Ireland without misgivings. The fact that her husband's stepmother and sister, inevitably resentful of his eccentric marriage, were actually living in Dublin and had charge of his first wife's children, made matters much worse. Her unhappy memories, the chance of embarrassing meetings, an uneasy feeling that the more critical among her husband's friends must now be smiling unkindly at his lack of dignity and would to-morrow run with eager tittle-tattle to the angry dowager — these and other secret dreads, to which any woman in her position and with half her social sense would have been liable, cannot but have tortured her. This party in Henrietta Street was virtually her first encounter with a world whose polished surface must disguise jealousy and slander and contempt. She was sufficiently advanced already from the gay ignorance of girlhood to be aware of dangers and, if need arose, to smile them down; but experience had not yet taught her all its bitter lessons, so that after the guests were gone and when the strain of playing the happy, heedless bride was temporarily relaxed, small wonder if, for a little while, the Countess of Blessington wilted and became once more a tired and rather apprehensive Sally Power.

From Dublin, the bride and bridegroom drove northeastward to the town of Omagh in County Tyrone, some few miles beyond which lay the vast Blessington estate of Mountjoy Forest. This estate had an extent of over fifty square miles and, apart from foresters' and keepers' cottages, comprised two dwelling houses, one of which, near the hamlet of Rash, was known as "The House" and the other, about a quarter of a mile distant, as "The Cottage."

During the early years of the century Lord Blessington (or Mountjoy, as he then was) started extensive building operations on "The House", in which his stepmother had lived for a while after her husband's death. According to contemporary authority: "He expended about 1807 a great deal of money in enlarging the offices, building an extensive kitchen and wine cellar, and erecting a spacious and elegantly decorated theatre, and private properties and a suitable wardrobe of magnificent theatrical dresses. Professional actors and actresses were brought down from Dublin and even from London, for the private theatricals at Mountjoy Forest, but there were amateur performers also and two of the old tenants remember seeing his Lordship act 'some great parts.' . . . The quality who came down and remained at Rash during the performances, which generally lasted for three or four weeks each year, were entertained with great hospitality. The expenditure was profuse in the extreme for their entertainment and the fitting up and furnishing of places of temporary accommodation for them during their brief sojourn. The dwelling house of Rash was more a large cottage, with some remains of an older structure, than a nobleman's mansion."

Before the enlargements were completed, but not before they had cost many thousands of pounds, Blessington changed his mind, left the work unfinished and transferred his attention and furniture to "The Cottage", which lay on the other side of the river and had been used only as a hunting lodge.

The building and adornment of this "Cottage" had already gone some way, when in 1818 the new Countess paid her first visit to Mountjoy. An entirely new drawing-room had been built, forty feet long, twenty-eight feet wide and twenty feet high. This room had been given a superb Italian ceiling, a marble mantelpiece — also of Italian workmanship — two carved mirrors of immense size and a new floor of polished bog oak. The dining room, part of the Earl's earlier enlargement, was also provided with a new and handsome ceiling. The entrance portico and other features had been restored and beautified. Also lavish advance preparation had, as usual, been made for her reception. The lady's private sitting room was hung with crimson silk velvet fringed with gold; furniture of a most unsuitable richness filled the house.

Marguerite handled a difficult situation with discretion and good sense. Her husband's follies had been committed in her honour and she must show a right appreciation of his fond enthusiasm. On the other hand, they were in themselves inappropriate; and she had already made up her mind to direct into other channels the purposeless extravagance which even during the last few years had reduced his income by nearly one quarter. She was not averse to having money spent in her honour; but, for reasons easily understood, she preferred that such money as was to be spent should be spent on the delights of fashionable life in London and on the Continent, rather than in Ireland. So, while showing a pretty gratitude for his thoughtfulness and behaving with natural unaffected kindliness toward the tenants and employees of the estate, she gradually turned his mind from the idea that Mountjoy was to be in any sense their home; that other, more exciting experiences could be bought in England and abroad; and that the embellishment of "The Cottage" might at any rate be suspended until the pattern of their joint lives had had more time to show itself.

In this matter fate was to take her only too thoroughly at her word. Although her husband was to pay other visits, make other plans for building his Irish home, nothing permanent was ever achieved, and Lady Blessington herself was never to see Mountjoy again.

CHAPTER IV

St. James's Square

1

THE autumn of 1818 saw Number 11 St. James's Square open to society. From the beginning, it was evident that the Countess of Blessington had so gravely transgressed against the code of her kind that she was not to be "visited." Ladies of fashion were not necessarily averse to sexual irregularity, and willingly tolerated such frailty as did the transgressor social credit. Peeresses known for their accessibility to royalty could give parties to which their less ingenious sisters crowded eagerly. Even non-royal intimacies could be so contrived as to give great satisfaction to toadies and gossip-mongers. But that an Irish nobody, who had lived in the country house of an ordinary commoner and then, by means unknown but certainly sinister, had snatched a titled and wealthy husband from under the very noses of matchmaking mammas, should now presume to act the smart London hostess, was an outrage alike to morals and to society.

And in other respects also Lady Blessington was distasteful to her female competitors. She was more beautiful than they, more intelligent and pleasanter company, with the result that clever men seemed actually to prefer an evening in her house to one spent in an atmosphere more hallowed but more tedious.

Admittedly the circumstances were unusual. Had Blessington been a man with any ambition beyond amusement or one more sensitive to the influence of the community on the individual, he would have felt the falseness of his wife's position, and either have forced the issue in order to remedy it or have insisted on a way of life which reminded her less continually of her ostracism. But the finesse of social relationships was beyond his heedless comprehension; and because he himself would much rather fill his house with amusing talkers, and was only interested in women as decoration, as stage colleagues, and as cheerful company, he was undisturbed by the absence from St. James's Square of ladies of birth and breeding, if indeed he noticed it at all.

Admittedly, also, Lady Blessington had in secret much to bear in the way of slights, cuts direct in public places, and the misery which any woman must suffer at pointed exclusion from the company of her fellows. But she had no alternative save to endure, seeing that behind her was an isolation even more miserable, at her side a husband gaily unconscious of her difficulties, and in front of her a prospect of luxury, beautiful possessions, and the admiration of clever men. Her task was obviously to pretend indifference to her outlawry, and, by pretending hard enough, in time to make her indifference real.

It was not long before the lavish entertainment and the distinguished conversation offered at Number 11 St. James's Square gave to the Blessington parties a special reputation of their own. They combined politics, literature, painting and *sans-gêne,* in a way unknown in other houses. Their splendour of appointment brought with it neither formality nor ostentation. The Earl was completely without arrogance and would show off his fine house and his beautiful wife to any one ready to be interested, with a child's unself-conscious delight in a collection of new toys. As for the Countess, she already showed that instinct for pleasant friendliness (a friendliness which was never so casual as to seem insincere or so eager as to be impertinent) and that talent for prompting others to talk, which were to distinguish her throughout her life. Wherefore, with neither master nor mistress inclined to pomposity or rudeness; with magnificent rooms; superb food and drink; and a company to which at one time or another belonged nearly every man of individual attainments in London, it was no wonder that the Blessingtons' dinners and soirées soon became a feature of the metropolitan scene.

2

A mere catalogue of the notabilities who frequented the house in St. James's Square would convey as little of the spirit of that house as do the "social" columns of a modern newspaper of the gatherings they advertise. Unluckily (and in contrast to Lady Blessington's later salons in Seamore Place and at Gore House) little beyond a visiting list survives of this first period of her London hospitality. It is recorded that of politicians, Palmerston, Castlereagh, Earl Grey, Canning, Erskine and Brougham; of writers and artists, Moore, Rogers, Galt, Lawrence, Wilkie and Varley — were more or less regular guests. But only two or three of these troubled to write down details of their experience.

Joseph Jekyll, whom Samuel Rogers called "the Yorick of our time", makes brief mention of a dinner party in April, 1820, and shows that the Countess had already a taste for literary lions:

> The gallant Blessington has bought Heathcote's house. He gave us a banquet last week composed of *beaux esprits*. Miladi is a beauty, leaves her card at my door in a morning; keeps an album and desires all her literary friends to write in it to perpetuate their autographs.

Galt provides an agreeable glimpse of old Doctor Samuel Parr, the famous classical scholar, awaiting in full canonicals in the drawing-room at St. James's Square the return of his host and hostess and, in consequence, his dinner. He had been invited early, because of his special habit of dining before the usual time, and had then been forgotten. Galt set himself with anxious zeal to charm away the old man's irritation, which he achieved so successfully that the apologetic arrival of the Blessingtons an hour later found the eccentric Doctor and the

Scottish novelist chuckling loudly over Edinburgh memories. After his belated dinner was eaten and while still at table, Doctor Parr, as was his habit, produced his long clay pipe. This notorious instrument required for its proper exploitation a basin of water; but the Blessington dining room, though adequately watered, was unprovided with basins. Unabashed, the Doctor heaved his ageing bulk from his chair, chose from the sideboard a decorative chalice of pure gold and, putting it at his feet, signified that, though not ideal, it would serve his purpose.

Doctor Parr became comparatively intimate with Lady Blessington during the three years of her first London residence. He it was who first spoke of her as "most gorgeous" (the phrase has deservedly survived), and also prophesied that with her shrewd and masculine mind she would be even more impressive in middle age than while in the lovely splendour of her youth. This prophecy was fulfilled, for youthful beauty needs sex appeal to give it meaning, but middle age relies on charm and on experience.

Another anecdote shows that the conversation at a Blessington party could, if desired, be as unconventional as the table manners. Canning and Lord Grey were provoked by a marble statue of a woman, which stood in one of the drawing-rooms at St. James's Square, into a discussion of the points of beauty of the female foot. Grey liked a plump and fleshy foot, Canning preferred slimness and form. Unable to agree — and feeling perhaps that female anatomy was more properly an artist's speciality than a politician's — they appealed to Sir Thomas Lawrence. He supported Grey and, when Canning was obstinate, offered to fetch the Countess and prove his point by demonstration. Canning declared laughingly that in the face of such evidence, he would swear black to be white.

Lawrence's lovely painting of Marguerite Blessington, reproduced as frontispiece to this book, is one of his best-known portraits. It was included in the Royal Academy Exhibition for

1821 and caused something of a sensation. One more than ordinarily articulate person was privileged to see both portrait and original at once. Chance brought Lord Blessington, with his wife on his arm, to view the picture at the moment of its inspection by P. G. Patmore, father of Coventry Patmore, a literary journalist of repute and for some years editor of the *New Monthly Magazine*. Writing in *Bentley's Miscellany* nearly thirty years later,[1] Patmore recalled the incident. "I have seen no other so striking instance," he says, "of the inferiority of art to nature as in this celebrated portrait of Lady Blessington. As the original stood before it, she fairly 'killed' the copy, and this no less in the individual details than in the general effect." He goes on to describe the appearance at that time of her whom he calls "perhaps the loveliest woman of her day"; and begins by commenting on the complete absence from her manner of any consciousness of beauty, of any desire to court notice or to pose for admiration.

He proceeds: "There was about her face, together with that beaming intelligence which rarely shows itself upon the countenance till that period of life" [*i.e.*, the late twenties, such being Patmore's estimate of the lady's age], "a bloom and freshness which as rarely survive early youth, and a total absence of those indefinable marks which thought and feeling still more rarely fail to leave behind them. Unlike all other beautiful faces that I have seen, hers was, at the time of which I speak, neither a history nor a prophecy . . . but an end and a consummation in itself, not a means to, or a promise of, anything else."

Tom Moore has been mentioned as one of the frequenters of Number 11 St. James's Square, and his voluminous diaries contain several references to the house and its owners. These are mainly interesting as evidence that to a habitual (and slightly servile) visitor to Holland House, the peculiar atmosphere of

[1] Vol. XXII, pp. 162–175. The essay was reprinted in "My Friends and Acquaintances." 3 vols. 1854.

the Blessington ménage was baffling and uncomfortable. Moore, like Rogers and Luttrell, was an old-style haunter of the houses of the great. In order that aristocracy should not turn away the light of its countenance, he was prepared to go far in outward humility, in expressions of gratitude and in parlour tricks. None of these was required of visitors to St. James's Square. Marguerite Blessington was ready to welcome Moore and to admire him for what in his actual work seemed good; she was equally ready to criticise or to make fun of him for carelessness or for tufthunting.

In what was, to him, a salon of a new kind, Moore found himself ill at ease, and his diary contains amusing self-betrayals. In July, 1819, he described Lady Blessington as dabbling in politics and as taking him home after the Opera, in order to beg his help in converting Lord Lansdowne to the Opposition. One can hardly blame a courtier of the formidable Lady Holland for taking his hostess with an extreme and careful seriousness, but it must have amused Marguerite to observe the grave deliberation with which her quizzing was received. Another entry in Moore's diary, of nearly three years later, shows him wholly at sea with the seeming-solemn nonsense which she and her intimates were beginning to introduce into social small talk. "Called at Lady Blessington's," he writes on May 5, 1822, "who is growing very absurd. 'I have felt very melancholy and ill all this day,' she said. 'Why is that?' I asked. 'It is the anniversary of my poor Napoleon's death.' "

This was so palpably a mischievous pastiche of Lady Holland's notorious Napoleon mania that Moore may conceivably have felt the pin prick and decided to laugh it off; but one prefers to imagine him quite insensitive to the satire and hurrying off to more familiar and more portentous places, gently malicious over the follies and affectations of the hated Lady Blessington.

3

And what, during these half-brilliant, half-frustrated years of London hospitality, were the normal occupations of Lord

Blessington? From one point of view he had none at all. Volatile, erratic, in a perpetual scurry of easily negligible engagements, he played little part in those aspects of public life which are recorded for posterity, and only occasionally crop up in contemporary comments of the obscurer sort.

Sydney Morgan had caricatured him cruelly as Lord Rosbrin in her novel "Florence Macarthy", published in 1818, representing him as stage-struck to the point of lunacy, always dressing up in flamboyant fancy costume and with a mind like "a tablet, upon which memory — the genius of fools — had made some traces." But Sydney Morgan was prejudiced. Herself a professional actor's daughter, she had been "taken up" by the Abercorns, and in consequence despised equally the amateur Thespian and those members of the Irish peerage who were inferior in rank and length of tradition to her very august protectors. A more friendly portrait of this elusive, ridiculous, but rather engaging peer is to be found in Galt's novel "Sir Andrew Wylie", (1822) the second edition of which is dedicated to Blessington in return for his having served as model for Lord Sandiford.

Redding describes him as "a weak creature, whose after-dinner conversations, when the wine was in, became wretchedly maudlin." Gronow speaks of him as "a very good amateur actor"; and his passion for theatricals earns him a place in an amusing poem called "Whig — Ass — urance", published in the high Tory scandal-sheet *John Bull* on December 17, 1820, and February 7, 1821, and satirising the notabilities of the Whig party:

> Lord Blesinton's a stage struck ass —
> — umer of Lothario
> But by his talents, wit or grace,
> (Had he but eyes to find his place)
> He's fitter for Paddy Carey O!

And the following year in the same paper:

> To manage the stage
> The actors engage
> And to play Master Ford is Lord Blesinton's rage.

On a third occasion, *Bull's* satirist led off a poem on the Whig party with Blessington, and in such a way as to lay rather cruel emphasis on his squint and to give (as much by hazard as by design) an apt impression of the purposeless energy which characterised him:

Blesinton hath a beaming eye
  But no one knows for whom it beameth,
Right and left it seems to fly
  But what it looks at no one dreameth.

The Earl's eyes — bright, strenuous, futile and undisciplined — seem to have impressed the Tory gutter-journalists, for in a scurrilous attack on the Duchess of St. Albans, published in the *Age*, a comparison is drawn between the immobile eye of the Duchess' coachman and one of Lord Blessington's, which moved "upward and downward spirally."

And yet, with all his ineffectiveness, extravagance and bustle, Blessington was not really a fool. He possessed the great quality of endearing himself to his few intimates, and if he had only given himself a chance seriously to develop one or two interests instead of dabbling frenetically in a dozen, he might have prolonged his own life and made good use of the prolongation. His liberalism was genuine and generously expressed. He was one of the founder-members of Robert Owen's British and Foreign Philanthropic Society, started in London in 1822 and designed to carry out Owen's plan of Villages of Coöperation. As an Irish landlord, he was humane and open-handed; and as will be seen, his belief in Catholic Emancipation was to bring him at top speed, though in ill health, from Paris to London and back again on purpose to record his vote in the vital Division of 1829. In fact Lord Blessington was so nearly an individuality, that his failure to be one altogether is an important element in the tragic evanescence of his whole ménage. Perhaps if he had inherited a smaller fortune . . . if his marriage could have been one of passion and not merely one of amiable connoisseurship . . . if the fascinating d'Orsay had never come to St.

James's Square and set his ill-balanced senses reeling . . . if his only son had not died . . .

So many "ifs"; so many tricks of fate . . .

4

It was on an evening in the autumn of 1821 that Alfred d'Orsay was brought to one of the Blessington parties by his brother-in-law, the Duc de Guiche. He was just twenty years of age — slim, athletic, amazingly handsome — and his full name was Gillion Gaspard Alfred de Grimaud,[2] Comte d'Orsay et du Saint Empire. He had come to London for the first time in the spring of 1821 with his sister Ida, Duchesse de Guiche, and her husband. The de Guiches had English affiliations. The Duc had held a commission in an English regiment, and his sister had married the heir of Lord Tankerville and was at this time Lady Ossulston. Wherefore, when he first met the Blessingtons, the young Count had already made an appearance in certain English houses, collected a little troupe of admiring imitators and won notice in the Row by his exquisite clothes, outré horsemanship and gay insolence of manner. He had an easy and rather impertinent charm which enraged persons of a certain type but was irresistible to others.

Of the former class was the redoubtable Lady Holland, with whom d'Orsay had already made sensational contact. Seated next her at dinner, quite shortly after his arrival in London, he behaved with what she regarded as unsuitable self-possession in any foreign visitor, and in so young a man as outrageous. Accordingly (for she delighted to put down what she considered conceit in her inferiors), she dropped on the floor first her napkin, then her fan, then her fork, then her spoon. Each time the young Frenchman retrieved the fallen object with courteous suavity but continued quite unabashed to chatter his broken English. Finally Lady Holland knocked her wineglass off the

[2] Alternatively "Grimod."

table. D'Orsay turned to a footman behind him. "Put," he said, "my *couvert* on the floor. I will finish my dinner there. It will be much more convenient to miladi."

It can hardly be doubted that this story had reached St. James's Square, where it would be greatly relished. The arrogant rudeness of aristocrats of Lady Holland's type was an offense to Lady Blessington, and she would have desired to make the acquaintance of any young foreigner who had so admirably put bad-mannered rank in its place. When, therefore, Alfred d'Orsay came to her party and bowed over her hand, he was made welcome. It was the beginning of an association which was to last until death.

Early in 1822, Marguerite Blessington's first book was published — a seventy-page octavo, anonymous and entitled "The Magic Lantern or Sketches of Scenes in the Metropolis." It contained four essays, describing an auction in an expensive private house; a walk in Hyde Park; a visit to the Egyptian Tomb; and an evening at the Italian Opera. The writing is undistinguished but without affectation; the matter trivial enough. Evidently two or three years spent in constant conversation about books with writers and critics, in regular reading of the latest publications, had suggested to her ladyship that she also should try her hand at authorship and, by setting down simple descriptions of life as she observed it, should express some of her own ideas on society and manners.

The result, though negligible as literature, is not without interest. There is, for example, a melancholy irony in the first essay, which describes a fashionable throng dawdling through the desolate rooms of a once hospitable mansion, fingering the objects labelled for sale, criticising their owners, sneering unkindly at the misfortunes which have overtaken them. Precisely such a selfish throng were, years later, to trail through Lady Blessington's own abandoned home and, in curiosity, greed and heedlessness, to pry into the secrets of Gore House.

It seems that in the early summer of 1822, Lord Blessington contemplated a visit to Ireland and that Galt, among other friends, encouraged him to make it. But the Countess pleaded ill health. Her dislike of the very idea of Ireland had grown stronger during her three years in London and she declared that if her husband went, he went alone. Blessington, ever changeable, thought that perhaps in such a case he would not go, after all. Then Galt wrote the Countess a long and remarkable letter which, inasmuch as it proved unavailing, shows that the ill health was but an excuse and that the lady was obstinately determined to have done with Ireland once and for all. Writing from Liverpool on July 27, 1822, Galt said:

> On Monday evening I was so distinctly impressed with the repugnance which your ladyship feels at the idea of going to Ireland, that I entered entirely into your feelings, but upon reflection I cannot recall *all* the reasonableness of the argument — a circumstance so unusual with respect to your ladyship's reasons in general that I am led to think that some other cause at the moment must have tended to lend the energy of its effect to the expressions of your reluctance.

It is permissible to picture the reception of this letter. The Countess sits brooding in her boudoir, the quarto sheets upon her lap; the Earl, wrinkling his fresh, good-natured face into a semblance of deep thought, paces up and down the soft Aubusson carpet. She is adamant; she will not go. He is worried; but will not go, either. And at this moment a servant announces the Count d'Orsay. It is not his first morning visit and he is already gaily at home in his friends' luxurious house. Something in the atmosphere checks his cheerful greeting. "Miladi is not well? The good Blessington is anxious?" The charming youth is all sympathy. With a presumption which he contrives to disguise as flattering familiarity, he takes Galt's letter from the lady's knee and quickly reads it. "But, my dear Earl, with our delicious Countess suffering . . . !" How fortunate that he should have called that very morning, for he came to propose a little plan. Or do these dear people feel that they really ought to go to Ireland? Marguerite shivers (that grave of memories!). And Alfred sees the clouding of her eyes. He becomes voluble. Listen! He must return forthwith to France. But he is tired of his regiment, tired of being a lay figure, all pipe clay and clanking swords. Listen again. If his charming friends will decide to take a foreign tour, will stop a little while in Paris . . . then travel southwards . . . at Avignon, if all goes well, he will meet them. Then Italy perhaps . . .

The voice floats tunefully across the room. Italy! Sunshine and freedom and beauty and release from these boring English, with their fake virtue and their heavy pride of rank. Marguerite turns with clasped hands to her husband. Oh, let us go! Let us go!

The Earl looks at her one moment; then at Alfred. The excitement and freshness of organising a trip abroad sets his imagination racing; also at Avignon that lovely boy will visit them once more — perhaps join their party.

The affair is settled. The Blessingtons will leave London for the Continent.

CHAPTER V

ALFRED D'ORSAY

"SO MANY 'ifs'; so many tricks of fate. . . ."

And, in truth, there was never a tale which showed fate more clearly in the rôle of evil trickster than the tragi-comic tale of Charles, Earl of Blessington, his household and his dynasty. Like water which bubbles up from nowhere, glitters for a while in the sunshine, and then, soaking away through treacherous sand, is no more seen, the little group whose thirty years of surface splendour was in effect the history of the Blessington peerage, lived their dazzling hour, seemed for a while the brightest, gayest things in nature, only one after the other to fade, to vanish and to leave no trace behind. Fate's share in the sorry fantasy was to provide that each one of them came to prominence with the seeds of transience already sown; further, so to tangle their lives and impulses that the result was a mere raddle of irrelevant disorder.

First, their innate impermanence. Blessington was the flustered plaything of his own money power and prematurely collapsed under the strain of crazy prodigality. His wife — half of whose heritage of womanhood had been sacrificed to her father's brutal greed — made gallant showing of the other half; until at last the odds — spiritual, social and material — became too great and conquered her.

And d'Orsay, the Earl's fancy boy and protégé . . . ?

Maybe the origins of this exquisite youth, by their very bizarrerie, excuse his fatal influence on those who loved him best. Certainly they go far to account for them. If Blessington was ruined by the impact of wealth too early inherited on a nature too easily unbalanced, if Marguerite was doomed to years of gilded sham because her father was a savage fool, Alfred — alike in his disastrous charm and in his ultimate futility — was the inevitable product of heredity unto the second generation of those who made him.

He was the son of General Count d'Orsay, an officer of the Army of the Empire and, as befitted one who owed his advancement to Napoleon, a convinced Bonapartist. General d'Orsay's origin was ordinary enough. His father was a plebeian of mercantile genius, by name Grimaud, who skilfully exploited the chances of profit offered by the protracted confusion of the Revolutionary Wars. With the fortune thus made, M. Grimaud married a Netherlandish aristocrat and bought the property and title of the Count d'Orsay. Alfred's grandfather, in short, was a *roturier* who could afford ennoblement.

His mother had origins less respectable but more brightly coloured. She was the daughter, by the Duke of Würtemberg, of an Italian adventuress, known successively as Anne Franchi, La Belle Sullivan, and Madame Craufurd. Child of a tailor in Lucca, Anne Franchi went on the stage as a dancer in early youth and actually married about 1768 a member of the troupe to which she belonged. But her beauty and spirit made friends for her beyond the footlights; and sometime during the 1770's she was put among her furniture by the Duke of Würtemberg, who had so relished her public performances that for two years he paid her to give private ones. Whence the female child who, ingeniously baptised "Eleonore de Franquemont", became later the wife of General d'Orsay and the mother of Alfred.

At the end of her two years of ducal favour (each of which had left its pledge behind) Anne Franchi appeared in Paris under the protection of a certain Chevalier d'Aigremont. But the Chevalier was deficient either in character or in funds; and his mistress was soon stolen from him by an engaging Irishman called Sullivan, who was a member of the Sullivan family prominent in the service of the East India Company during the closing decades of the eighteenth century. To India Sullivan and Anne Franchi duly sailed, where the young lady's wit and beauty gained her a certain reputation and the tacit permission to call herself by her protector's name. But once again it was not long before she decided to transfer her favours. This time her choice was impeccable. Quintin Craufurd, on the point of retiring with a huge fortune from the service of John Company, crooked his finger at the lovely Sullivan. They returned together to Paris, where the cultured nabob collected books and pictures and statuary, and frequented the Court of Marie Antoinette, while "Madame Craufurd" spent his lavish revenues on dress, on social enjoyments and on her two little "Franquemonts", toward whom Quintin behaved with genial affection. This was early in the 1780's, and for nearly ten years the ménage went its pleasant way. Then, however, Craufurd rashly involved himself in a plot to smuggle the King and Queen from France — the plot which ended so miserably at Varennes. He was himself in Belgium when the actual attempt was made and in consequence escaped prison and a revolutionary tribunal; but automatically he had become an exile, his collections in Paris were sequestrated and sold,[1] and he found himself an emigré with only three *objets d'art* still in his possession — his faithful Anne and her two now adolescent children. Inasmuch as their money came from sources unaffected by the French Revolution, the Craufurds contrived to pass the next ten years agreeably enough in the various centres of emigré society. Brussels, Frankfurt and Vienna were successively their home, and while Quintin wrote books and essays, Madame Craufurd made good use of the opportunities of worldly experience afforded by these various sojourns. In 1802 peace was signed at Amiens, the Consulate was instituted, and persons of royalist colouring might once again return to Paris in safety. By this time Anne had become as essential a part of her lover's life as ever a lawful wife could be.

[1] Several of the statues still adorning the Tuileries and the Place Louis Quinze belonged to the Craufurd collection.

She was now nearly fifty — admirably preserved, at once witty and sympathetic, with a daughter respectably married and a grandson; above all she was disinclined for further adventuring. Craufurd was ten years her senior and equally prepared to settle down. So the two were married; and with an intensity which showed that there were to be no two ways about it. One day they were married in the British Embassy; the next they were married in the English church; the next they were married by a Catholic priest at St. Germain-en-Laye. "Madame Craufurd" was now Madame Craufurd indeed.

Within ten years of this triple wedding Lord Blessington was also to marry one woman three times. Near St. Germain-en-Laye the widow of Lord Blessington and the grandson of Madame Craufurd were to be buried side by side. It was an odd tangle of coincidence, whose strands — originally quite independent one of the other — were destined to entwine in the cruellest yet gaudiest of knots.

Madame Craufurd's grandson had been born at Paris in the autumn of 1801, while she and her Quintin were still living in luxurious exile. The father, General d'Orsay, was a very handsome man; the mother had something of her own mother's witty charm. So the child was all but inevitably good-looking and intelligent, his elements of uncertainty being those of character and principle.

The d'Orsay household was of modest means; and had its members been left to build their own lives, they might have proved useful though undistinguished representatives of the Parisian bourgeoisie. But the prospects of the General's children (there was a daughter Ida, younger by a year than Alfred), were wholly changed by the return of the Craufurds to Paris, their formal marriage and their impressive establishment as figures in high society. Quintin Craufurd could afford to live on a grand scale, and despite his English origin kept skilfully on good terms with the reigning Bonapartes during the years of the Empire. But it was after Waterloo that his real chance came. When English visitors flocked once more to Paris, he found himself the most important individual link between France and England then resident in the French capital. He was consulted over every matter of social policy and was personally responsible for arranging the purchase by the British Government of the house in the Faubourg St. Honoré which is still the British Embassy. Inasmuch as that house was the property of the Princess Borghese (née Pauline Bonaparte) Craufurd did a good turn to his old friends as well as to his new by his tactful handling of a difficult negotiation. He died in November, 1819, in a blaze of contemporary renown which makes the more remarkable the transience of his memory.

During these years of brilliant hospitality and growing social prominence, Madame Craufurd was ever mindful of her daughter and her grandchildren. In consequence, Ida and Alfred d'Orsay passed their childhood and adolescence in a world to which, but for their grandmother, they could hardly have aspired. They were lavishly provided for; brought forward early and often; and, thanks to their extreme beauty, became the pets of many a smart drawing-room at an age when they had better have remained out of sight in the schoolroom.

Gronow saw Alfred at one of his grandmother's receptions in the Rue d'Anjou in 1816, and the fifteen-year-old boy was already noteworthy for his distinguished appearance and easy manners. Nor was he less of a prodigy in outdoor sports. He can hardly have been more than fifteen when Lord William Pitt Lennox observed him at a "meet" in the Bois de Boulogne, mounted on a "first-rate Leicestershire hunter, with a simple English saddle and bridle" — specially sent to him from England. The lad was among those "who took part in the 'lark' home, across country. Albeit unaccustomed to go across country, he was always in the first flight and made up by hard riding what he lacked in judgment."

His sister Ida rivalled him in social precocity. When barely seventeen she married the Duc de Guiche, son and heir to the Duc de Gramont, and took her place at once among fashion's "younger set." Henceforward the younger d'Orsays were completely absorbed into that cultivated, expensive and highly decorative society which flitted engagingly between London and Paris during the years following the Bourbon restoration.

When he was eighteen, Alfred's grandmother facilitated his entry into the Garde Royale. Influence was necessary to make the son of the Bonapartist General d'Orsay welcome at a Bourbon mess; but the Craufurds were — if not all-powerful at Paris — at any rate powerful enough for that. Whether the dazzling newcomer was quite so welcome when he displayed the dressing case, the set of gold plate, the gold-mounted harness and the other costly equipment with which the ornate taste and somewhat exaggerated fondness of his grandmother had furnished him, can reasonably be doubted. Indeed, to dispel the resentful scorn of his brother officers must have been the first serious test of Alfred's social nerve. How far he passed that test will never be known; but it is possible that his readiness to send in his papers within four years of having been gazetted was in part a wish to escape the critical brusquerie of military superiors.

Such the origins and such the upbringing of the exquisite youth who, on his very first visit to the Blessingtons' London house, was so immediately sympathetic to his hosts that a lasting intimacy between the trio seemed almost to be ordained.

In the fact that it so seemed lies the essential clue to the mystery of their relationship. The completeness with which Alfred d'Orsay, the Earl of Blessington and the Countess Marguerite understood and liked one another cannot be explained by the arguments used hitherto. It has been assumed that d'Orsay and the Countess fell in love; that Blessington was a complaisant dupe; and that the story developed into the ordinary story of a rich, myopic cuckold, a guilty wife, a dashing young lover who contrived simultaneously to enjoy the husband's money and the lady. Given the personnel of this particular drama, so naïve a plot cannot be accepted. Marguerite, when she first saw d'Orsay, was very little more than thirty years old and in the spring of her mature beauty — that is to say, she was neither an excitable young girl to be dazzled by a handsome youth nor a woman within sight of fading, whose love chances (did she covet any) were likely to diminish with every year which passed. Further, she had not lived a life either cloistered or uneventful; and even her enemies admitted that she had plenty of mother wit.

Is it conceivable that a clever woman, who well knew the penalties of social irregularity, would have been such a fool thus early in her career of luxurious enjoyment as to risk losing all she had won for the sake of a wanton amourette? Further, again, there is evidence that she was fond of her husband and grateful to him, so that only if she were so passionate that a continual change of lovers was necessary to her would she have committed the offensive folly of betraying him under his very nose. As to which, enough has been said already to show that only by regarding her as virtually unresponsive to sexual emotion can her life and character be interpreted.

Wherefore, so far as Marguerite was concerned, it may be taken for certain that she did not fall in love with d'Orsay, nor ever, in the sexual sense, come to love him. She liked him enormously; she enjoyed his company, his intelligence, his conversation and his decorative qualities; and she desired instinctively to keep him at her side. Wherefore throughout her life she sought to protect him from the consequences of his own recklessness, and when, after her death, he mourned "a kind and loving mother", he was expressing as literally as possible the spirit of their many years of intimacy.

And then Lord Blessington. Here again the conventional

theory of deceived husband and faithless wife wrecks on the facts of personality. The Earl was eccentric, frivolous and full of extravagant whims; but he was not the traditional dotard to be unaware of a young wife's treachery or, knowing it, to be fondly tolerant. Even if his physical possessiveness were weak, his connoisseurship was very strong; and he would as violently have resented any one tampering with his household's fairest ornament as would any amateur of beauty resent unauthorised handling of his most treasured *objet d'art.* His fondness for d'Orsay also probably had its origin in this same connoisseurship; although there cannot be much doubt that the affection of the forty-year-old Blessington for the twenty-year-old Alfred soon developed a sexual element of its own.

Finally d'Orsay himself — how easily can he be adjusted to the tale as generally told? Up to a point, more easily than either of the others. He must have realised, even in his middle teens, that money was the secret of a gay and elegant life, that he excelled at elegant gaiety, but that he had no money of his own now and few prospects of money in the future. He lived on his grandmother's largesse and was not kept ignorant of the fact that he owed that largesse to his good looks, his athletic powers and his personal charm. He saw his sister married to a man of wealth and fashion; he became part of her set and was expected to live on the scale of her husband and friends. How was it to be done? Even a devoted and generous grandmother could not be expected to provide cash indefinitely, particularly as the money she gave him was her husband's and there were other claims on the Craufurd residue. Further, when in 1819 Craufurd died, it was found that his widow, though left comfortably off, was no longer a millionairess. What then? Inevitably Alfred d'Orsay must capitalise his only assets, sell his looks and his fascination to the best possible advantage. His relations would have realised this and one suspects that the de Guiches brought him to London with the idea of exploring the market. If anything good were discoverable anywhere, it would surely be in England, where was the war-wealth of an exhausted Europe.

But suppose that there were an obstacle to this natural solution of Alfred's difficulties. A normal youth, with his exceptional advantages, would have chosen the richest heiress in society and married her. Alfred did not do this. Why? I suggest that he neither married an heiress nor showed any sign of trying to do so, because he was impotent.

This, surely, is the secret of Alfred d'Orsay, the clue to his character, the genesis of his strange career? Combined with his peculiar type of physical beauty — the build and stature of an athlete, the face of a woman — it explains his popularity with men, his lack of appeal to women. His masculine friends were many; but despite all the gossip to the contrary, there is no real evidence that normal women admired or even liked him.

Further, only impotence could have endeared him so immediately to Lady Blessington. It reacted on his character in just the manner she liked best. It made him unaggressive and kindly; it increased his sensitiveness to the suavities and savours of good breeding. Thus it seems little short of a miracle that two persons, so congenial in taste and character, because so similar in physical incompleteness, should have been permitted by circumstance to join forces.

Finally, if we believe him impotent, we begin to understand the curious compounds of egoism, fastidiousness and impersonal amiability which entitles him to be called (for want of a better word) a dandy.

Dandyism and its implications are examined in a famous essay written by Barbey d'Aurevilly, about 1860, and reëxamined, more satisfactorily, in another essay by Baudelaire published a few years later.[2] The former, while losing much of its merit as a study of a social type by the naïve nationalism which

[2] "Du Dandysme et de Georges Brummell." Paris. 1861.
"Le Peintre de la Vie Moderne (L'Art Romantique)." Paris. 1868.

underlies its argument, nevertheless contains passages relevant to our present problem; the latter is more detached and more generally significant. The two, if read in conjunction, help us to relate d'Orsay's individual and difficult psychology to the complex psychology of his time.

Barbey d'Aurevilly begins by distinguishing between love (of another), pride (in oneself) and vanity (which feeds on the reflection of one's own personality in the eyes of others). Masculine vanity he subdivides into that which measures success by the extent to which it wins women's admiration, and that engendered by an intense inner egoism requiring neither conquest nor flattery but only, within the limits of its ambition, unchallenged sovereignty. This last he describes as "English vanity" or dandyism, which, in his view, found its final and most perfect expression in George Brummell. Barbey finds the egoism of the English more absolute than that of any race since the Romans; the French he considers innocent of egoism. Deftly he points his moral thus:

"Everything universal and human has its name in Voltaire's language; other things have to be imported into that language. That is why the word Dandyism is not a French word."

He proceeds to an interesting definition of this dandyism: "Some have imagined that Dandyism is primarily a specialisation in the art of dressing oneself with daring and elegance. It is that, but much else as well. It is a state of mind made up of many shades, a state of mind produced in old and civilised societies where gaiety has become infrequent or where conventions rule at the price of their subject's boredom. Nowhere has the conflict between convention and consequent ennui been more violent than in England . . . and on the day when in England victory goes to one side or the other, dandyism will either be modified or will cease to exist, for it is the direct result of the endless warfare between respectability and boredom. . . ."

In other words, dandyism is an individual and hypercivilised revolt against the rules of a social order which the rebel hates but reveres. He continues to observe these rules and, while resenting, obeys them; but he just sufficiently exaggerates their tenor most subtly to flout them and, even while obedient to them, subjects them to his own caprice.

Read now Baudelaire's definition of the same phenomenon — a definition in many ways very similar but, because it is not so much concerned to prove that no Frenchman was ever a dandy as to explain dandyism itself, more detached and more illustrative of social history as opposed to racial peculiarity:

"The dandy regards neither love nor money as an end in itself. He leaves these gross passions to more ordinary mortals and unlimited credit is wealth enough for him. Dandyism is not, as many seem to think, an exaggerated love of fine clothes and material comfort. These things, to the perfect dandy, are mere symbols of his own spiritual aristocracy. . . .

"What then is the impulse — it has become almost a religion — which has created the lofty caste of dandies? It is primarily a desire to be individually original, but always within the limits of polite social convention. It is a kind of self-worship, which can dispense with the need of finding happiness in others — in women, for example — and can even do without illusions. It is the love of startling others and of never being startled oneself. A dandy may be bored, he may even be ill and in pain. But he will keep smiling all the time with Spartan serenity.

"It will be seen that in some respects dandyism resembles both religious faith and stoicism. But a dandy can never be a man of coarse fibre. He might commit a crime, but to commit one for some trivial motive would dishonour him irretrievably. A strange faith! And yet for those who are both priests and worshippers, the complex life to which they gladly submit — from possessing and wearing perfect costumes for every moment of the day to the exercise of the most exigent and dangerous of sports — is only a sort of penance undergone to strengthen the will and discipline the soul. . . .

"Dandyism makes its appearance at times of transition, when

democracy is only half powerful or when aristocracy is already tottering but has not yet fallen. At such times a few men — déclassés, disgusted or merely bored — will sometime play with the idea of founding a new band of aristocracy, and one all the more difficult to destroy because it will be based on qualities and gifts which toil cannot acquire or money buy. Dandyism is the last gesture of the heroic in an age of decadence . . . it is a setting sun, magnificent but without warmth and full of melancholy."

It is not difficult to see d'Orsay taking shape from the mists of these generalisations. Barbey would forbid him to do so, and devotes a special footnote to the purpose:

"D'Orsay, that 'lion' in the fashionable sense, was not a dandy at all. To call him one is to mistake him. His nature was something infinitely more complex, larger and more human than this English dandyism. Let us repeat that lymph — that heavy liquid which never froths save under the lash of vanity — is the basis of dandyism, and in d'Orsay's veins ran the red blood of France. He was at once full-blooded and highly strung, with broad shoulders, a deep chest and a beauty which won hearts. His very handshake was wholly different from the aloof greeting of the dandy. D'Orsay was a being of genuine good-heartedness, while any such warmth of feeling is unknown to dandyism. It is true that he had a sense of clothes, but it was deep and instinctive and never ostentatious."

Barbey's argument amounts to this — that dandyism is an English product; d'Orsay was a Frenchman; that therefore d'Orsay was no dandy.

The syllogism will serve as part of the comparison between d'Orsay and Brummell to which it belongs; and its logic rests to some extent on the fact that Barbey accepts the legend of d'Orsay's many loves, and in particular his love for Lady Blessington. But what if d'Orsay's relations with Lady Blessington be recognised as inevitably platonic? The neat sequence of argument is turned topsy-turvy and proves the opposite. It is true that the dandy type as defined both by Barbey and Baude-

ALFRED D'ORSAY

After an original drawing by Aubry

laire is more an English type than a French one. The English are colder and more afraid of their emotions than the French; for this reason they are more continent. Libertinism is not a dandy quality, involving as it does a surrender of oneself to others and periodical relaxations of one's remote and studied calm. Wherefore few Frenchmen would qualify as dandies, even if they wished to do so. But d'Orsay lacked precisely those qualities which unfit the French for dandyism. Through no fault of his own, he approximated to English rather than to French standards in respect to sexual enterprise. Which is one of the reasons why eventually he got on with Englishmen better than with his own countrymen, and why for the greater part of his life he lived in England.

It also explains his conformity, with certain variations peculiar to himself, to the dandy type. He did not regard love as an end in itself, because he did not regard it at all. He did not regard money as an end in itself, and in literal fact only needed credit to be perfectly happy. He achieved individual distinction because he took infinite pains to do himself all the justice possible. Never was man less coarsely fibred and his fineness was as spiritually inherent as his distinction. Often in distress, he never allowed it to appear when social obligation or the presence of others bade him conceal it.

Conversely his selfishness was so complete that through no chink in its perfect harness could consideration for the feelings of other people penetrate. He went the way he wished to go, not disregarding the interests of his fellows, but serenely and genuinely unaware of them. Finally, he lived in just such a time of transition as is described by Baudelaire, and in the midst of just such a society torn between boredom and prudery as is described by Barbey d'Aurevilly. He helped Lady Blessington to flout, but at the same time to subscribe to, the rules and modes of the latter. Then, as the former passed and a new stability of manners succeeded the uncertainty of the transition, he sank below the horizon, "magnificent, but without warmth and full of melancholy."

BOOK TWO

FANFARE

CHAPTER I

The Blessington Circus

On August 25, 1822, Lord and Lady Blessington, with the latter's youngest sister Mary Ann Power and a horde of attendants, left London for France. They were seasick, visited Rouen and reached St. Germain-en-Laye on August 30. The Countess in her journal comments with conventional delight on the forest of St. Germain and on "the sunbeams glancing through its umbrageous shades"; she also declares that she could wander for hours along its stately avenues, reflecting on the glittering pageants in the olden time and on the mighty changes that have since occurred. "Here," she writes, "all remains the same. The same blue sky looks down on the gigantic trees; the same air rustles their leaves; and the same greensward offers a carpet to the feet. But they, the proud, the gay, where are they?"

After two days' sojourn she left the little town with regret. Her mortal remains were to return after twenty-seven years never to leave again. One likes to think that her trite but gracious spirit still hovers over the forest; still from the rising hillside where her body once was laid watches the changing colours of the trees.

She was in Paris for her thirty-third birthday and reveals incidentally that she had been there twice before. No record survives of these earlier visits, which must have been made in company with Jenkins. They seem to have been spent mainly in enthusiastic though somewhat facile study of the pictures in the Louvre — a study now further prosecuted to the greater glory of Claude Lorraine, Titian and Giorgione, but with emphatic disapprovel of Rubens' taste in models. Moore was in Paris and took the Countess riding on the "Montagnes Russes", a switchboard in artificial ice, copied from Petersburg and set up in the Tivoli Gardens after the allied entry into Paris in 1815. She found "the extreme velocity with which one is hurried along an agreeable excitement." She went shopping; visited in several houses; and was somewhat fluttered by the tendency of the hotel servants to walk in and out of her bedroom at all hours, without showing any sense either of their audacity or their good fortune. Meantime Blessington was engaging a cook once in the employ of Napoleon, buying a travelling kitchen of fantastic elaboration and in other ways bustling expensively about the city.

The departure of the Blessingtons from Paris on September 12 caused such a disturbance in the hotel yard and neighbouring streets that one onlooker compared the cortège to a regiment setting out for war. Another — more happily — christened it the "Blessington Circus." Byron had travelled to Italy some three years before with seven servants, five carriages, several wagons full of furniture and books, and a number of animals and birds — designed, some for food, others for company. Lord Blessington cut out the live stock and preferred to buy furniture *en route*; but his retinue of servants was enormous, his *batterie de cuisine* sufficient to feed a club; while the various travelling carriages — with mattresses, pillows, *chaises longues*, picnic appliances, restoratives, toilet accessories, changes of clothing, writing desks and books — have never yet been numbered. The Countess was slightly self-conscious at the ostentation of their cavalcade and takes refuge in her diary in mournful reflections on the chains which luxury forges for its votaries. Nevertheless, she has the candour to admit that she would with regret have resigned her special barouche — a double-springed sleeping carriage, with soft cushions, eiderdown pillows, a bookcase, a canteen of plate and glass and "innumerable other little comforts." Happily she was not called upon to do so.

At last the loading was done, the travellers installed. The Blessington Circus — all shining harness and new paint, unwieldy, slow-moving and desperately costly — lumbered through the narrow streets of the Faubourg St. Denis along the road to Fontainebleau.

A week in Geneva; a few days in Berne, Zurich, and Lucerne; then Geneva again; Lyons for four days; and on October 17, Vienne. The lady's journal is that of an ecstatic sight-seer, but one whose common-sense femininity is ever awake to the shortcomings or merits of food and lodging. The inn at Vienne is declared so dirty and ill-managed that even the precaution taken by the Earl's courier to reserve almost the entire building for the accommodation of milord and, presumably, the installation of the ex-imperial chef with his saucepans and scullions, could not turn squalor into comfort. Nevertheless an adequate compromise was somehow made; for the party remained over three weeks in Vienne, and the Countess found that, by taking more than her customary exercise and fresh air, she soon had as good an appetite and slept as well as ever.

On November 9 the cortège moved on. Grenoble; St. Marcellin; Valence; Montelimart; Orange; and, on the 20th, Avignon. In this city a long sojourn had been planned, and the Blessingtons settled themselves into the best hotel and prepared to go into society. During the three months of their stay in Avignon, they went everywhere, met every one, saw everything. Most important of all, they welcomed Alfred d'Orsay to their private party. He had resigned his commission, said good-bye to his relations in Paris, and henceforward was a member of the Blessington household.

Seeing that for the next eight years of her life Lady Blessington's journals are our principal sources of information, it is essential to realise their nature. Undoubtedly they were originally kept from day to day, but they were none of them made public until some years after the events described.[1] When their author decided to publish, she not only revised but, one suspects, largely rewrote the contents of her notebooks. On the one hand discretion, on the other a desire to produce something saleable, made a very thorough refurbishing necessary. In consequence, the journals in their printed form are doubly palimpsest. Their basis is what actually occurred; this was then modified to remove evidence of the writer's immediate companionship at certain stages of her foreign residence and to eradicate those incidents and personal encounters which, as matters turned out, could only have been remembered with embarrassment; finally, the elements in the journals most likely to appeal to the public on whose favour the books' success depended, were deliberately written up and given the quality and perspective essential to popularity.

This double manipulation of her diary material first becomes unmistakably evident at Avignon. The change in the personnel of the party is not even hinted, and the whole record becomes a blend of practical good sense and engaging but always elusive intimacy, which it is impossible not to admire. From this moment onward until nearly the end of "The Idler in France" (until, that is to say, a few months before her permanent return to England in 1830), her journals seem like an answer to the prayer of some modern circulation-monger. She writes as one domesticated Englishwoman to ten thousand others. She instinctively comments on precisely those things most likely to interest her audience, partly of set policy, but largely because they interest her also. She is skilfully prodigal with titled acquaintances and glimpses of the life luxurious; yet she never hesitates to describe her house-hunting, her sewing of curtains,

[1] The "Conversations with Lord Byron" (relating incidents which took place in 1823) were published in 1834; "The Idler in Italy" (covering the years 1822–1828) in 1839; and "The Idler in France" (1828–1830) in 1841.

her moments of active efficiency in domestic economy and housewifery, and is always sweetly loyal to the morals and decorum of the British fair.

Had the "Woman's Page" of to-day existed a century ago, Lady Blessington would have been the most sought after editress of her time. She was herself "news"; she was lovely, titled, and familiar with the habits of the *ton;* she could be gently daring and at times even a little coarse, particularly when describing the customs, absurdities and adventures of vulgarians, tourists and other stock "comics" in the diarist's repertory. But no stauncher champion existed of the delicacy, dignity and orthodox morality of English womanhood, while she could always be relied on to judge every situation from the point of view of good feminine common sense. Her prolonged stay in Avignon gave her an opportunity of studying and describing French manners, of which she took full advantage. Her journal deals successively with the relations between mistress and servant and between young men and young women in society; with the superiority of French conversation over English; with the sociability of the French; with their talent for acting. Being naturally of cosmopolitan sympathies, she had no illusions as to the quality of English conversation vis-à-vis that of France. The heavy formality, the snobbery, the stiff inarticulateness of London life, had already provoked her to discreet rebellion; and she took every chance of praising the French for excelling precisely where her countrymen fell short. But every now and again she speaks a timely word for British propriety, interpreting propriety in a way magnificently Anglo-Saxon for illogicality and opportunism. Thus, when praising the unself-consciousness and vivacity of French amateur acting she observes: "English ladies, however highbred, always retain a certain timidity (and it is one of their greatest charms) which precludes that perfect ease so essentially necessary in dramatic exhibitions."

A few pages farther on, she is busy with the clothes and deportment of Frenchwomen of breeding:

In England people form truly erroneous opinions of French manners and customs. There, those who have never resided in France, suppose that in it a much greater latitude in respect to demeanour prevails than with us; but I consider that here a stricter attention to decorum, in externals at least, is exhibited. I am far too patriotic to admit that this reserve and decorum arises from, or indicates, a superiority of the French ladies over our own in moral worth or real modesty, for in these qualities none can exceed ours. . . . But to strangers who behold only the surface, the impression produced by the extreme reserve of young French women is that they are more carefully brought up than ours are and impose a greater restraint on their male acquaintances.

A much greater degree of prudery, if it may be so called, is exercised in France than in England with regard to dress; the robes of ladies of all ages conceal much more of the bust and shoulders. Ill-natured people are not wanting who declare that prudence has more to say to concealment than modesty; the French busts and shoulders being very inferior to the English. Of the former I have had no means of judging, but of the latter all must pronounce that they are charming.

February 16, 1823, saw the departure of the Blessington Circus from Avignon. Her ladyship and Miss Power were loaded with "cakes, bonbons, orange-flower water and bouquets of flowers" as parting presents; while there was an addition to the cortège — only second in importance to the Count d'Orsay — in the form of an Arab charger called Mameluke, which the Countess had borrowed from the colonel of a regiment stationed at Avignon, had herself ridden up the steep and slippery road to Villeneuve "to the wonder of many spectators" and, by the ready indulgence of her husband, had subsequently acquired.

Aix-en-Provence; Marseilles; Toulon; Fréjus; Cannes. On March 5 the party arrived at Nice and settled down for a stay of two weeks. The Countess expresses with some force her opinion of Nice as a wintering place for invalids. It is cold, treacherously exposed to wind, and only too numerous in the streets are "those who bear about with them the visible symptoms of approaching dissolution." Also the streets are unclean and the main square cheerless and filthy. That she was only able to have a private sitting room by paying extra for another bedroom and having the beds removed lost to Nice its penultimate chance of her approval. "Comfort," she cries, "England is thy dwelling place! There thou art wedded to good taste, and worshipped as the penates of happy homes; but rarely art thou encountered in other lands, where grandeur strives in vain to compensate for thine absence."

Matters improved after a few evenings of conversation about English literature with the Duc de Vallombrosa, and the Comte Andriani; but all the good was undone by a visit to the grotto at the Château Neuf, "the mouth of which is so small that it can only be entered by a person's crawling, not on the hands and knees but perfectly prostrate — a posture as uneasy as it is unseemly." One is therefore not surprised to find the party leaving Nice the next day for Mentone, and even deciding, beyond that town, to risk the Cornice road on mule-back, rather than wait for the snow to clear from the Col de Tende.

What became of the rolling stock and personnel of the Blessington Circus is not recorded. Clothes and personal belongings were presumably loaded on to mules; superfluous servants were discharged. But the double-springed sleeping carriage; the *batterie de cuisine;* the trail of passenger and luggage coaches — were they sold off for what they would fetch in the forlorn spaces of the great square at Nice? Were they presented to the resident nobility? We do not know. Maybe Lord Blessington did not know either; or care. He had had the fun of buying them; had used them for some months and was already busy with plans for a prolonged Italian residence. Mameluke, of course, was jealously preserved and joined the cavalcade. It is possible that d'Orsay rode him.

Ventimiglia; Oneglia; Noli; Voltri. Lady Blessington takes leave of the mules, speaking warmly of their sure-footed patience and amenability. "Coaches of the country" are obtained, and the last short stretch of the six months' journey from London to Genoa is undertaken in a fervor of excited anticipation:

"Desirous as I am to see Genoa the Superb, I confess that its being the residence of Lord Byron gives it a still greater attraction for me. His works have excited such a lively interest in my mind and the stories related of him have so much increased it, that I look forward to making his acquaintance with impatience. . . . I long to compare him with the *beau ideal* I have formed in my mind's eye and to judge how far the descriptions given of him are correct."

CHAPTER II

CONVERSATIONS WITH LORD BYRON

1

THE nine weeks spent by Lady Blessington in Genoa have been more often and more closely chronicled than any other period of her life. During this time she and her husband were in frequent contact with Byron; her printed record of "Conversations" with the poet is the best known and most satisfactory of her own works; and, almost without exception, subsequent commentators on Byron's life and character have paid tribute to her shrewd and sympathetic portrait of a man whom Ethel Colburn Mayne well describes as "the most *ondoyant et divers* of human beings."

When on March 31, 1823, the Blessingtons arrived in Genoa, Byron had only been settled there for a few months. He had left Pisa under something of a cloud; had refused to make an experimental voyage from Leghorn to Genoa in the schooner *Bolivar* (which Trelawney a little officiously had caused to be built for him); but had gone to Genoa direct and, late in 1822, had there established himself in a villa called Casa Saluzzo at Albaro above the city. The Countess Guiccioli, her father and brother, occupied part of the same house.

Byron's notoriety as a rebel against England and her customs, the scandalous failure of his marriage, and the consequent legends of his debauchery and godlessness had been for years the favourite themes of London gossip-mongers who (characteristically enough) were at the same time loud in admiration of his poetry. No words were bad enough for Byron; and yet there were not words enough to say all the foolish, gloating things which must be said. The English were possessed by Byron. They hated and feared him; but they could not let him alone.

Lady Blessington was no less intrigued by his personality than were other ladies of fashion, but for better reasons. She was, in the first place, a genuine student of letters, and whatsoever fault one may find with her literary tastes, they were her tastes and based on her own reading. Therefore she knew Byron's poetry, as well as its reputation, and admired it. Secondly her husband had been on good terms with Byron during the years from 1812 to 1814. The two had met here and there in London; and because Blessington, with the unself-conscious geniality of his nature, had treated the poet as an ordinary being, instead of with the awkward or censorious reserve which most Englishmen showed in his presence, their acquaintance, though never intimate, had been a friendly one. To the Countess he would have spoken favourably of Byron's personality, and so have made her as readily inclined to meet the man as to claim acquaintance with the notability. Finally, she was predisposed to sympathy with any one whom English society had virtually driven abroad by its arrogance and disapprobation.

Doubtless she spoke of him to Moore in Paris; probably Moore, between doses of "Montagnes Russes", promised to advise his friend of the Blessingtons' descent on Italy, of the Earl's desire to renew an old acquaintance, of her ladyship's cordial admiration of his genius. Her journal contains ever more numerous and excited references to the coming encounter, as the Circus moves irresistibly southward. On the very evening of her arrival in Genoa the prolonged overture to her actual meeting with Byron mounted to its climax:

"And am I indeed," she wrote in her diary, "in the same town with Byron? And tomorrow I may perhaps behold him!!!! I never felt before the same impatient longing to see anyone known to me only by his works. I hope he may not be fat, as

Moore described him at Venice; for a *fat poet* is an anomaly in my opinion. Well, well, tomorrow I may know what he is like; and now to bed to sleep away the fatigues of my journey."

To-morrow came. With her husband, her sister and d'Orsay, she was driven up the hill to the Casa Saluzzo. Lord Blessington sent in his card. The ladies sat in the carriage and waited.

"They had not," says Harold Nicolson, in his book on Byron, "long to wait. But a few minutes had passed before they heard the sound of shambling footsteps on the gravel of the courtyard. And there, lounging towards them, came a pale little man without a hat and with wisps of auburn-gray hair tumbling over the back of his collar. He undulated towards them with that swinging gait which is the mark of those afflicted with the peculiar form of lameness known as Little's disease. 'You may have thought me,' he drawled, 'quite as ill-bred and *sauvage* as fame reports, in having permitted Your Ladyship to remain a quarter of an hour at my gate; but my old friend Lord Blessington is to blame; for I only heard a minute ago that I was so highly honoured. I shall think you do not pardon this apparent rudeness unless you enter my abode, which I entreat you will do.' "

They did; and sat a long while in Byron's study, looking over the garden toward the sea, talking of common friends and English mischief-making and a little of the poet's earlier life. When Lady Blessington opened her diary again, to make her entry for April 1st, she wrote, "I have seen Lord Byron; and am disappointed."

Not thus had she pictured the author of "Childe Harold." "Her disillusion" (to quote Harold Nicolson again) "was inevitable. She expected something sinister, poignant, and possibly fat: she found something sinuous, appallingly affable, and thin. So thin, in fact, that his tawdry Venice clothes hung round him like a sack, and bulged over his little martyred feet and his little dimpled hands. She had expected something promethean and recondite: she found something soft, sociable, and chatty. 'No,' she confided to her diary, 'the sublime passages in "Child Harold" and "Manfred" cannot be associated in my mind with the lively, brilliant conversationalist that I this day saw. *They* still belong, in my fancy, to the more grave and dignified individual that I had conceived their author to have been: an individual resembling Philips' portrait of Byron, but paler and more thoughtful. I can imagine the man I saw as the author of "Beppo" and "Don Juan." He is witty, sarcastic, and lively enough for these works; but he does not look like my preconceived notion of the melancholy poet. Well, I never will again allow myself to form an ideal of any person I desire to see; for disappointment never fails to ensue.' "

The following day, when Byron made a return call at the Blessingtons' hotel, things were no better. Two days later he dined with them; the next day and the next they rode out in his company, paid him more visits. Still preconception lingered and warred rebelliously with fact. This ingratiating, tawdry figure in ill-fitting clothes, talking incessantly of his own rank and (surely in the circumstances an indecorous theme?) of the aristocratic connections of the Guiccioli's husband, refused to harmonise with any one of half-a-dozen conceivable Byrons. The Countess did not flinch from writing down her irritation and perplexity:

"I never met anyone with so decided a taste for aristocracy as Lord Byron, and this is shown in a thousand different ways." Again: "Were he but sensible how much the *Lord* is overlooked in the *Poet,* he would be less vain of his rank; but as it is, this vanity is very prominent, and resembles more the pride of a parvenu than the calm dignity of an ancient aristocrat." Again: "I should say that a bad and vulgar taste predominated in all Byron's equipments, whether in dress or in furniture. His bed at Genoa was the most gaudy and vulgar thing I ever saw; the curtains in the worst taste, and the cornice having the family motto '*crede Biron*' surmounted by baronial coronets. His carriages and his liveries were in the same bad taste, having an affectation of finery, but *mesquin* in the details and tawdry in the *ensemble;* and it was evident that he piqued himself upon them by the complacency with which they were referred to."

In this comment was revealed the true — one might almost say the hereditary — Lady Blessington. Her mother was a Desmond; and in the really old families of Ireland persisted a tradition that all people of gentle blood were equals, and that titles were mere embellishments, permissible to those who fancied them, things of indifference to the rest. She had an instinct for gentility; and that instinct was jarred by the vulgarity which Byron inherited from his mother and made him proud to be that little thing, a "lord." As if it mattered! . . . Years afterward, in a letter to Bulwer-Lytton, she was to refer to "a sort of silent respect for myself" which had always influenced her attitude toward the world. Surely Byron, with all his genius, should have had a self-respect even greater?

But for his genius' sake and because she pitied him, she forgot the posturer in the poet; he, conquered by her swift inexigent intelligence, forgot the female in the sympathetic feminine. There developed between them an intimacy of a kind quite personal to themselves, which not only transcended the niceties of polite behaviour, but brought to Byron the only really tranquil friendship with a woman that he ever experienced.

This latter fact is of more interest to posterity than it was to Byron himself. Indeed, the very ordinariness of his relationship to Lady Blessington would naturally have obscured its significance; and apart from a "first impression" of her appearance in a letter to Moore and two rather amusingly offhand references in letters to Lady Hardy, he left behind no record of his opinion of the personality of his new acquaintance.

"Your other allies," he wrote to Moore on April 2, "whom I have found very agreeable personages, are Milor Blessington and *épouse*, travelling with a very handsome companion, in the shape of a 'French Count' (to use Farquhar's phrase in the 'Beaux Stratagem') who has all the air of a *Cupidon déchainé*, and is one of the few specimens I have seen of an ideal of a Frenchman *before* the Revolution. . . . Miladi seems highly literary, to which, and your honour's acquaintance with the family, I attribute the pleasure of having seen them. She is also very pretty, even in a morning — a species of beauty on which the sun of Italy does not shine so frequently as the Chandelier. . . . Mountjoy seems very good-natured, but is much tamed since I recollect him in all the glory of gems and snuffboxes and uniforms and theatricals and speeches in our house . . . and sitting to Stroelling, the painter, to be depicted as one of the heroes of Agincourt with his long sword, saddle, bridle, Whack fal de, etc. etc."

Six weeks later he wrote to Lady Hardy a letter in rather a different strain. He is comically insistent on his own disinclination to philander with his new friend. His hint at her absorption in her "Parisian appendage" is a little ungenerous; his complacent description of the Guiccioli's jealousy more than a little naïve.

Genoa, May 17th, 1823

There be here and have been for some time past the Earl and Lady Blessington and a Parisian *ami* of the Family's (Comte d'Orsay), to all of whom, as friends of Thos. Moore and Blue besides, I have been presented and all that. The Parisian is very young and a beauty, of which last advantage he is fully aware, but he is not at all disagreeable and I should suspect that the women find him more formidable than dreadful. Miladi is the Miladi of whom Lawrence made a picture that set all London raving, as you may have seen in the papers. She is also an authoress, hath written three books and will I suppose write thirty in due course of time and tide.

As they were friends of Moore's and have been civil to me, I could not easily (in my usual way) escape being occasionally with them, especially as they are equestrians and I met them frequently in my rides about Genoa; but this has plunged me into a bit of dramatic trouble, for "La mia dama", Mde. la Comptesse G., was seized with a furious fit of Italian jealousy and was as unreasonable and perverse as can well be imagined. God He knows she paid me the greatest compliment, for what little communication I had with this new Goddess of Discord was literally literary, and besides that, I have long come to years of discretion and would much rather fall into the sea than in Love any day of the week. Her Ladyship was extremely well guaranteed from any presumed observation of my inclination by her Parisian appendage, and would only have changed for the worse, which would neither have suited her or me.

Madame Gi (who never saw her) wont allow her to be pretty and *will* allow her to be not young. I dared not form a judgment on the subject before a person who argues with all the insolence of four and twenty. I send you this gossip that you may laugh at it which is all that it is good for, if it is good for so much.

Lady Hardy was in Florence when this letter reached her, and evidently in reply permitted herself to comment on Byron's new friend with more hostility than accuracy. She may well have been repeating gossip heard in British ministerial circles, for the then representatives of His Majesty at the Florentine court were not among Lady Blessington's admirers. Byron in his next letter is still so anxiously concerned to disclaim more than a very casual acquaintance with the Blessingtons, that he does not attempt even to express incredulity at his correspondent's tittle-tattle.

June 10th, 1823

To return to our Irish Aspasia, I did not know that she had been Post-Mistress of Cahir, but I had heard that she had been a mistress of some kind or other before she espoused the Earl of Blessington. Her slightest acquaintance with me was of the most decorous description; the poor woman seemed deranged with ennui, entirely bored with her Lord and a little sick of her Parisian Paladin also, though why I could not perceive, for he is not only remarkably handsome but certainly clever and apparently amiable — but it was hinted that his temper was not good, in fact that he was exigeant, though I saw few signs of either. I saw very little of them, especially latterly, and now they are gone."[1]

[1] These portions of letters from Byron to Lady Hardy are extracted from a series of such letters first printed, with a commentary by John Gore, in the *Cornhill Magazine*, Vol. LXIV, New Series, 1928.

2

Both these letters of Byron's were written toward the end of the Blessingtons' tour in Genoa, and must certainly be taken into account when gauging the degree of intimacy to which he and the Countess really attained. When, years afterward, she published her "Journal of Conversations with Lord Byron", her enemies declared she had invented practically the whole book and that she had hardly known Byron at all. It is easy to see that they could base their argument on these very letters to Lady Hardy or (if others were written) on others of the kind. But we know enough of the incidents of the relationship between Byron and the whole Blessington party to realise that their meetings were more frequent than he would have had Lady Hardy believe. Further, quick-witted though Lady Blessington was, she can hardly be credited with the capacity to produce a considerable volume of purely imaginary "conversations" which could be accepted by students of a century later as convincing interpretations of Byron's attitude of mind.

The truth lay surely between the two extremes of contention, and a good deal nearer to Lady Blessington's end than to that of her enemies. She may slightly have dramatised her familiarity with the poet for the purposes of self-assertion and to make her book more popular; but he most certainly understated the frequency of his meetings with her and her party, and to the freedom and candour with which he talked, her book bears witness.

"The Journal of Conversations with Lord Byron" — an octavo of over four hundred pages — is remarkable both for its contents and its technique. Whether by the good fortune which sometimes attends artlessness or by a careful achievement of simplicity which would have meant the exercise of considerable art, Lady Blessington succeeded in combining in one continuous and coherent narrative her own impressions of Byron's personality and his observations and opinions on a great variety of themes. The book runs on with hardly a break, passing from an estimate of his character to prolonged verbatim reporting of his spoken words, thence to a brief summary of one of their discussions, thence to further analysis of his thwarted and contradictory nature. The individuality of the authoress is at once skilfully subdued yet everywhere in control. She keeps Byron in the limelight all the time, yet it is clearly at her bidding that he turns to right and left, discusses this or that. The questions which she asks him have the unobtrusive dexterity of the best kind of social proficiency; she is not afraid to make fun of him, even to reprove insincerity or deliberate bitterness; but although he is often annoyed with her (and once so angry that he abruptly turns his horse and rides away) he always recovers his temper quickly and surely, and likes her the better for her frankness and courage.

It is possible, reading the account of her handling of Byron, to guess at the secret of her skill as a hostess. As with him, so, at the head of her own table, she would direct conversation yet submit to it. She was not only a brilliant listener; she could also make sure that her vis-à-vis said something worth listening to.

She did more than charm her guests; she stimulated and at the same time disciplined them. They were encouraged to talk of themselves and their work; but the moment they began to strut or deliberately to assume a cynicism or a flippancy out of harmony with their real nature, she would bring them to their senses, now with a quiet smile, now with a gentle but disconcerting question, occasionally by a direct remonstrance. Further (and this also the "Conversations with Byron" demonstrate), she had a rare gift of understanding the complex characters of clever men. Throughout the book one is struck by the balanced judgments which she passes on Byron's psychology, the sureness with which she distinguishes between his genuine feelings and his self-protective readiness to sneer, to wound and to shock. His exhibitionism neither deceived nor revolted her; it merely made her the more sorry for him, the more determined to release the true character of genius from the bonds of its self-consciousness.

And perhaps even more remarkable than the perceptiveness of Lady Blessington's reading of Byron is the fact that her judgments are for the most part very well expressed. For skill and sympathy in her interpretation of her fellow creatures we are more or less prepared; but we hardly anticipate such clarity in describing complex states of mind as in this book she achieves. Her very use of words is different — apter and more relevant — than that displayed in her novels; the reason being, of course, that in recording conversations she was getting as near as is possible in a printed book to actual talk. And at talk she excelled, a matter which P. G. Patmore puts beyond doubt. He declares that these recollections of Byron are as much superior to all her other works as they are themselves inferior to her own spoken words:

> The printed "Conversations" *with* Byron [he says], characteristic as they are both of him and herself, are flat and spiritless — or rather marrowless — compared with Lady Blessington's own *viva voce* conversations of him, one half hour of which contained more pith and substance than the whole octavo volume. Talking not writing was Lady Blessington's forte. After reading any one of her books (except the "Conversations") you could not help wondering at the reputation she enjoyed as the companion of the most accomplished and brilliant writers, statesmen and celebrities of the day. But the first half hour of her talk solved the mystery at once.

A reading of the "Conversations", therefore, helps to convince us that the *intelligence* of Lady Blessington, which has otherwise survived more in rumour than in evidence, was a genuine intelligence. Then if, in addition to shrewdness and good sense, one can imagine serene vivacity of manner and charm both of voice and of expression, one is within reach of understanding the fascination she exercised over those who were her friends.

3

The period of Byron's intimacy with Lady Blessington naturally brought him as frequently into contact with the Earl and with d'Orsay as with the lady herself. To Blessington he paid a striking tribute, which is duly recorded in the "Conversations":

"I never saw the milk of human kindness overflow in any nature to so great a degree as in Lord Blessington's," he said one day. "I used, before I knew him, to think that Shelley was the most amiable person I ever knew, but now I think Lord Blessington bears off the palm. . . . I do assure you I have thought better of mankind since I have known him intimately."

As for d'Orsay, he was soon on terms of the gayest familiarity with the poet. Letters from Byron to Lord Blessington show that the latter, on the second day of their stay in Genoa, asked Byron if he would be willing to read d'Orsay's journal of his recent sojourn in England. The manuscript was lent and returned to the Earl in three days with the following letter:

April 5, 1823

I return the Count d'Orsay's Journal, which is a very extraordinary production and of a most melancholy truth in all that regards high life in England. I know, or knew, personally, most of the personages and societies which he describes; and after reading his remarks, have the sensation fresh upon me as if I had seen them yesterday. . . . The most singular thing is *how* he should have penetrated *not* the *fact* but the *mystery* of English ennui at two and twenty. I was about the same age when I made the same discovery in almost precisely the same circles — but I never could have described it so well. *Il faut être français* to effect this.

But he ought also to have been in the country during the hunting season, with a select party of distinguished guests, as the papers term it. He ought to have seen the gentlemen after dinner (on hunting days) and the soirée ensuing therefrom — and the women looking as if they had hunted, or rather been hunted . . . and I could have wished that he had been at a dinner in town which I recollect at Lord Cowper's — small, but select and composed of the most amusing people. The dessert was hardly on the table, when, out of twelve, I counted five asleep. . . .

Altogether your friend's journal is a very formidable production. Alas! our dearly beloved countrymen have only discovered that they are tired, and not that they are tiresome. . . . I have read the whole with great attention and instruction.

The writer of the journal was so delighted with this august approbation that he immediately offered to present the entire manuscript to Byron, who replied (still to Blessington):

April 6

I have received a very flattering note from Count d'Orsay . . . I would not on any account deprive him of a production of which I really think more than I have even said . . . but whenever it is completed, it would give me the greatest pleasure to have a copy. . . . By changing the names, or at least omitting several, and altering the circumstances indicative of the writer's real situation, the author would render it a most amusing publication. His countrymen have not been treated with such deference in English recent works as to lay him under any great national obligation of forbearance; and really the remarks are so true and piquant, that I cannot bring myself to wish them suppression. . . .

I beg my compliments to Lady B., Miss P. and your Alfred. I think since his Majesty of the same name there has not been such a learned surveyor of our society.

From this beginning the friendship of poet and paragon proceeded apace and happily. Alfred was continually at the Casa Saluzzo; he drew Byron's portrait and that of the Guiccioli's brother; he gossiped enchantingly of the dull formality of social England, using his talent for highly malicious satire to feed the phobia of the exiled poet.

What actually became of d'Orsay's journal is not certainly known. It is said that he himself destroyed it, lest it give pain to many whom in the meantime he had come to view, if not more affectionately, at any rate with a greater appreciation of their qualities. But from the reflection of its mischievous brillance in the mirror of Byron's appreciative mind, we can guess what d'Orsay's journal was like, and continue to hope that somewhere it survives.

The daily occupations of the Blessington party while at Genoa are sufficiently recorded in the Countess' books to make detailed repetition unnecessary. Riding, sight-seeing, water parties, the opera, evenings of literary talk, occasional visits from English residents or from naval men for whom Genoa was a port of call, frequent excursions and continual conversations with Byron — these stand out as the special events of a life of tranquil idleness. How long, if Byron had not already begun his preparations to go to Greece, the lady would have been content to remain in Genoa, cannot be known; but it is doubtful whether in any event she would have lingered. Her decision to stay on at an inn rather than set up a private establishment suggests that she wished to be free to move on when time seemed ripe. She resisted Byron's suggestion (expressed in a few foolish lines of verse) that they should buy or rent a derelict villa called "Il Paradiso" and settle as his neighbours; but fell in more readily with the idea (also probably Byron's, who needed funds for his journey) that the Earl should purchase the *Bolivar,* which had been laid up in the harbour by Trelawney and there remained. An arbitrator fixed the price; whereupon Byron asked more and got it. The Countess was greatly taken with the yacht's marble baths and velvet couches, but is careful to note in her diary that the poet "has written much on board this vessel, which gives it its chief value, in my eyes at least." She also remarks that Byron "is certainly fond of money"; and narrates a little tartly that when, in response to urgent entreaty, she consented to sell him her horse Mameluke, he tried to beat her down from a hundred guineas to eighty pounds. "How strange," she observes, "to beg and entreat to have the horse resigned to him and then name a price less than he cost."

The last meeting between the poet and the Countess' party occurred on June 2. Byron wept and distributed a number of souvenirs which he had brought with him in little parcels. The Earl got a book, d'Orsay a print of Bartolini's bust of Byron, and Lady Blessington his Armenian grammar with autograph annotations. The last rather bleak memento is not specified in her journal, where it is suavely disguised as a *gage-d'amitié*. The poet followed his lavish distribution of gifts with a request for some personal trinket of the countess' own. She took a ring from her finger and gave it to him. By now the emotional atmosphere was sufficiently charged to sweep even Byron's prudence away. He took a pin from his stock and begged her to accept it. Next morning she received a note, asking for the pin back and sending a chain in its place. With the chain came a ring for d'Orsay. "It is formed of lava," said Byron, "and so far adapted to the fire of his years and character." The compliment was none the less apt for being double-edged.

4

News of Blessington during these idle but crowded weeks in Genoa is very scanty. Doubtless, having introduced his wife and his friend to Byron, he hustled about, playing now host, now equerry, to all of them; he also seems to have tried his hand at a little writing (early in May Byron wrote to d'Orsay that he was "deep in Milor's manuscript and would do him justice by a diligent perusal") and probably at this period was conceived his historical romance "De Vavasour", which came into the world some three years later and without the smallest éclat. But under the genial and rather silly mask which was his ordinary wear, he had a mind and, one presumes, a spirit capable of satisfaction or despair. How did he see himself in relation to those whose lives he had now bound up so closely with his own? To what future, if to any, did he look for all of them?

One would suppose, if ever at all Blessington looked private facts in the face, that he did so at Genoa. Only four days after his arrival there, he received news from home than which none could have been more personally shattering or more grievous. His only legitimate son by his first wife, Luke Wellington Gardiner, Viscount Mountjoy, had died a week earlier in his tenth year. Charity and reason alike suggest that by these sad tidings he was, for a while at least, stricken to the depths of his vacuous but amiable soul. In this moment of bitterness, surely even Blessington must have looked inward on himself and on the futile record of his life. There was no longer an heir either to title or estates; the prospect of another from such a marriage as he had now made must have been negligible, if indeed it had ever existed. Not the gracious loveliness of his wife, or the ready sympathy of Byron, or the luxury of their surroundings, or the sunshine aglitter on the sea, can have lightened for the wretched man the blackness of a sudden misery, or have prevented the awful realisation that he at least was one whose name was writ in water.

Unluckily no mood of Blessington's, even a mood of gravity, could last for long; and it is to be feared that his recovery of heedless good spirits had a tainted source. Where the Countess and Byron and the pleasant idleness of Genoa had failed to comfort him, d'Orsay succeeded. The fascination of the young man's beauty, which had earlier exercised a half-playful domination over the weak-minded Earl, now (one can only conclude) had utterly enslaved him. Perhaps Alfred saw his chance and took it; perhaps Blessington, in the grip of his crazy infatuation, carried the youth by storm. Whosesoever the initiative and the fault, matter moved swiftly to an ignoble end. On the morning of June 2, just as the party was leaving Genoa and not three months after Mountjoy's death, Blessington added to his will a codicil so extraordinary as to merit verbatim reproduction.

CODICIL

Genoa, June 2nd, 1823

Having had the misfortune to lose my beloved son, Luke Wellington, and having entered into engagements with Alfred, Comte d'Orsay, that an alliance should take place between him and my daughter, which engagement has been sanctioned by Albert, Comte d'Orsay, General, etc. in the service of France, this is to declare and publish my desire to leave to the said Alfred d'Orsay my estates in the city and county of Dublin (subject, however, to the annuity of three thousand per annum, which sum is to include the settlement of one thousand per annum to my wife, Margaret, Countess of Blessington, subject also to that portion of debt, whether by annuity or mortgage, to which my executor and trustee, Luke Norman, shall consider them to be subjected), for his and her use, whether it be Mary (baptised Emily) Rosalie Hamilton, or Harriet Ann Jane Frances, and to their heirs, male, [or to] the said Alfred and said Mary, or Harriet, for ever in default of issue male, to follow the provisions of the will and testament.

I make also the said Alfred d'Orsay sole guardian of my son Charles John, and my sister, Harriet Gardiner, guardian of my daughters, until they, the daughters, arrive at the age of sixteen, at which age I consider that they will be marriageable.

I also bequeath to Luke Norman my estates in the county of Tyrone, etc., in trust for my son, Charles John, who I desire to take the name of Stewart Gardiner, until he shall arrive at the age of twenty-five, allowing for his education such sums as Alfred d'Orsay may think necessary, and one thousand per annum from twenty-one to twenty-five.

Done at Genoa, life being uncertain, at eight o'clock on the morning of Monday, June the second, one thousand eight hundred and twenty-three.

BLESSINGTON [2]

Of the children mentioned in this document, Emily Rosalie and Charles John were born of Lord Blessington's first wife while she was still Mrs. Browne, and were therefore bastards. Harriet, one year older than the boy who had just died, was born of the same lady, but in wedlock. She was therefore the Earl's only surviving legitimate child. By the codicil Alfred d'Orsay became principal legatee (for the Dublin property, even with Lady Blessington's annual three thousand pounds deducted from

[2] This text has perforce been transcribed from Madden's book, as the original codicil cannot be traced. It is therefore impossible to say whether the contradictions between it and the will made later in the same year are due to Blessington's drafting or to Madden's inaccuracy.

it, outvalued Mountjoy Forest by about five to one), guardian of the surviving boy, and was offered his choice in marriage of the two girls, neither of whom he had ever seen, and who at this date were respectively twelve and eleven years old.

So far-reaching were to be the effects on the lives of three of the persons concerned of this precipitate and rather shocking codicil that its origins cannot, as hitherto, be merely taken for granted.

The facile interpretation is that Lady Blessington and d'Orsay originated the idea and pressed it on Blessington until he yielded. This theory, however, will not bear examination. D'Orsay, certainly, was later to show himself capable of an extreme meanness when driven into a corner and momentarily desperate; but for such long-distance plotting as this he never betrayed either the instinct or the inclination. He was naturally a lily of the field — sweet, elegant and volatile; and at this early stage of his career would have looked forward with smiling confidence to many years of indolent delight.

That Lady Blessington was responsible for a scheme at once ruthless and inefficient is still harder to believe. Even if we assume her capable of conspiring with a lover to secure a husband's fortune, it is out of character for her to have coöperated in anything so crude. Further, had she been able to persuade her husband to so sudden and drastic an alteration of his will, she would have devised not only more subtle but, from her own point of view, more profitable means of gaining her end. The codicil was queerly restrained in its provision for her personal fortune; and when three months later Blessington visited England and signed a completely new will on the lines of the codicil, her annual jointure was actually reduced from three thousand pounds to two.[3]

Least credible of all is it that Blessington could be tricked,

[3] Lord Blessington's will is printed verbatim as Appendix II. It is a vital document, since without a knowledge of its provisions, many subsequent events are unintelligible.

flattered or bullied into so bizarre a disposal of his property. He was by no means a doting simpleton; and though he delighted to waste money on those he loved, he never showed any sign of permitting them to waste it without his collaboration. Wherefore it seems almost certain that the codicil was of Blessington's independent devising, that his wife had no part in it save the acceptance of an accomplished fact, and that what really happened was this: —

The Earl was infatuated with d'Orsay and wished to do something for him. He realised that unless the young man were provided for, he would be compelled to look elsewhere for livelihood, and the prospect of losing his company was intolerable. But behind his fondness for d'Orsay lay a strong sense of family and a determination that, even though his heir were dead, his descendants should ultimately possess his wealth. What more likely than that he saw in an arranged marriage between Alfred and one of his daughters an ingenious means of rewarding his favourite and at the same time of securing to his children or their children the reversion of his property? Whether or no he was aware of d'Orsay's disability is immaterial. If, as one would expect, he knew of it, the planning of the codicil would achieve its end without offending any one; if he did not, it could be taken literally and still work out as he desired.

Finally it should be remembered that, to the cosmopolitan and unemotional minds of Blessington and his wife, there was nothing amiss *per se* with a marriage of convenience. Into the bargain, and by the standards of the time, the arrangement would be very advantageous to the girl d'Orsay ultimately chose. She would enjoy a fortune and get for husband the most charming young man known to her father and stepmother. What better could a young woman ask than to find her future thus brilliantly and considerately planned?

In those circumstances it seems the fairest assumption that the Genoa codicil was planned by Blessington, welcomed by d'Orsay, and dutifully accepted by Lady Blessington, whose only share in the whole affair was a stipulation that the child bride be left alone for the first four years of her married life.

Unfortunately she made one inevitable, though as matters turned out, disastrous miscalculation. She failed to foresee that scandal would so irrevocably link her name with d'Orsay's that when, in a few years' time, he actually became the husband of Lord Blessington's daughter, the world would assume them guilty of a stratagem of a peculiarly ugly kind. Even her plea that the girl enjoy four years of immunity from sex-experience was turned to her discredit and humane consideration taken by gossip for jealousy.

Thus the tragedy of little Mountjoy's death was not a tragedy for Blessington alone. Like many another incident in the tale of this doomed household, its evil influence spread to each member in turn and left its stain. If Mountjoy had not died, d'Orsay would not have contracted his *pastiche* marriage with Harriet Gardiner; if d'Orsay had not married Harriet Gardiner, half the scandal which later went the round of London, and much of the bitter enmity felt and expressed by the stepmother and sister of Lord Blessington toward his widow would have been stilled; most important of all, the life of Lady Blessington, both materially and spiritually, would have been easier and more serene. She notes in her journal that a presentiment of evil seized her, when she saw riding into the inn yard the courier who brought the news. It was a truer presentiment even than she knew.

CHAPTER III

IDLERS IN ITALY

1

ONCE the party had taken the road again and were moving southward, the Countess' diary reverts to its normal tact and sweetness. Her interlude as companion and comforter to genius was over, and she was once again the titled gossip under contract to a Woman's Page. Clothes, local customs, a little sightseeing, filled the pages of her notebooks. At Lucca, on June 6, she records "the celerity with which *Le Petit Courrier des Dames* voyages, and enables the female aristocracy of Lucca who cannot visit that emporium of fashion, Paris, to look somewhat like its fair denizens" — but three months out of date. "Seeing the fireflies flitting about the garden in myriads, my *femme de chambre*, true to the instinct of her *métier*, observed that it looked like a dark robe covered with spangles." At Carrara, the mass production of busts of Wellington warms the diarist's patriotic heart. "Long, long may England," she exclaims, "preserve the original, and glory in his achievements!"

On June 8 they came to Florence, where they remained for three weeks. The British minister to the Florentine court was Lord Burghersh (later Earl of Westmoreland) and the one perfunctory reference to him in Lady Blessington's record of this her first Florentine sojourn indicates (as we know from other sources to have been the case) that she was definitely unwelcome to society under his ministerial régime. Lady Burghersh was a woman of severe social principle, who later contrived to copy out portions of Byron's memoirs and then, curiosity satisfied, to destroy her copy with much public indignation. Virtue so ingenious and so inquisitive could be trusted to detect an equivocal Mrs. Farmer behind the legitimate splendours of Lord Blessington's wife.

On this occasion Lady Blessington's Florentine notes are brief, and more definitely than usual those of a mere tourist, to whom monuments rather than personalities are the main objectives. She sight-sees and wanders through the streets. Her taste in art leans more than ever toward florid sentiment. Michael Angelo's "Holy Family" she finds "hard and laboured in the colouring", but Raphael, Correggio and Guercino enchant her with "their simple innocence, their natural grace, their charm." With true journalistic flair, she treats the nude both with emphasis and with gentility. The Medici Venus has a modesty which "precludes the feeling of embarrassment with which women contemplate a nude statue in the presence of men." Not so, however, the celebrated Venus by Titian, which "breathes an atmosphere of sensuality." "The Venus de Medici," she concludes, "must always charm women; the Venus of Titian men."

From Florence to Rome, via Siena, Radicofani and Orvieto, was a journey of five days. The travellers' first sight of the Eternal City is recorded with suitable emotion, but they only stayed a week and the Countess' experiences are summarily told. She implies that the season was too late for Rome and speaks of the oppressive heat and "evil prophecies dinned into my ears of the malaria." Nevertheless, there is reason to think that the discomfort of the Roman hotel had something to do with her impatience. "All the appliances to comfort, or rather to luxury," says Madden, "which had become necessary to Lady Blessington, had not been found in Rome. Her ladyship had become exceedingly fastidious in her tastes." So once again they packed into their train of carriages and proceeded across the desolate marshes to Terracina. On July 17 they rumbled into Naples, where for no less than two years and a half Lady Blessington was to remain.

Her husband, on the other hand, had hardly got his party to their destination and arranged to establish his wife in a magnificent palace at Vomero, belonging to Prince Belvedere, before he was off again to London, arriving at the end of July. He had political business in the matter of Catholic Emancipation, but his journey seems to have been prompted as much by a sudden revival of interest in plans for developing Mountjoy Forest as by public duty. Also he desired, by making a new will, to implement the codicil devised at Genoa.

The shadow of his heir's death had wholly passed away. In the excitement of the journey through Italy; in the amusement of authorising purchases in Naples of upholstered sofas and chairs, carpets, curtains, beds, plate, glass and goodness knows what, in order to make habitable a palazzo already fully furnished; in the delicious company of Alfred d'Orsay — the Earl's fitful intelligence had been first soothed, then stimulated to new schemes for crazy innovation. He passed through London rapidly and early in August was at Mountjoy.

On his way across town he called on his old friend, Charles Mathews, the actor. Mathews' son, then a boy of twenty, had just completed four years as articled pupil to the Gothic-revivalist architect Pugin, and, in the expectation of a place in the office of the great Nash, was temporarily at home. He had designed a picture gallery and a small library in the Gothic manner for his father, and by chance Lord Blessington caught sight of these and other drawings and liked them. On the spur of the moment, once arrived in Ireland, he decided to give the lad the chance of acting as architect at Mountjoy, and wrote to the father to send him posthaste to Omagh. Within a week of their first meeting, the pair of them were utterly absorbed in plans of visionary splendour.

Young Mathews may well say in his autobiography that "for a couple of months I led a charmed life." The experience indeed had all the qualities of fantasy. A boy just out of school, his head full of wonder-buildings and with a large share of hereditary delight in playing a part and sensing the fancies of an audience, found himself alone with a reputed Midas of uncontrolled enthusiasms, who asked nothing better from his sudden protégé than that scheme should outbid scheme and costs be piled on costs. Young Mathews was shrewd enough to realise that Blessington fancied his own talents as an architect and looked to his new companion for encouragement, plus a little technical knowledge, rather than for criticism or instruction. It appears that Benjamin Wyatt, son of the designer of Fonthill and Ashridge and himself responsible for the rebuilding of Drury Lane Theatre, had already provided the Earl with plans for an outsize castle; but having made the mistake of standing on his architect's dignity and of refusing to consider his client's emendations, he had been paid his preliminary fee and not again disturbed. Mathews made no such blunder. With an exuberance equal to that of his employer, he planned and planned again. They ran hither and thither through the woods and fields of Mountjoy, choosing first one site and then another.

At last the place was chosen. Labourers were set to cut the turf; the future mansion lay in outline before the Earl's excited eyes. Mathews next asked for piles of stones six feet high, wherever in the outer walls a window was to be made. It was essential to judge the view as it would be seen from every ground-floor room. The piles were raised. Gravely, and enjoying every minute of the experiment, the young architect scrambled precariously to the top of one pile after another. Alas! from one side of the house it was impossible to get a desired glimpse of a stone bridge spanning the river, while on the other side the prospect was seriously damaged by a considerable hill. He reported these misfortunes to his employer, who gave immediate instructions for the course of the river to be diverted and the hill to be removed. At the same time an unwanted wood was cut down and the slopes of "a large bare mountain very disagreeable to have always staring us in the face" were planted with a hundred and fifty thousand larches specially brought from a nursery garden.

By the end of August, Blessington felt that he was ready to submit his plans for castle building to his wife. He therefore proposed an immediate return to Naples and to take young Mathews with him. The boy's parents joyfully consented, and on September 21, in the Earl's carriage and four, the pair drove out of St. James's Square for Dover and Italy.

It is amusing, through the eyes of Charles Mathews, to watch Lord Blessington travelling across Europe and to wonder whether, under the determined gaze of his highly cultivated wife, he pretended a zeal for galleries and monuments which he certainly did not possess. "Lord Blessington was not a walker," says Mathews; "was a hater of sight-seeing and moreover a late riser, breakfasting in bed and reading his book or newspaper there till late in the day. So we saw little of him except when travelling or at mealtime." Fortunately for the young man's natural curiosity, Colonel Sir Charles Sutton, a soldier who had served with distinction in the Portuguese Army, was also of the party; and he good-naturedly visited galleries, churches and ancient buildings in Mathews' company. At Geneva, on September 30, they met by chance Lady Blessington's younger sister Ellen, at this time Mrs. Home Purves, with her five children. In their company was the Rt. Hon. Charles Manners Sutton, Speaker of the House of Commons, a relative of Blessington's soldier friend and a widower. He also was accompanied by his children and attendant governesses.

About 1810 Ellen Power had married John Home Purves, a Scot of good family; but for reasons as to which contemporary authority observes a rather pathetic discretion, had parted from him forever in this very year 1823. One might assume that Manners Sutton had met the beautiful Mrs. Purves at the moment of a distressful collapse of her married life and, partly out of courtesy, partly out of pity, was escorting her to some foreign destination of her own. But inasmuch as when

Blessington, in his impulsive way, pressed the whole party to return with him to Naples and there remain indefinitely, they immediately agreed to join forces, their companionship would appear to have been both leisured and purposeful. The obvious explanation is, of course, that Manners Sutton had run away with Purves' wife and that both had already found the happiness which was to last their lifetime. They were formally married five years later (Purves died in Florida during 1827) and lived in great contentment until 1845, first as Mr. and Mrs. Manners Sutton, later as Lord and Lady Canterbury.

The Blessington cortège now consisted of four heavy travelling carriages, one of them a crowded nursery, and its movements from place to place produced something of the scurry which marked the progress of the original Circus. The party had lingered a whole month in Geneva, but made the journey from there to Milan in three days. Here Mrs. Purves and her friend decided after all to part company with Lord Blessington. He expressed lively regret and, so ingrained was his habit of easy generosity, begged that if and when they returned to London, they would use his home in St. James's Square as though it were their own. The offer was not forgotten, and Mrs. Purves, at any rate, was to live there in comfort for nearly two years.

Leaving his sister-in-law in Milan, Lord Blessington, after buying a new carriage, crossed the mountains to Genoa, whence in defiance of bad weather and floods he pressed on toward Spezia. But at a miserable little town called Borghetto a river in spate was frankly impassable. The Earl and his friends must await the falling of the flood.

"The wretched hut called inn," says Mathews, "was almost without furniture and wholly without sashes to the windows. Four bare walls formed our sitting room, but without any fastening to the door, so that we were constantly intruded upon by any stray pigs that chanced to be passing by. The bedroom was about ten feet square and contained three beds. This we gave up to Milord, bringing two of the beds into the *salle-à-manger,* which, in the end, turned out the more comfortable room of the two, for unluckily the public staircase, leading to the kitchen above us, was exactly over Lord Blessington's bed, and the tramp was uniformly kept up the whole night, so that he never was allowed to slumber for a moment."

"I shall never forget," he goes on, "the appearance of his room. It was the acme of misery, and yet with a comic side to it. A small truck-bed in a little alcove at the farther end, over which was the staircase, whose creaking boards completely banished sleep; Lord Blessington, in a large flannel night-cap, with a travelling-shawl over his shoulders, sitting up in bed, with his books and drawings strewed around him, his breakfast by his side, served in the silver accessories of his travelling kit; a poor little rickety table, set out with all the profusion of costly plate and cut-glass bottles of his emptied dressing-case, with brocaded dressing-gowns on the broken-backed chairs, and imperials piled on imperials, almost reaching the ceiling, and actually filling the room. It was a splendid subject for a picture."

We must be grateful to young Mathews for this tale of travellers' misfortune, which is among the most attractive of the few surviving anecdotes of Blessington for his own sake. The miserable but humorous figure, propped against pillows and surrounded by the extremes of opulence and squalor, is much more nearly a credible Blessington than any other which history has troubled to record. Away from the gracious despotism of his wife, he became once more the happy-go-lucky bohemian who in earlier days had been the boon companion of actors and actresses, who now, rather like a schoolboy on the loose, welcomed discomfort for the fun of laughing back at it when it was over.

Even Mathews' later reminiscences of his fairy godfather have not quite the buoyancy of this particular memory; for once they reached Naples and the Earl became again the fortunate husband of a brilliant wife, the focus alters and we are asked to smile indulgently at Blessington rather than to like him.

The travellers arrived at the Palazzo Belvedere late in November. "The house," says Mathews, "was the perfection of an Italian palace, with its exquisite frescoes, marble arcades, and succession of terraces one beneath the other, adorned with hanging groves of orange trees and pomegranates."

The Countess gives her own description:

"The Palazzo forms three sides of a square, the fourth being an arcade, that connects one portion of the building with the other. There is a courtyard and fountain in the centre. The windows of the principal salons open on a garden, formed on an elevated terrace, surrounded on three sides by a marble balustrade and inclosed on the fourth by a long gallery, filled with pictures, statues and alti and bassi relievi. On the top of this gallery is a terrace, at the extreme end of which is a pavilion with open arcades and paved with marble. This portion commands a most enchanting prospect of the bay."

The house's internal splendour would have alarmed any but an intrepid amateur of luxury. Lady Blessington is undismayed:

"The walls of all the rooms are literally covered with pictures: the architraves of the doors of the principal rooms are of Oriental alabaster and the rarest marbles; the tables and consoles are composed of the same costly materials. Besides five *salons de reception* on the principal floor, the palace contains a richly decorated chapel and sacristy, a large *salle de billard* and several suites of bed and dressing rooms. An abundance of the finest and rarest porcelain vases, rock crystal, malachite and agate ornaments are piled on the marble tables and consoles; and now that curtains, carpets, and other adjuncts to comfort are beginning to be placed, the palazzo is assuming an aspect of English elegance joined to Italian grandeur, that renders it a delightful residence."

Fortunately there was no servant problem. Neapolitans were engaged and so far as possible disguised as London footmen. Their obstinate habit of wearing earrings was graciously condoned. The Countess was pleased to discover that her chef would contract to supply so many meals per day at so much a head. At the end of the week a bill was presented, checked by the major-domo and handed to Lord Blessington's banker for settlement. The quality, in fact, had nothing whatsoever to do except amuse themselves and either to improve their minds or gratify their senses.

With such possibilities, the party's method of enjoying their fabulous paradise was remarkable for its pleasant gaiety and good breeding. They were a queerly assorted community, and the deportment of wealthy Anglo-Saxons settled abroad is often the more unrestrained for its freedom from national disapprobation. But Lady Blessington was genuine in her liking for a suave and civilised existence; and it cannot be denied, save by those who are enemies on principle to riches and lotus-eating, that under her skilful sway life at the Belvedere palace, for all its lavishment, was both urbane and intelligent. Each member of the household was at his or her best in the surroundings provided by the Earl's exuberant generosity. All were good friends, and most tastes and interests were held in common.

"Lady Blessington," says Mathews, "then in her zenith, formed the centre figure of the little group. Count d'Orsay was the model of all that could be conceived of noble demeanour and youthful candour, with a gaiety of heart and cheerfulness of mind that spread happiness on all around him. . . . Miss Power, Lady Blessington's youngest sister, was somewhat demure in aspect, of quiet and retiring manners. Lady Blessington has been described as a peach-blossom, and Miss Power as a primrose by her side."

The young architect was made immediately and easily welcome; for the Countess, then and always, had a real genius for putting visitors at their ease. He slipped forthwith into the daily life of his hosts.

"In one corner of the large saloon stood Lady Blessington's table, laden with books and writings; Count d'Orsay's in another, equally adorned with literary and artistic litter, Miss Power's and mine completed the arrangement, while Lord Blessington strolled and chatted from one to the other, and then dived into his own sanctum, where he divided his time between fresh architectural schemes for his castle in the air and the novel of 'De Vavasour', on which he was busily engaged."

The days passed in reading, writing, drawing, charades and friendly chaff. For exercise, the menfolk rode horseback, walked, swam and fenced. Lady Blessington was no athlete and was content to control the time-table of the establishment. She took exactly one and a half hours to dress in the morning, and the moment of her appearance was the moment of déjeuner. Inasmuch as the time of her waking was announced to the household, every one knew where he was, and comfort and punctuality were automatically secured. After the meal, some or all of the party would visit galleries or ruins or points of view; if the weather were bad, they would settle to their books, letters or diaries; or try impromptu acting; or play billiards. Dinner was as frequently without guests as with them, and quiet evenings of talk and cards brought them to midnight and bed.

At meals the Countess took the head of the table with her husband on her left, d'Orsay on her right and Mathews and Miss Power opposite. The food was elegant but moderate in quantity. The men were all of them sparing with their wine. Indeed, excess of any kind was wholly out of harmony with the tone of the household. Lady Blessington, within a few weeks of having settled in Naples, had created the particular social atmosphere which, until the end of her life, was to remain her speciality and her distinction.

Even the practical joking (in an age when this form of humour took an extreme and often brutal form) was always friendly and considerate. To amuse Miss Power, who had a bad illness and a long convalescence, Mathews dressed up as the doctor and paid solemn visits to her bedside. Afterward he came downstairs and continued to parody the genuine practitioner to the great mystification of casual visitors. He would also concoct with d'Orsay imitations of well-known people, and one or the other of the young men would appear at meals or on the terrace in the most unexpected rôles, to the delight of Lord and Lady Blessington and the astonishment of their guests. Among themselves, jokes were continuous. When it became known that Lord Blessington always cut his own hair with scissors, it was decreed that the ceremony should regularly be carried out before a solemnly attentive family audience. Sometimes notice was suddenly given that dinner would be taken in fancy dress, and there was a general scurry for impromptu costumes. Mathews described one such occasion to his mother:

"Lady Blessington was dressed as an old lady in an embroidered silk gown, a cap, and a quantity of curls in front powdered. You never saw such a darling as she was altogether. Miss Power was dressed in a pair of my white trousers, buff waistcoat and blue frock coat, with beard, mustachios, eyebrows made with cork, as a young Spanish gentleman. I was disguised as a nice old doctor, bald and powdered, with white silk stockings and large buckles."

Exception rather than rule, during these months of tranquil pleasure, were prolonged excursions to places of interest or evenings of thronged salons, when resident and visiting notabilities came to enjoy the good company and comfort of the Belvedere palace. Naturally these occasions are fully recorded in the Countess' journal, while the daily round is virtually undescribed. In consequence, an impression is given of ceaseless entertaining, which not only distorts this actual Neapolitan reality but has helped to create in the minds of posterity an idea that Lady

Blessington had no resources within herself, and was throughout her life a dazzling hostess but nothing more. The impression is mistaken. Her years in Hampshire had taught her both to improve her hours of solitude and to enjoy them; and never afterward — whether in Italy or in London — did she live habitually in a crowd, or for the sake of social occasions. This being so, it is easy to realise that the traditional isolation of her later London period has come to be overstressed. She was happiest with one or two congenial companions, each of whom had some intelligent interest to pursue; with whom, over meals or after dinner, she could discuss the mental adventures of the day. As society was then constituted, she found this selective and instructed companionship more easily among men than women. Gossip bored her, and her sense of the proprieties was decades ahead of that of other ladies of position. Therefore, deliberately she formed her own circle in her own home, and found many compensations for being always a hostess and seldom a guest.

Of course, it is undeniable that up to a point she came to make a virtue of necessity. She would bluntly have been refused access to many of the more censorious London houses and was not so foolish as to expose herself to deliberate rebuff. But there were undoubtedly women of fashion and rank who would have visited her and made her welcome, had she sought their company. That she did not, that she was genuinely indifferent to the conventional amusements of society, was largely due to the agreeable seclusion of her prolonged sojourn in Naples.

Only once, during the whole thirty months of this sojourn, did serious disagreement cloud the serenity of her circle. Down below the palace, in the harbour, lay the yacht *Bolivar*, under the command of a solemn cockney braggart, called by courtesy "Captain" Smith, whose tales of his own prowess in every clime and grumbling nostalgia for the cosy bar-parlours of the Old Kent Road were among the favourite jokes of his employer's party. Blessington, always an extremist, was so persistent in his plans for sailing that he became a bore. He was, however, far too dependent on companionship to like going out alone, so a compromise had to be arranged. For a while, the others took it in turn to humour him, but when Doctor Madden (the future biographer of Lady Blessington) came to stay in Naples and showed (or rashly pretended) that he really enjoyed spending hours on the sea with the yacht-crazy Earl, they gladly surrendered all claim to rivalry. One day, however, Madden was not available. The heat was terrific, and Blessington's suggestion of a trip to Castellamare was received unfavourably. The Countess and Miss Power said it was too hot. D'Orsay bluntly refused to risk the ennui of being becalmed for several hours and have to listen to the captain's trumpetings. Mathews declared he had a sketch he particularly wished to make. The excuse was injudicious, for Blessington's vexation was rising with the temperature. He snapped back that he hoped for once Mathews would really do his drawing, for according to d'Orsay, he always carried a sketch-book about and never put anything in it.

From this trifling retort developed a portentous quarrel between Mathews and d'Orsay, with talk of a duel and letters from seconds and severe reproofs to every one concerned from the outraged Lady Blessington, in whose presence the young men had so far forgotten themselves as to exchange high words. Eventually, after four days of tension, the silly storm was stilled by Blessington himself, who was not only the first to recover his temper but the only one to see the absurdity of the whole affair. His letter to Mathews, who had retired with great dignity into the city and put himself in the hands of Madden, is at once sensible and pathetic. At last the two youths met, shook hands, embraced and all was well. But Lady Blessington had the last word. After the reconciliation, she took d'Orsay to task so severely for his part in the contretemps that he burst into tears. Thus ended what Madden describes as "an occurrence of an unpleasant nature, which was attended with some grave results."

In May, 1824, about a month after it had occurred, the death of Byron at Missolonghi became known at the Belvedere palace. The party had just returned from a fortnight's excursion to Salerno, Pæstum, Beneventum and Vesuvius, accompanied by the renowned but ludicrous archæologist, Sir William Gell, who had already — and with magnificent pomposity — acted the learned cicerone when Lady Blessington visited Pompeii.

All were grief-stricken at the news. "I can hardly bring myself to think," wrote the Countess in her journal, "that Byron is indeed gone for ever. A thousand circumstances, trifling in themselves but associated with our *séjour* at Genoa and constant intercourse with him, are recurring to memory. We have been recalling every word, every look of his during our last interview. I have been reading over the notes of his conversations with me and could almost fancy I heard his lips utter the words."

Throughout the summer this melancholy sense of personal loss persisted. In October, a disagreement with the owner caused Lord Blessington to leave the Belvedere palace for the Villa Gallo at Capo di Monte. The new house was less splendid than the old; but although the Countess regretted her large and lofty rooms, she admitted that one winter at Vomero had been enough, and that something more easily warmed and in stouter repair was sensible preparation for the next.

The change of residence involved no change in the party's way of life. The same cheerful intimacies, the same modest but steady stream of visitors, the same quiet pursuit of art, literature and exercise, continued at the Villa Gallo as at the Belvedere palace.

In December, 1824, young Mathews returned home. His parents and his career had need of him, and only the gushing fondness which Mrs. Mathews at that time expressed for Lady Blessington (she played turncoat later) had reconciled the former to their son's prolonged absence abroad. Even the pretence of professional activity had vanished for the young architect. The plans for Mountjoy had been shelved, if nothing worse; and the Countess, who had now even less intention of returning to Ireland than before, had temporarily turned her husband's mind to other things. So back to London Mathews came, pursued by affectionate and amusing letters from d'Orsay, which show that the mischievous humour — half-nonsense, half-raillery — of the Blessington group was as "modern", as far in advance of its time, as were their social ideas of pleasurable existence.

While Mathews was thus kept in mind of his lotus-eating friends in Italy, he was spending his leisure hours in St. James's Square, developing a pleasant amourette with Louisa, the beautiful fifteen-year-old daughter of Mrs. Home Purves. Charles and Louisa drifted happily through a period of youthful romance, reading Italian, drawing, learning music and sitting hand in hand at the play or on the splendid sofas of Lord Blessington's London house. But very soon after the young girl "came out", the sweet illusion faded. Some say her mother forbade her to see more of Mathews or to think of him with love. In any event, she married a man called Fairlie, while still well in her teens. Louisa Fairlie was to have more than her share of struggle and unhappiness, but all who knew her spoke of her gentleness and courage.

Meantime at Naples the months were slipping by. Blessington began to get restless and even urged a return to London. But the others were too happy in their tranquil and luxurious exile, and finally in August, 1825, the Earl once again journeyed home alone. We read of him in Moore's journal, entertaining the poet at dinner on August 9 and 13, and introducing him to Alfred's father, General d'Orsay, and to the latter's aide-de-camp, a gentleman whom Moore found dull. On both occasions the Speaker was of the party. Presumably dinner at St. James's Square had been a habit of his for long enough.

Blessington was not long before starting for Ireland, and wrote to Mathews to say he would travel through Wales in company with his surviving son, Charles Gardiner, and his two French friends. The young architect hurried to meet them at Holyhead. At the inn in the early morning, having been directed to Blessington's room and told that the Earl was to be called at 4 A.M., he decided to impersonate the servant. Singing loudly, he burst into the room at the appointed hour, to find a perfect stranger gazing at him in sleepy alarm. It was the elder d'Orsay. Mathews stammered his excuses.

"Oh!" said the General, "I made sure you were a Frenchman, by your gaiety," and insisted on the calling process being repeated in the right room.

"By jove, it's Mathews!" cried Blessington; and they all had breakfast in cheerful amity.

Shortly afterward the Earl and his friends went on board the packet. Mathews waved them out of sight, then mounted his horse and rode sadly away. It was raining heavily. This, strangely enough, was to prove his last sight of the wayward, open-handed, genial peer, whose kindness — and that of Lady Blessington also — Mathews at least never forgot or denied.

Details of Blessington's activity on this second visit to Mountjoy have not survived. His plans for castle-building had been quashed, and it must be presumed that he was concerned with business of landlordism; with paying rather nervous respects to his stepmother and sister; and with receiving financial reports from his agents. These last can hardly have been very favourable, for the Earl was spending as recklessly as ever. But family coldness and business pessimism were not taken seriously or else were conveniently forgotten. He was back in Italy early in the autumn, as cheerful, as prodigal and as erratic as before.

2

In February, 1826, the long sojourn in Naples came to an end. For about three weeks the party stayed in Rome, pursuing archæology under the joint guidance of their old friend Gell and of another equally learned but less comic antiquary, Edward Dodwell, who had a fine collection of antiquities and a singularly beautiful young wife. The contrast between this lady and a female mummy much prized by her husband provoked Lady Blessington to kittenish comment of an inevitable kind:

> When Mr. Dodwell was showing us his fine collection of antiquities today, he directed our attention to a female mummy, declaring that the Egyptian dame must have been one of the most perfect beauties ever seen. At that moment my eyes were fixed on his beautiful wife who stood by him, offering in her own person one of the most faultless models of loveliness ever beheld; and the arch smile that played round her lips seemed to say that living beauties might be found to compete with the dead one.

In March they came to Florence. The Burghershs were away; and in their absence Strangways was acting minister, with, as second in command, Blessington's stage-struck young friend, Lord Normanby — who on the death of his father became Earl of Mulgrave, and was later created Marquis of Normanby. Constantine Henry Phipps, by courtesy Viscount Normanby, was at this time in his late twenties. He had published his first novel, "Matilda", a year earlier and his second, "The English in Italy", was shortly to appear. He was a young man of attractive manners, with a passion for theatricals, a very good opinion of his own charm, and a wife both witty and intelligent. His novels were of the "silver-fork" school and are still readable in their racy though superficial way; his acting and sense of theatre seem to have been genuinely first-rate; but as a statesman and diplomat (he became in turn Governor of Jamaica, Lord Privy Seal, Viceroy of Ireland, Secretary for the Colonies and for Home Affairs, and in 1846 Ambassador to Paris) his talents were hardly equal to his opportunities, although he had greater difficulties to overcome than were at the time admitted and never came openly to disaster. He ended his official career with something of an anticlimax, as minister at the very Florentine court where in 1826 he was merely an attaché.

Normanby's clothes and affectations were those of an English dandy of the twenties and thirties — that is to say, he cultivated the artificial and often ridiculous foppery of Disraeli, Bulwer or Ainsworth. In 1835, Doctor Maginn, who preferred stimulants to rouge as an embellishment to masculinity, pilloried Normanby (who was by then Mulgrave and Viceroy of Ireland) in Fraser's "Gallery of Illustrious Literary Characters." He presented a painted, curled, oiled and padded gentleman — poverty-stricken, sponging and mean. Of course, Irish politics had their share in prejudicing the Doctor against the, at that time, dispenser of "Castle Government", but his rudeness was mainly an expression of the natural dislike of bohemian Grub Street for the airs and graces of highbrow Mayfair. The portrait was both brutal and venomous; yet it was clearly something of a likeness, for its subject was later widely nicknamed "Mantalini Normanby", and must as late as 1840 still have been a thing of whiskers, lisping talk and gorgeous dressing gowns. The actor Macready, with his usual resigned but conscientious severity, also found cause for censure:

> Lord Mulgrave is a man of some talent, but I begin to suspect it is not of great depth or extent. He is good-tempered, but particularly selfish and very vain, which renders any services he may confer on others indulgences of his own self-love and not benevolences. He is a man of the world, in its sordid acceptation, and a man likely to be very popular with those who see little of him. His manners are most agreeable.

But there was another and a charming side to Normanby, which neither Maginn nor Macready could have been expected to appreciate. He had something of the easy good nature of Lord Blessington — at any rate, to the extent of liking people to enjoy themselves and of helping them to do so — and with his theatrical enthusiasm went real talent. In his Palazzo San Clementi, he had built a private theatre; and we have the evidence of young Mathews, who was made welcome there during 1828, that it was as smoothly managed and as perfectly equipped as any professional theatre in Europe. To the Blessingtons Normanby must have seemed an almost ideal substitute for the censorious Burghersh. He shared their tastes; his wife shared their sense of humour; and his considered modishness was, to them at least, no offence. His craze for acting suited both Blessington and d'Orsay; his wife's witticisms and elegant *calèche* delighted the ladies. Wherefore no longer was Florence an affair of cathedrals, museums and lazzaroni, but a social stage whereon intellect, gaiety and fashion played their several parts.

But after nine months, Blessington's health and her ladyship's weariness of bustle and parties suggested that they proceed elsewhere. They travelled northward and spent some weeks in Genoa (where "every object recalled poor Byron" and there was an opportunity to transform an earlier acquaintance with Lord John Russell into a warm and lasting friendship) and late in December came to Pisa. Here were living d'Orsay's sister and her husband, the Duc and Duchesse de Guiche, with whom intimacy quickly developed. In her journal of these months, Lady Blessington speaks of the quiet of Pisa with genuine appreciation:

> The mode of passing the time at Pisa is more rational than most other places, for though it may be urged that we are all at liberty to dispose of our hours as best suits our inclination, still the interruptions consequent on a town residence preclude the enjoyment of diurnal occupation so agreeable, if not necessary, to those habituated to it. The mornings here are not broken into by visitors; so that the hours from breakfast until it is time to ride or drive into the country are wholly at one's own disposal. The evenings are devoted to visits. We meet in my house and one or two others, without the ceremony of a formal invitation. Literature, the fine arts and the peculiar usages of the different countries to which the individuals composing this friendly circle belong, form the usual topics of conversation. Politics are never named, and scandal is banished.

They had been four months in Pisa when, one June morning at breakfast, a visiting friend declared he must suddenly hurry to Florence, because poor Walter Landor was lying there ill. Now Blessington had known Landor in the old days and, the moment he heard the name, proposed with his usual quick generosity that he also should drive to Florence to visit the invalid. Many years later Landor wrote a description of their meeting: [1]

> My servant entered my inner drawing-room where I was lying on a sofa and announced Lord Blessington. I said I knew no such person. He immediately entered, saying: "Come, come Landor! I never thought you would refuse to see an old friend. If you don't know Blessington, you may remember Mountjoy." I should not have remembered Lord Mountjoy. He used to be somewhat fat for so young a man; he had now become emaciated. In a few days he brought his lady "to see me and make me well again." They remained at Florence all that year. In the spring and until the end of autumn I went every evening from my villa and spent it in their society.

Thus began one of the steadiest and most sympathetic intimacies, not only of Lady Blessington's life, but of Walter Savage Landor's also. He was already over fifty years of age when they met, with behind him a record full of turbulent extravagance and brilliance thwarted by temper. Of a good Staffordshire family, he had passed through Rugby and Oxford with triumphant scholarship, but continual social catastrophe. He was defiant of authority, professed extreme radical views, and was perpetually in violent conflict, both with his tutors and his fellow students. Having been virtually removed from school and then sent down for a year from college, his relations with his father, who would have preferred his son's abnormal talents tempered with an element of social common sense, became strained, and Walter left home on a small allowance. But in 1805 the father died, and Walter found himself a man of means and his own master. He used both money and liberty with

[1] *Athenæum*. February 17, 1855.

characteristic recklessness. He went to Spain to fight in the Spanish army against the French; returning, he bought a large estate in Wales and spent many thousands in the practice of what he took to be enlightened landlordism. In 1811 he met a pretty girl at a dance in Bath, married her out of hand, and within two years had started a crescendo of repentance. Meantime his life in Wales was becoming rapidly intolerable. He quarrelled with the neighbouring gentry who disliked his views, and with his own labourers who resented his imperious temper. Disgusted with Britain, and financially in difficulties, he removed to Jersey, leaving his Welsh property to deteriorate still further in the hands of incompetent tenants.

From Jersey he wished to go to France, and when his wife demurred, departed alone and declared he would never see her again. They were ostensibly reconciled a few months later and travelled from one place to another, until in 1821 they settled in Florence.

Why, during 1826, Blessington had never thought to connect the Florentine Landor with his old friend is a mystery, for he must have heard tell of the handsome and dignified Englishman, who lived in the Palazzo Medici with his bewildered and rather peevish wife and their four little children. Landor had become something of a local institution in Florence. His great mental attainments; his devotion to children and to dogs; his indifference to outward appearance; his continual disputes with all and sundry, were everywhere notorious. One can only conclude that the bad relations which always existed between him and officialdom so wholly excluded him from the favour of ministerial circles that the Blessingtons, if they heard speak of him at all, were given the impression that he belonged to an altogether inferior creation and was not at all the kind of man Lord Blessington would have known in the past.

But now that contact had been made, it became quickly evident that, however violent and eccentric Landor may have seemed to others, to the Blessingtons he was both sympathetic and stimulating. The Countess was always more attracted to persons of intellectual eminence than to mere aristocrats; and being herself unusually well informed of significant novelties in contemporary literature, was equally equipped and disposed to welcome her new acquaintance.

"Of Landor's genius," she writes in her journal, "his 'Imaginary Conversations' had, previously to our meeting, left me in no doubt; of the elevation of his mind and the nobleness of his thoughts I had learned to form a just estimate."

To Landor, her familiarity with his work must have seemed almost miraculous. Although a second edition of the first two volumes of "Imaginary Conversations" had been published by Colburn in 1826, the work had hardly attracted attention outside the small circle of its author's literary and critical friends; and it is doubtful whether there was a fine lady in London who could claim even to be aware of the book's existence. Yet here was Lady Blessington, for years resident in Italy, who had not only heard of his book but had actually read it! Landor's usual defensive dignity softened forthwith to gentle courtesy.

The Countess' journal continues:

> The high breeding and urbanity of his manners which are very striking, I had not been taught to expect. His avoidance of general society and his fearless courage in following the dictates of a lofty mind had given the impression that his manners were, if not somewhat abrupt, at least singular. But the only singularity I can discern is a more than ordinary politeness towards women — a singularity that I heartily wish was one no longer.

Blessington also seems to have struck up a friendship of his own with Landor, of a kind more seriously significant than the jolly but casual acquaintanceships with which he filled his life. He was described by Landor, in a letter to his sister, as "a most delightful and well-informed man", and it may well have been that, feeling himself liked for his own sake and not merely for his money, Blessington, in his response to Landor, permitted more of his mental capacity to appear than often he felt to be desirable. Forster, in his "Life of Landor", prints a letter written by Blessington (undoubtedly from Rome late in 1827) which shows the Earl interested and knowledgeable in public affairs and possessed of a pleasant humour.

It must have been delight in Landor's company which decided the Blessingtons to prolong this their third visit to Florence. In any case, no alternative attraction is evident. The Burghershs were back; and to revisit galleries and churches would require a sojourn of several months. The Countess settled her household in the Casa Pecori, a pleasant villa on the banks of the Arno. Here, as he has himself recorded, Landor came constantly, to discuss classical and modern books and authors with her ladyship; politics and politicians with Blessington; his children and his dogs with the party as a whole. In August he moved his family to Fiesole, where almost at once his wife and two of the children fell victims to malignant fever. Lady Blessington immediately drove out from Florence, packed the other children into her carriage, and took them back with her, keeping them at the Casa Pecori until all risk of infection at home was over.

When the sick children were at last out of danger, their father was near collapse with anxiety and sleeplessness. Blessington therefore persuaded him to sail to Naples and back in the *Bolivar*. The trip restored Landor to health, and also enabled him to see many beautiful and interesting places which previously had been but phrases in his learning. It is not surprising, with such thoughtful kindness on one side and, on the other, a gratitude all the stronger for having taken root in a mind predisposed to suspicion and reserve, that the friendship between Landor and the Blessingtons was by the end of the year unshakeable.

It was forthwith to have a chance to prove itself. Four years had passed since Blessington in London had made the will which offered d'Orsay one of his daughters as the price of a fortune. The girls were now sixteen and fifteen years of age, and the Count must choose his bride or risk the loss of his inheritance. He was in no mind to do the latter and decided, with significant prudence, to marry the legitimate younger daughter rather than the elder one. So Lady Harriet Gardiner, a pale nervous child of less than fifteen and a half and abnormally young for her age, was brought from her school in Ireland to Florence and confronted with her appointed husband.

That the Blessingtons should seriously have intended to celebrate this indefensible marriage under official auspices in Florence showed a misapprehension of the atmosphere of the English community which, on the part of the Countess at any rate, is very unexpected. But such an intention existed; and can only be explained on the supposition that even yet she had not realised the extent to which her name and d'Orsay's were discreditably linked together. That she should have been thus unaware is quite comprehensible, for not only had she made few contacts with her countrymen, but her own feeling for d'Orsay was so completely free from any emotionalism, that serious misinterpretation of their friendship would hardly occur to her as possible.

So when her husband and d'Orsay suggested that they put matters in train for the wedding to be celebrated, she probably agreed without any foreboding of disaster. D'Orsay began with the French minister whom he knew well, by whom he was well received. But when Blessington, with his genial self-assurance, made bland application to the English minister, he was immediately snubbed. In fairness to Lord Burghersh, it must be realised that the proposal, as it would have been presented to him, was a monstrous one. He would naturally accept the current belief that d'Orsay and Lady Blessington were lovers. When invited to authorise the marriage of the former to the latter's half-grown stepdaughter, what else could he have thought, save that a complaisant husband, an adulterous wife and a handsome lover had agreed to cloak their evil-doing behind the bridal trappings of an innocent child? So he determined to wreck the whole scheme, and the method adopted was ingenious. Since a dual ceremony — Catholic and Protestant — was necessary, he insisted to the French minister at Florence that the Church of England rite must have precedence. The demand was the more damaging in that the French minister was not only a personal friend of d'Orsay but also of the Blessingtons, was frequently at their house, and as frequently welcomed them to his. Thus Burghersh contrived simultaneously to be offensive to France, to the Catholic religion, and to the French minister's chosen intimates; and, by producing a deadlock and talk of an international incident, to checkmate what seemed to him an unsavoury and intolerable intrigue. At this point Lady Blessington most imprudently intervened. Still lulled in false security, she went in person to see the minister and remonstrate, taking the child bride with her. Burghersh, who could hardly have asked for a better opening, was, we are told, very rude.

That official obstruction should have culminated in personal insult set the whole of the Casa Pecori in a flutter. Landor was furious and wrote off to Lady Blessington:

> I have said on other occasions that nothing could surprise me of folly or indecorum in Lord Burghersh. I must retract my words. That a man educated among the sons of gentlemen could be guilty of such incivility to two ladies is inconceivable, even to the most observant of his behaviour throughout the whole period of his public life. From what I have heard and known during a residence of six years at Florence, I am convinced that all the ministers of all the other Courts in Europe have never been guilty of so many unbecoming and disgraceful actions as this man. The only person for whom he ever interested himself was a notorious gambler and profligate who had been expelled from the Tuscan Lucca states. And now his conscience will not permit him to sanction a father's disposal of his daughter in marriage with the very man who deserves her most.

To some purpose, indeed, had Landor become a Blessingtonian.

As for the offended principals, they left Florence immediately and went via Rome to Naples. There, under the régime of a more tolerant minister, the disagreeable farce of marriage turned Harriet Gardiner into the Countess d'Orsay. The ceremony over, the whole party returned to Rome, whence d'Orsay wrote an insulting letter to Burghersh, telling him he did not know his job, and another letter to Landor, saying he would like to cut off Burghersh's nose. In this atmosphere did d'Orsay begin his married life.

3

Settling down in Rome was only accomplished after some difficulty and much expense. In her description of what occurred, Lady Blessington, whose journal is silent about the contretemps in Florence and the whole business of the d'Orsay marriage, breaks out into fluent and confiding domesticity. She deplores the barren discomfort of the so-called furnished houses offered at huge rents to visiting foreigners; indicates nonchalantly her own standard of living, and then sets her audience purring by a brisk display of housewifery.

> I have occupied the whole day in house-hunting and never beheld less tempting habitations than those I went over. Not one offered a single room in which a person accustomed to comfort could say or fancy — "here I can manage to render the apartment liveable." I have at length found an abode in the Palazzo Negroni, of which I have engaged the two principal floors at one hundred guineas a month, for six months certain. . . . The suites of rooms are good; but the furniture of the whole would not be sufficient to arrange two of them with comfort, so we must look out for furniture to be hired. This will, I am told, cost about twenty pounds a month.
>
> But murmuring will not render things any better; so courage! and tomorrow I will try if with the aid of countless yards of white muslin for clean window curtains; innumerable table covers (with which we are always provided) to conceal the ill-polished wood; and some dozen of eiderdown pillows, smartly cased, to lay along the hard backs of the miserable, half-stuffed sofas, I can render the three saloons habitable.

Apart from their appeal to readers of her diary, these domestic activities may well have served to turn her mind from the discomfort of recent events. The white scared face of little Harriet d'Orsay might seem less reproachful in its pallor, once the snowy muslin hung thick and stiff about the windows. The Countess also sought refuge from her conscience in lavish entertaining, and society flocked to the Palazzo Negroni. Talk was gay, books new and different, food and wine plentiful and exquisite. Thus passed the d'Orsay honeymoon — a honeymoon spent in a crowd, with the bride hardly speaking to any one and the bridegroom to every one but her.

In March, 1828, Madden, who had been in the Near East, stopped at the Palazzo Negroni on his way home to England. He was unpleasantly struck with the manifest unhappiness of Harriet d'Orsay:

> There was no appearance of familiarity [he says], with anyone around her; no air or look of womanhood, no semblance of satisfaction in her new position. She seldom or ever spoke; she was little noticed. I think her feelings were crushed, repressed, and her emotion driven inwards by a sense of slight and indifference, and she became strange and cold and apparently devoid of all vivacity and interest in society.

The interpretation of this unhappiness is rather more complex than might appear. It is impossible to believe that the child was actually ill-treated. No one of the dominant trio in the Blessington household was capable of direct cruelty; nor was there profit to any one of them in making an already difficult relationship more difficult still by unfriendliness or aloof frigidity. The contrary indeed; and that the atmosphere so soon became one of discomfort and embarrassment was surely due as much to Harriet's own angry bewilderment as to cold-shouldering or unkindness from her father, her husband or her stepmother.

Harriet would have spent her last year or two in Dublin — years more intensely "noticing" than any in her life hitherto — in an atmosphere charged with bitter dislike and suspicion of Lady Blessington and of d'Orsay. Her grandmother and her aunt may well, in the outspoken manner of the Ireland of the period, have talked in front of her of the shameless adventuress who had captured her rich and foolish father and was now flaunting herself in Italy with a handsome young Frenchman in her train. Even if Lady Mountjoy and Miss Gardiner did not actually talk their minds in the child's presence, there would have been a feeling of constraint in the house, sudden silences when she entered a room, above all eager and reckless gossip among maidservants and grooms — all of which would leave their mark on the quick impressionable curiosity of fourteen and fifteen.

When she arrived in Naples she was, one may be certain, greeted by her stepmother with that sweeping confident charm which had never failed to win its victory, — never until now, when it came up against the obstinate and resentful terror of immaturity and was repulsed. Lady Blessington would be patient. She would be sweet, tender, cheerful, sympathetic. But the child would pass from blank unresponsiveness to *farouche* animosity, becoming the readier to bite a kindly hand for its very kindliness. At last the stepmother would give up trying. They would all give up trying. Possibly the father, in one of his quick rages, would box the girl's ears for a sulky little fool, who had not even the grace to be civil to her new mother.

And poor Harriet would shrink into herself, finding what solitude she could, hating to be noticed yet hating still more to be ignored, watching the man who was her husband in laughing attendance on the radiant beauty of her stepmother; crying perhaps at night, when the longing for Dublin and for her grandmother's familiar home became too poignant to be borne.

Some such a youthful Harriet as this prepares us for the Harriet of maturity; some such a reading as this of Lady Blessington's failure to win over her stepdaughter helps us to guess at the uneasy dread — half shame, half fear for the future — which must have underlain her gaiety in the Negroni Palace and sent her the more eagerly to seek distraction in furnishings and in society.

But if conscience could be stifled, scandal could not; and there can be no doubt that the affair of d'Orsay's marriage soon had repercussions in general society. The Burghershs would not have been silent about the incident in Florence; and the connections between Florentine and Roman residents were close and various. One suspects that folk began to look askance, even to murmur. Lady Blessington's journal, as the spring of 1828 goes by, becomes rapidly more perfunctory and less informative. Then suddenly in May, after a eulogy of the Guiccioli who had just arrived in Rome, she bluntly states: "Tomorrow we leave the Eternal City — perhaps to see it no more."

Why? Whither? She does not say. And we realise that her silences have for some few months been more significant than her words.

They travelled quickly via Ravenna, Ferrara and Padua to Venice, where they stayed a few weeks, and the Countess, by yielding to an importunate Jew and purchasing the inkstand of the last of the Doges, began her collection of objects which had once belonged to famous folk. From Venice they drove to Vicenza, Verona, Milan, Bologna, Modena and Parma. In the last-named town they narrowly avoided a meeting with the Burghershs, who were paying a ceremonial call on the grand duchess. The moment threatened awkwardness. Even in her diary Lady Blessington scurries from the scene. Passing through Piacenza they came for the last time to Genoa. By a strange coincidence they saw in the street a young English girl, whose resemblance to Byron was so striking that the Countess' quick eye at once remarked it. Enquiry revealed that the girl was none other than the poet's daughter Ada, of whom five years earlier he had so often spoken to Lady Blessington.

The stay in Genoa ended with a characteristically lavish compliment paid by Blessington to his wife. There was landed from a ship just arrived from England a *calèche* which the Countess was begged to accept. Months ago the Earl had heard her admire the *calèche* in which Lady Burghersh drove about Florence.

He had written home to have an exact replica made and shipped to Genoa. Probably he hoped, by this rather touching gesture, to make up to her for the rudeness she had suffered from Burghersh and his wife — rudeness for which, likely enough, he had at the time been made to suffer. The Countess was enchanted with her new carriage; and a few days later the whole party crossed the frontier into France *en route* for Paris.

CHAPTER IV

Paris and Widowing

Back along the Riviera to Marseilles came the swollen cortège of Milord. Its bulk was as great as ever — greater, maybe, with all the books and statues and pictures and vases which her ladyship's collecting fervour had gathered during six years in Italy. It had also another "drawing-room" passenger in the person of the Countess d'Orsay.

On the road once more — behind her Rome and its uneasy memories, in front the gay indifference of fashionable Paris — Lady Blessington's diary regains something of the old serenity and discursiveness. Nîmes, with its amphitheatre, its Maison Carrée and other monuments, its smart crowds and purposeful accomplished officers, is warmly approved. The antiquities, also, are tastefully commended for their cleanliness, which is so considerable that "in examining them in the interior or exterior, no risk is incurred of encountering aught offensive to the olfactory nerves or injurious to the *chaussure.*"

After Nîmes, Beaucaire, and Tarascon and Arles. This last is described by Lady Blessington with unusual directness and selective sense; also, to a far greater extent than any other place she visited, it has remained unchanged from that day to this. She is struck with the curious combination of "streets as clean as those of Holland, with inhabitants neat and tidy in their attire" and "houses for the most part old and dilapidated." The friendly courtesy of the Arlesiens impressed and charmed her; and when she left (after the unaccustomed experience of simple fare and simple lodging, both first-rate of their kind) she declared that "Arles is certainly one of the most interesting towns

I have ever seen, whether viewed as a place remarkable for the objects of antiquity it contains, or for the primitive simplicity of its inhabitants and its picturesque appearance."

From Arles their route lay through St. Rémy (for the sake of the Triumphal Arch and the Tomb of the Julii) to Lyons. Thence, without further descriptive comment, they travelled to Paris, where they arrived in June, 1828, and put up at an elegant but noisy hotel in the Rue de Rivoli, overlooking the Tuileries Gardens.

Their first Parisian visitors were the de Guiches, themselves not long home from Italy; and Lady Blessington is so overcome with the beauty, distinction, charm and domestic virtues of these gifted beings that she sweeps her fascinated readers off their feet with the torrent of her reiterated admiration. Throughout the twenty-seven months of the Paris journal, the virtues and graces of d'Orsay's sister Ida and of his brother-in-law, the Duc de Guiche, are set forth in wearisome superlative. We are told of the Duchesse "sparkling in diamonds and looking so beautiful that she reminded me of Burke's description of Marie Antoinette"; of the Duchesse "in simple white peignoir and her matchless hair bound tightly about her classically shaped head, enacting the part of *garde malade* to her children who have caught the measles"; of the Duchesse on a sledging party, "wrapped in a pelisse of the finest Russian sable, her fair cheeks tinged with pink by the cold air and her luxuriant silken curls falling on the dark fur that encircled her throat." We are introduced to the Duc, "more *distingué* than any one else — the perfect *beau idéal* of a nobleman"; to the Duc "released from his attendance at court, hurrying into the sick chamber of his children and their languid eyes lighting up and their feverish lips relaxing into a smile at the sound of his well-known voice." All of that and more. Lady Blessington described her daily round in Paris as having included "journalising from one till four." The phrase was apter than she guessed.

Under the ægis of the entrancing Ida she goes shopping; and

the details given of where to buy and what, the hints about price, the coy references to pleasing men, the shuddersome jokes about bills and Benedicts, are perfectly designed to snare that particular public on which, when the journal was finally prepared for publication, she had her skilful eye. The right note is struck and brilliantly maintained. Titled diarist and untitled readers are all wholesome British girls together, but the diarist is a little grander and richer and freer and more brilliant than the rest.

The weeks pass. Intimacy with the de Guiches leads naturally to friendship with Madame Craufurd, and through her good offices to the acquaintance of half of Parisian society. The British ambassador, Lord Stuart de Rothesay, dines with her; every kind of visiting notability, English and foreign, bows over the Countess' hand. They go to a military review where is Charles X and other royalties, and the cue for respectful but homely flattery is neatly taken. They see Taglioni's début; and Mlle. Mars; and Malibran. They attend several theatres, and Lady Blessington makes a number of interesting comments on the menacing enthusiasm of the Paris crowd for plays with revolutionary implications. To what extent, in her subsequent editing, she credited herself with forebodings which were in fact after the event, is uncertain; but that she actually witnessed the three or four plays described and noted the response of the cheaper seats to every suggestion of social violence and upheaval can hardly be doubted. Evidently signs were already to be seen that the second Bourbon experiment was nearing its end.

They visit Montmorency, where the sight of Rousseau's hermitage persuades her ladyship that Rousseau's life story — his great talents being unaccompanied by goodness — is "one of the most humiliating episodes in the whole history of literary men and the most calculated to bring genius into disrepute." They also visit Orsay and view the château, built under Charles VII and pillaged in the Revolution. Either Lady Blessington was ill informed as to the actual origins of the contemporary family of

LORD BLESSINGTON
(1828)
After a drawing by d'Orsay

d'Orsay; or else, with more dexterity than candour, she deliberately telescoped the Counts d'Orsay of her day with those of pre-Revolutionary times. Whatever its impulse, her description smothers the parvenu Grimaud in the breeding and ancestry of his wife, and so gives him a traditional background to which, in his wildest dreams, he would never have aspired. Genealogical discretion no less memorable marks her comments on the Hôtel d'Orsay — the Paris mansion of the same family, which also (and no wonder) suffered in the Revolution. On this dwelling Grimaud spent his millions in true *roturier* fashion, the climax of costly blatancy being a device by which (in Lady Blessington's words) "on the folding doors of the state drawing rooms being thrown open to admit company, certain pedals connected with them were put in motion, and a strain of music was produced, which announced the presence of guests, and the doors of each of the drawing rooms when opened took up the air and continued it until closed." "The effect," she adds, "was greatly admired, though I believe owing to the great expense, the mode was not adopted in other houses."

Naturally Lady Blessington had not been long in Paris before setting up an establishment of her own; and this mansion seems to have marked the zenith even of Blessingtonian extravagance. The house chosen was known as the Hôtel Ney (it had been the property of Napoleon's marshal) and stood on what is now the Quai d'Orsay and on the site of the Rue de Solférino. Its windows looked over the Seine to the Tuileries. The grounds were large and surrounded by a high wall; an avenue of fine trees led from the *porte-cochère* to the main entrance of the house. Vast plate-glass windows; innumerable mirrors; Corinthian columns, pilasters and cornices, all gold and imitation marble; carved chimneypieces in real marble; painted walls and ceilings, and a huge conservatory — were the decorative features of this overwhelming and admittedly expensive home. It was unfurnished; and having signed a lease for a year, the Blessingtons went out to find a suitable upholsterer. They found one so resourceful and so rapid that the Countess likens him to a magician and, on paying a visit to the new house only a few days after work had been started, "could hardly believe her eyes", so complete was the transformation.

But the best was still to come. The upholsterer, with playful but firm civility, refused to let her ladyship inspect either her bedroom or dressing room. Milord had devised a special decorative scheme, which should be revealed when ready, but not earlier. She pouts and gracefully submits. Two days later:

"The secret is out, the doors of my *chambre à coucher* and dressing room are opened and I am delighted with both. The whole fitting up is in exquisite taste, and as usual, when my most gallant of all gallant husbands interferes, no expense has been spared."

The latter of these two statements at any rate would appear to be correct. Here is the bedroom:

> The bed, which is silvered, instead of gilt, rests on the backs of two large silver swans, so exquisitely sculptured that every feather is in alto-relievo, and looks nearly as fleecy as those of the living bird. The recess in which it is placed is lined with white fluted silk, bordered with blue embossed lace; and from the columns that support the frieze of the recess, pale blue silk curtains, lined with white, are hung which, when drawn, conceal the recess altogether.
>
> The window curtains are of pale blue silk, with embroidered muslin curtains, trimmed with lace inside them, and have borders of blue and white lace to match those of the recess.
>
> A silvered sofa has been made to fit the side of the room opposite the fire-place, near to which stands a most inviting *bergère*. An *escritoire* occupies one panel, a book-stand the other, and a rich coffer for jewels, forms a pendant to a similar one for lace, or India shawls.
>
> A carpet of uncut pile, of a pale blue, a silver lamp, and a Psyche glass, the ornaments silvered to correspond with the decorations of the chamber, complete the furniture.

Here is the dressing room:

> The hangings of the dressing-room are of blue silk, covered with lace and trimmed with rich frills of the same material, as are also the dressing-stools and *chaise longue,* and the carpet and lamp are similar to those of the bedroom.

A toilette table stands before the window, and small *jardinières* are placed in front of each panel of looking-glass, but so low as not to impede a full view of the person dressing in this beautiful little sanctuary.

And here the bathroom:

The *salle de bains* is draped with white muslin trimmed with lace, and the sofa and *bergère* are covered with the same. The bath is of white marble, inserted in the floor, with which the surface is level. On the ceiling over it, is a painting of Flora scattering flowers with one hand, while from the other is suspended an alabaster lamp, in the form of a lotos.

The verdict of its joyful occupant on this repulsive interior is that "the effect of the whole suite is chastely beautiful. Lord B. has all the merit of the taste, and the upholsterer that of the rapidity and excellence of the execution."

Lord Blessington would also have had the bill; and it is only necessary to consider for a moment how many tens of thousands of francs this crazy installation must have cost, to appreciate the following comment made years later by the usually uncensorious Madden:

The gilt [*sic*] frame-work of the bed resting on the backs of the large silver swans it does not do to think of, when visiting the Mountjoy estate that did belong to the Earl of Blessington, when one enters the cabin of one of the now indigent peasantry, from the sweat of whose brow the means were derived that were squandered in luxury in foreign lands. Lord Blessington, when fitting up the Hôtel Ney in this sumptuous manner was coöperating with others of his order in laying the foundation of the Encumbered Estates Court Jurisdiction in Ireland.

Indeed one could feel only disgust for a spendthrift so selfish, so fantastic and so sterile, were one passing judgment on a man of normal human impulses. But Blessington was not normal. Always the queerest tangle of acuteness, good nature, self-indulgence and absurdity, he was also — in one respect at any rate — definitely insane. He was incapable of relating his personal extravagance to any general principle, either of economics or social duty. Undoubtedly a generous and thoughtful landlord when landlordism was in his mind, he was also sincere and liberal in his patriotism. His concern over the distresses of Ireland and his desire to alleviate them were enlightened and genuine; but to connect his country's misery with his own wasteful absenteeism was something outside his reasoning capacity.

Madden prints a letter of his written in 1824, which speaks of Ireland's "impoverishment in money and talent" and England's "superabundancy of the one and sufficiency of the other if she will apply her materials to our good." "Admit Catholics to the houses of parliament and the bench," the letter continues, "at the same time establishing throughout Ireland a gendarmerie, not for political but for policial purposes. Make the nobility and gentry live on their estates or sell them."

The very naïveté of the Earl's illogicality disarms criticism; he was helpless in the grip of his own squandermania — as helpless as were to be those who came after him in the grip of its consequences. And the time for consequences was now close at hand.

In April, 1829, he received a letter from London urging him to be in the House of Lords to support the Catholic Emancipation Bill, which the Duke of Wellington was about to introduce. Although in poor health, he had too real an interest in the subject to be content merely to send his proxy. He travelled to London, recorded his vote, presided at a dinner in support of the Covent Garden theatrical fund, and in May was back in Paris again.

"Lord B. arrived yesterday," writes his wife in her diary, "and, Heaven be thanked! is in better health. He is delighted at the Catholic question having been carried."

But in the next sentences she shows an inability to relate cause and effect little less obstinate than Blessington's own.

> How few, with estates in a province where so strong a prejudice is entertained against Roman Catholics as exists in the North of Ireland, would have voted as Lord B. has done? If there were many

such landlords in Ireland, prejudices — the bane of that country — would soon subside. Lord B. came back laden with presents for me. Some of them are quite beautiful and would excite the envy of half my sex.

The lease of the Hôtel Ney was running out and could not be renewed, but the Earl, with his usual zeal, was delighted to start house-hunting once more. Lady Blessington favoured a mansion in the Avenue de Matignon. "It is newly built and freshly and beautifully decorated but Lord B. does not think it good enough." Nevertheless, he could discover nothing better, and her ladyship's choice was finally adopted. "It will be beautiful when completed," she remarks, "but not to be compared with the Hôtel Ney." The apparent inconsistency is quickly explained. The house was indeed perfectly new and elegantly decorated; but "it has been found necessary to build an additional room!" So not only upholsterers but builders also were sent spinning to the scene. "The builders seem to be as expeditious as the upholsterers," notes the complacent Countess, "and adding a room or two appears to be as easily accomplished as adding some extra furniture. One is made to pay dearly, however, for this facility and expedition."

While the room was being built, the garden was under drastic treatment.

Deep beds of earth inclosed in green cases line the sides of the terrace, and an abundance of orange trees, flowering shrubs, plants and flowers are placed in them. At the end of the terrace, the wall which abounds it has been painted in fresco with a view of Italian scenery; and the wall forms the back of an aviary with a fountain which plays in the centre. A smaller aviary, constructed of glass, is erected on the end of the terrace close to my library, from the window of which I can feed my favourite birds; and this aviary as well as the library is warmed by means of a stove beneath the latter.

The time for moving into the new house was very near. "Already," writes Lady Blessington, "we begin to feel the unsettled state peculiar to an intended change of abode." She is gathering her knick-knacks, arranging her books for packing, discussing with her sister where this statue shall stand and where this vase. A restlessness and lack of purpose slowly pervades the house. Down the long perspective of mirrored rooms, soundless and infinitely multiplied, the slight drab figure of Harriet d'Orsay flutters like an unhappy moth. Change is in the air — change and the menace of graver things.

After luncheon on Saturday, May 23rd, Blessington complained of feeling unwell. He took a draught and found some relief; but immediately afterward, with a strange imprudence, ordered his horse. It was very hot, and in the full blaze of early afternoon he rode up the Champs Élysées, his servant in his train. An hour later they brought him home, stricken speechless with apoplexy. Throughout Sunday he lay insensible, while doctors, nurses and a distracted household fought their hopeless fight. Early on Monday morning, the tortured breathing ceased. The first and last Earl of Blessington was dead; and those whom in fond kindness he had made but by a kindness overfond had marred, were left behind. Their problem was to make what compromise they could, with a world whose terms even for tolerance and flattery were strictly cash.

The calamity of her husband's death threatened utterly to overwhelm Lady Blessington. There is no reason to doubt the sincerity of her personal grief, nor is it uncharitable to assume that material fears blended with sentiment in her extreme of lamentation. She dragged through the now hateful task of moving house and then fell ill. There is a gap of four months in her journal; and when she resumes her entries in late September, 1829, she writes of her loss with the simplicity of genuine feeling. Indeed, from now onward to the end of her stay in Paris, her whole diary is much more subdued, its style quieter, its reflections briefer and less ornate. She is confronting her new situation and prospects. Every day she is realising more clearly that her time of sheltered luxury is over, and that henceforward she must be a business woman, to whom social elegance has ceased to be a hobby and has become a profession.

Of the many letters and messages of condolence which she received, those from Landor were probably the most heartfelt and certainly the best expressed:

"Everyone that knows me," he wrote in one, "knows the sentiments I bore towards that disinterested and upright and kind-hearted man, than whom none was ever dearer or more delightful to his friends."

In another:

> So many hopes are torn away from us by this unexpected and most cruel blow. I cannot part with the one, of which the greatness and the justness of your grief almost deprives me — that you will recover your health and spirits. If they could return at once, or very soon, you would be unworthy of that love which the kindest and best of human beings lavished on you. He told me that you were requisite to his happiness and that he could not live without you. Suppose then he had survived you? His departure in that case could not have been so easy as it was, so unconscious of pain — of giving it or leaving it behind. I would most wish such a temper and soul as his, and next to them such a dissolution. Tho' my hand and my whole body shake as I am writing it, yet I am writing the truth.

And that his words to the widow were not mere surface emotionalism, a private comment, pencilled in the margin of the manuscript of an unpublished "Imaginary Conversation" — a conversation between the dead Earl's father and Lord Edward Fitzgerald — is evidence sufficient:

> Scarcely is the ink yet dry upon my paper, when intelligence reaches me of Lord Blessington's sudden death. Adieu, most pleasant companion! Adieu, most warm-hearted friend! Often and long and never with slight emotion shall I think of the many hours we have spent together, the lighter seldom ending gravely, the graver always lightly. It will be well if my regret at your loss shall hereafter be quieted by the assurance that, delighted by you among the many, I was esteemed and beloved among the few.

The body of Lord Blessington was taken to Dublin, where it was buried in the family vault in St. Thomas's Church in Marlborough Street. There is no record that any of the Paris party accompanied his remains to their last resting place. It is almost inconceivable that they should have done so, seeing the bitterness felt by the dead man's stepmother and sister toward his widow and toward d'Orsay. Thus, even the final scene of Blessington's sojourn in this world had the forlorn splendour of a ceremony without a heart. His Dublin relatives committed him to the tomb, then turned to listen with dismay to the provisions of the will and to the sorry tale of mortgages, debts, falling rentals and general decay, which was the account rendered by his man of business. In Paris the little group, who only now realised to what an extent their lives centred on Blessington, crouched uneasily in the freshly painted salons of the house in the Avenue de Matignon, the house whose beauties had been so eagerly and lavishly anticipated, the house which now was but a costly incubus. It was a queer beginning to a lease — the queerer in that at the same moment an epoch both in their individual lives and in the public history of France was drawing to an end. On the near horizon of their privacy, scandal was hovering; already, in the slums of the Faubourg St. Denis, the spirit of revolution was astir.

CHAPTER V

Scandal

The actual début of the d'Orsay-Blessington scandal — its emergence from gossip into the tangibility of ink and paper — was curious enough. There had of course been talk about the Countess' past and some cold-shouldering during her first sojourn in London; but these had been confined to the more rigid upholders of social etiquette and had not had time to become at all general. During the Blessingtons' long absence abroad, comment and curiosity had faded, and might well have been permanently stilled but for the fatal matchmaking which turned Harriet Gardiner into the Countess d'Orsay. This project must have been known to the Dowager Lady Mountjoy before it was actually carried through, and inasmuch as she would naturally attribute it to the influence of her stepson's second wife, it turned her dislike and suspicion of that lady into implacable hatred. She had ample opportunity of speaking her mind (the Charlevilles, for example, who were continually to and fro between Ireland and London, were friends of hers), and one can hardly doubt that, by the time d'Orsay was actually married, more than one influential household in fashionable London had drawn — and expressed — its own conclusions.

But even then, with Blessington still alive and the erring parties too far away to be infectious, disapproval would probably have remained behind closed doors, had not the creditable fidelity of the Speaker of the House of Commons drawn attention to a member of Lady Blessington's family and therefore indirectly revived interest in Lady Blessington herself.

It was about six months before Lord Blessington's death that his sister-in-law, Mrs. Home Purves, ended her prolonged occupation of his London house by regularising at St. George's, Hanover Square, her affectionate relationship with Charles Manners Sutton. Early in 1829, as the Speaker's wife, she opened the hospitable doors of the official residence in Westminster. She was (in Moore's words) "a hearty lively Irishwoman", generally popular and devoted to her husband's interests, so that only persons with peculiar reasons for sourness cared to asperse her character and record. But such persons existed, and here and there things were said. What was worse, they were not only said but written; and it is queerly significant of the gossip current in certain circles that of all people William Beckford — late Caliph of Fonthill, now a grandiose recluse in Lansdown Crescent, Bath — should have noted the Manners Sutton marriage, very soon after it occurred, in the embittered private notebook which he called his "Liber Veritatis." [1]

This strange record of spleen had its origin in Beckford's own thwarted desire for a peerage; and the resentment of one who had failed to gain a title against the many who had succeeded, fastened delightedly on every discoverable case of parvenu ennoblement or skilful husband-catching. There were many such (the acquisition of honoured names by war wealth or by feminine ingenuity being no less prevalent during the eighteen-twenties than a century later) and among them was this case of the Speaker's second wife. Under the heading "Rutland", Beckford wrote as follows:

> Like Macbeth when he stood in the False Cave by the Cauldron frothing with poison, we exclaim, "another and another still succeeds", but in the case we are going to mention we cannot cry out the last is like the former. Kind and indulgent excuses are found almost spontaneously for Youth; but when so mature and steady a character as the Speaker of the House of Commons, the ex-officio guardian as it were of public morals, and one so handsomely paid for being exemplary, demeans himself and his station by one of the least scrupulous or

[1] Edited from the original manuscript by Guy Chapman, and first published under the title "The Vision and Liber Veritatis", London, 1930.

delicate marriages even upon *modern record,* it becomes a public duty to point it out with the scorn and reprobation it merits. The Rt. Hon. Charles Manners Sutton, grandson of the 3rd Duke of Rutland, has thought fit before the altar at St. George's, Hanover Square, to make legally sure of Mrs. Purvis's (*sic*) affections and to bind that errant lady to him by the ties of the Church. In vain his daughters, offspring of a very different sort of an alliance, threw themselves at their parent's feet and implored him not to disgrace himself, tears and supplications were in vain. The speaker would have his way, would give his casting vote and Mrs. Purvis is at length nested, within the precincts of St. Stephens Chapel, a Peeress in embryo.

Not surprisingly, the attention of the author of "Liber Veritatis" passed from one erstwhile Miss Power to another, and his next entry, dated March 20, 1829, is headed "Blessington" and reads:

The lovely, accomplished Sister of this Lady [Mrs. Purves] after a trial of several years during the course of which the triumphs of her delightful temper were fully established, submitted also not very long ago to the form and ceremonies prescribed by the ritual. She is now the professed Countess of Blessington (an auspicious name) and that portion of her Ladyship's progeny, who may happen to enter this gay world since the close of her novitiate, will succeed to Estates and titles and the honour of descending as legitimately as could be wished from Luke Gardiner, an attendant of a former Lord Lieutenant of Ireland and the founder of the family. I must confess I am quite ignorant whether the (very possibly) virtuous parents of Lady Blessington and Mrs. Manners [*sic*] are still in existence. If they are, with what exultation must they contemplate the fortunate destiny of their fair offspring conducted at length after wandering through devious and flowery paths to a high and legal establishment.

Thus, even before Lord Blessington was dead, whispers against his wife had found their way into the secluded grandeur of Lansdown Tower, and were there set down in a book which Beckford was always going to publish but never actually did. Who shall doubt that the same whispers went Covent Garden-wards to Grub Street, were there made welcome, and filed away against a likely opportunity for profitable use? During August,

1829, that opportunity was judged to have arrived; and Charles Molloy Westmacott, the principal blackmailing editor of his day, decided to bring pressure on the now widowed Lady Blessington by judicious paragraphs in his weekly scandal sheet the *Age*.

On August 23, 1829, the following paragraph appeared in a "Letter from Paris":

> The Count d'Orsay, who a short time since married a daughter of the late Lord Blessinton (*sic*) continues to reside with his wife and noble mother-in-law, but for some reason or other their only visitant of rank is the Duchesse de Guiche — more it were not polite of us to tell.

This was followed, on September 27, 1829, by a "Letter to the Editor of the *Age*" signed "Otiosus":

> Alfred d'Orsay, with his pretty pink and white face, drives about *à la Petersham*, with a cocked up hat and a long tailed cream-coloured horse. He says he will have seventeen thousand a year to spend; others say seventeen hundred. He and my Lady go on as usual. The Duchesse de Guiche visits there in solitary womanhood; indeed she says it is a great bore and she can stand it no longer.

At what precise stage Westmacott sent the demand for money, which most certainly would have followed the first or second of these paragraphs, is not known. But evidently his offer to sell his paper's silence was either roughly rejected or ignored, for a fortnight later the tone of comment has changed from facetious insinuation to frank insolence. On October 11, "Otiosus" writes to the editor a description of a ceremonial fête:

> A little further is the Duc de Guiche whom his mother-in-law (who died of drinking brandy) used to call in her excellent German French *le beau bête*. He visits the club, while the Duchess visits Lady Blessington! What a ménage is that of Lady Blessington! It would create sensations, were it not for one fair flower that still blooms under the shade of the Upas. Can it be conceived in England that M. Alfred d'Orsay has publicly detailed to what degree he has carried his apathy for his pretty interesting wife, and has boasted

of his continence? This young gentleman, Lady Blessington, and the virgin-wife of 16 all live together. You must surely remember a lady who, some fifteen years ago, was *acting wife* to a Captain J. of some dragoon regiment. As he had nothing but his spurs and his whiskers Mrs. J. used to levy taxes on her friends, according to the system here called *les contributions indirectes*. Petersham introduced her to a lord, who like a fool married her.

This insulting passage was too outrageous to be ignored. It must have made a stir in London, for news of it reached the Avenue de Matignon immediately and Lady Blessington, on the advice of the British ambassador, wrote to her late husband's solicitor to start proceedings forthwith. The solicitor temporised. There were no grounds for action; better treat the *Age* with the contempt it deserved. By December nothing had been done. The Countess' circle in Paris were highly indignant, and certain officers crossed to London to make enquiries and, if opportunity offered, to take revenge. But by now Westmacott knew his business. He had been flogged more than once in his earlier, incautious days and was now carefully guarded from dangerous interviewers. Nevertheless, for some months he thought it prudent to keep silent. The original paragraphs had done their work, and Tory society, at least, was well infected with an anti-Blessington virus. If the lady would not pay, she must make up her mind to remain abroad. London, at least, was awake to the moral danger of her company. And just to make matters doubly sure, he inserted on March 7, 1830, one final comment:

The Count makes the most loving of *beaux fils* to his *belle mère* (*à la mode de Bretagne*). They are scarcely ever asunder. Lady Blessington is really a charming woman.

The immediate effect of Westmacott's little campaign on Lady Blessington and her household can be easily imagined. In normal circumstances and after the first shock of her husband's death had passed, she would have gone to England, for a while at any rate, in order to see to her affairs. Thereafter she would probably have returned to France, where she now had many friends and was well placed for seeing such Englishmen as she wished to see on their visits to Paris or on their way to Italy. But the autumn of 1829, when in the ordinary way she would have contemplated visiting London, was the time of Westmacott's most offensive mud-slinging. She was frightened and remained in Paris. By the new year, the position with regard to Blessington's estate, and the angry hostility with which she and d'Orsay were regarded by her husband's relatives, would have been well and disconcertingly known. She then decided to remain in Paris altogether, to live out the short lease of the beautiful new house and then move into quieter and simpler quarters. But once again circumstances defeated inclination. In the first place, it became more and more evident that she could not conduct the business arising out of Blessington's will (she had the d'Orsays' interest to guard as well as her own) at such a distance from London. Secondly, she realised that her own livelihood depended nearly as much on a profitable sale of the house in St. James's Square as on the annual two thousand pounds, which was all the cash income she could command; and no one could attend to the clearing of this house and to its disposal but herself. Thirdly, there were certain "painful circumstances" to which Madden alludes and at the nature of which a guess will in due course be made. Finally the unrest in the French capital, which had been visibly growing during the early months of the year, broke out in July into open and successful revolution. So, almost despite herself, she once more changed her plans.

During the actual upheaval she lingered in Paris; and her diary contains a vivid and interesting account of what occurred. She describes the first outbreaks of fighting; the incompetent complacency of the ministers of Charles X; the raising of the barricades; the growing lawlessness and mastery of the mob, and the final chaos when, the Bourbons having been ejected for a second time from the throne of France, their conquerors split into two factions, who hated one another more than the tyrants they had overthrown. At last the convulsion was over and some semblance of order restored; but Lady Blessington found the face of the city gravely altered. The de Guiches (and their parents, the de Gramonts), Madame Craufurd and the circle of pleasant, wealthy folk who had made up the society to which she and her husband had belonged, were temporarily eclipsed. The Duc de Guiche had been closely attached to the royal family and accompanied them on their flight into exile. His wife and her intimates were wisely unobtrusive during the period of transition. Even the shattered trees in the Champs Élysées were eloquent of changed and unfamiliar times. Thus a new and unfriendly Paris came to reinforce the practical arguments for a return to England; and, though her heart was heavy with reluctance and dread, Lady Blessington made up her mind to face forthwith the menace of a hostile London.

Was there ever any question of d'Orsay not accompanying her? The speculation is interesting. He was, oddly enough, as well served by the July revolution as his sister's family were damaged; for the d'Orsays had always been Bonapartist, and had suffered in Bourbon estimation for that very fact. Certainly Madame Craufurd, who had originally engineered her grandson's commission in the Garde Royale, had also succeeded in preserving Alfred and his father from active official hostility during the reign of Charles X. But while the revolution was in progress and after the Duc d'Orléans had accepted the crown and become King of the French, d'Orsay was several times recognised by street fighters or demonstrating crowds and loudly cheered, just for being d'Orsay. From the political point of view, therefore, he could comfortably have remained in Paris and, maybe, have found lucrative favour with the Bourbons' successors.

But his personal interest was more mixed. There is reason to doubt whether his wife was any longer a negligible quantity, to be disposed of as desired. As will be seen, her individual unacceptability to the new régime may well have had something to do with the household's move to London. Also his inheritance promised complications. On the one hand, he would have to rely on Lady Blessington to unravel on his behalf the complexities of English legal practice, and he was quite sensitive and intelligent enough to realise that his presence in London might still further inflame an already angry situation. On the other, although by the letter of the late Earl's will and on paper he was a man of wealth, there was already uncertainty as to the extent to which that wealth actually existed. So, though discretion suggested that the lady make her journey alone, that lady's urgent wish for his company, financial doubts, and maybe domestic difficulties also, weighted the scales the other way. Therefore he bowed to necessity and prepared for his second visit to England.

CHAPTER VI

Facing the Music

Two thousand pounds a year and the unexpired portion of a lease in St. James's Square (apart from her jewellery, effects, *objets d'art* and the furniture, plate and linen in the London house) were now the entire personal resources of the Countess of Blessington. They would have been adequate for retired elegance in Bruton Street or for continued though discreet residence abroad, but as basis for luxury of the kind to which she had now grown accustomed they were absurd.

Did she resent the will? We do not know; no word of comment on the circumstances in which she was left is passed in any of her books, nor in any of the manuscript material discoverable. Nor is it possible to gauge what had been in Blessington's mind when he allotted his wife so small a fraction of his ostensibly vast possessions. Did it never occur to him that they might be parted before old age had come and their joint lives had settled to a quiet dignity? Or was he asserting on paper an independence from her domination which to her face he could not achieve? Or was he punishing her for having in some way opposed his wishes — for her dislike of his house at Mountjoy, maybe; even for her presumption in claiming a share in d'Orsay's affection? Whatever its motive, the queer stinginess was to have results even queerer.

But not immediately. Indeed, she seems to have planned and carried out her assault on London with no financial qualms and, for twelve months at least, with no financial difficulty. How did she do it? One can only assume by pooling her own resources with those reputedly at the disposal of the Count and

Countess d'Orsay. She herself had been left little enough, but her stepdaughter and her stepdaughter's husband were part of her household; and they, at any rate on paper, were rich. Within twelve months of their marriage in 1827, twenty thousand pounds had been paid over for their account to trustees, and by the Earl's will, a further twenty thousand pounds were within twelve months of his death to be paid to the same trustees and invested for the d'Orsays' benefit. In addition, d'Orsay, as husband of Lady Harriet, would control the income from Blessington's Dublin estates, of which the annual rental value (less the widow's jointure) was nominally over ten thousand pounds.

Lady Blessington, therefore, in estimating the means at her disposal, would have added to her own jointure the interest on forty thousand pounds and a share of the d'Orsays' income from Dublin property, and have planned her life accordingly.

Her first act on arriving in London in November, 1830, was to sublet St. James's Square. Not only was the house too large for her needs, but its furnishings were less to her taste than the mass of cabinets, tables, china and ornaments which she had brought with her from Paris. She found a tenant in Windham's Club; but only at a profit of about five hundred a year over the rent she herself had to pay to the original landlord. When it transpired that this profit was to be subject to continual charges for repairs to a dilapidated building, she found the property more of a liability than an asset; and, two or three years later, did what she should have done originally — sold out her interest in the lease to the Blessington trustees.

Meantime she rented for her own use Lord Mountford's house in Seamore Place, Park Lane. Under d'Orsay's supervision and regardless of expense, the building was elaborately decorated and the necessary standard of comfort achieved. With this as her headquarters, she proceeded to make her bid for social leadership.

Lady Blessington had shrewdly gauged the problem which awaited her in London. Vested interests were already in possession, prepared to resent any newcomer and doubly to resent such a one as she. A widow, without assured position and recently the subject of slanderous gossip, she must rely on her own wits and her own courage to effect a lodgment in hostile territory. This done, she was confident that her skill as hostess would keep her there. Wherefore she summoned her courage and set her wits to work.

There must be no half measures. She would make a direct assault on the leisure hours of fashionable London, and she would provide entertainment of a kind elsewhere unobtainable. Long residence abroad had taught her so to combine luxury and mental stimulus as to produce the highest form of hospitality. The Englishmen who had visited her in Naples, Florence, Rome and Paris had left her in no doubt that her entertaining had a something which the greatest London houses lacked. Its atmosphere at once gracious and happy, at once elegant and friendly, enchanted the intelligent and disconcerted only those pompous or empty-headed persons whom she had no desire to see. She argued that if she could reproduce this atmosphere in London, her house would be unique and irresistible. She would attract precisely the friends she wanted and, secure in their admiring affection and behind her own dignified façade, would be able to live the life she wished to live, and worry not at all over the evil speaking of her rivals.

The three principal London hostesses to men of talent and wit were at this time Lady Holland, Lady Charleville and Lady Cork. The first was an old enemy. Although herself a remarried divorcée, she had been both free and caustic with her comments on the apotheosis of the dubious Margaret Farmer into the glittering Countess of Blessington, so that when the latter had left London in 1823, the two ladies were already vowed antagonists. Lady Holland ruled her salon by a domineering rudeness of manner; by her skill in keeping conversation general, and by her merited reputation for staunch friendship to those she liked. She was also greatly helped by her political traditions and by the popularity and kindly nature of her husband.

To compete with Lady Holland, Lady Blessington could only rely on her own more striking personal beauty, her unvarying good temper, her talent for rapid and amusing epigram, and her complete freedom from Whig associations. In this last she was unexpectedly assisted by the regrouping of parties consequent on the agitation for reform. The period of unrest which preceded the Reform Bill produced a radical sentiment among many men of family and fashion, who as thoroughly resented the mentality of the Whig oligarchs as that of their natural opponents, the Tories. Lady Blessington laid herself out to welcome these aristocratic radicals, and so secured for her salon Lord Durham, the Bulwer brothers, the young Disraeli and others, whom Lady Holland dared not receive, even if she would.

Lady Charleville, in her great house in Cavendish Square, was a more difficult matter. To begin with, she was a woman of general popularity; secondly, her avowed policy as a hostess was to reconcile possible hostilities, thus forestalling one of Lady Blessington's favourite maxims that the greatest cause of animosity between individuals of different classes or occupations is lack of acquaintanceship. But Cavendish Square's principal threat to the peace of mind of Seamore Place lay in Lady Charleville's Irish origins and connections. Married first to a well-known gentleman of County Louth, and second to Viscount Tullamoore (created Earl of Charleville in the peerage of Ireland in 1806) she was intimate with all the celebrities of contemporary Ireland. Among these, as Lady Blessington soon had reason to know, was the Dowager Lady Mountjoy, stepmother of the late Lord Blessington and his widow's implacable enemy. From instinct, therefore, Lady Blessington would have left Lady Charleville alone, neither commenting tartly on her mannerisms nor trespassing on her social territory; and if only the latter had not in a most peculiar manner become involved with the household in Seamore Place, the avoidance might have been mutual. As things turned out, however, Lady Charleville, though she and Lady Blessington never actually met, was to play an important part in the latter's London misadventures.

Between Lady Blessington and Lady Cork, there was less likelihood either of rivalry or of mutual forbearance. The now aged (and always eccentric) Countess of Cork and Orrery was rather a London institution than a London hostess. Usually referred to as "Corky", she was eighty-four years of age when Lady Blessington came to London, very short, very stout and splendidly flamboyant in her dress and *maquillage*. An intimate of Doctor Johnson and his circle during the seventeen-eighties, she had for half a century made a hobby of conversational entertaining. Since her widowing in 1798, she had lived at Number 6 New Burlington Street, and devoted her energies and intelligence to dinners and receptions, whither sooner or later anybody who was anybody (and many who were not) inevitably came. Universally laughed at but universally liked, she became more and more of an oddity as she grew older. Already in 1809 Lady Charleville in a letter to Mrs. Opie could say: "Poor dear Lady Cork's activity in pursuit of amusement is a pleasant proof of vivacity and spirit surviving youth." Yet twenty-five years later she was still at it. In 1834 C. R. Leslie, the painter, thus noted in his autobiography a meeting with her: "Lady Cork is very old, infirm and diminutive, dressed all in white, with a white bonnet which she wore at table. . . . Her features are delicate and her skin fair and notwithstanding her great age she is very animated. She was attended by a boy page in a fantastical green livery with a cap and a high plume of black feathers. The old lady, who was a lion-hunter in her youth, is as much one now as ever."

Lady Cork comes and goes through the volumes of Moore's diary, now complaining that the Regent would never come near her since Moore in the "Twopenny Post Bag" described him at one of her parties; now interrupting a rehearsal of "Comus" forcibly to unbutton the poet's waistcoat and stick a large pitch plaster on his chest, as remedy for the cold of which he had rashly complained; now greeting Lord Lansdowne on the occasion of a morning call: "Come in, come in! I am so glad you arrived at this moment! Only think — the grey parrot has laid an egg!"

This parrot was the original of Lady Sydney Morgan's amusing "Memoirs of a Macaw of a Lady of Quality",[1] from which we learn of Lady Cork's pink boudoir; of the continual crowd of guests, eminent and otherwise, which filled the house; and of the great evening when the conservatory was fitted up to look like a Brazilian forest, with tin palm trees, a stuffed alligator, and an artificial upas tree on which the macaw was solemnly enthroned to display his master trick of drawing out, clipping and smoking a cigar. He died in 1836 and his sorrowing mistress (she was six weeks short of ninety) wrote with her own hand to Lady Morgan: "Your old friend departed this life a few days ago; he is buried in my garden. He committed but one crime and only made a bit of an assault on George the Fourth's stocking. That was an *offence* merely. The crime was running away with a piece out of Lady Darlington's leg."

In 1831 during the agitation for reform, "she caused considerable indignation" (so Lady Charleville says in a letter to her daughter) "by hanging flags out of her windows inscribed: The Bill, the true Bill, and down with the Rich! — in other words playing *égalité*." On another occasion her guests at a dinner party all got rheumatism, because as an experiment she had removed the window sashes and stretched oiled silk across the opening, painted to represent the absent windowpanes.

It is said that a mild kleptomania took possession of Lady Cork during the last years of her life, and that considerate hosts would leave a fork or spoon in the hall for her to slip into her muff on departure. It is also said that she was the model for

[1] "The Book without a Name." 1841. Vol. I, pp. 257–316.

Lady Bellair in Disraeli's "Henrietta Temple" and for Mrs. Leo Hunter in the "Pickwick Papers." The former is possible; but the latter argues an association of ideas too indirect to be of much interest. The significance of Lady Cork lay in herself; and her lion hunting was merely one of many expressions of a vital and lovable personality. With her loud, genial voice, her unflagging spirits, her downright, outspoken talk and her good-humoured readiness to ridicule herself or any one else, she must, alike in manner and appearance, somewhat have resembled the late Amy Lowell.

With her eighteenth-century traditions, her privileged and unshakeable position, her racy indifference to opinions both private and public, Lady Cork would hardly of herself have troubled even to realise Lady Blessington's existence. But, thanks to her intimacy with Lady Morgan, she was made aware of the newcomer to Seamore Place and in terms highly charged with the malice characteristic of that voluble and indiscreet little "blue." Lady Morgan had transferred her dislike of Blessington to his widow, who had become (Archer-Shee tells us) her "favourite aversion", so that "to allude to Lady Blessington is like shaking a red rag in front of a bull and is sure to call forth some startling revelation in reference to her early career." Lady Blessington responded in kind, calling Sydney Morgan "old eighteen-penny" because her eyes were different sizes, like a shilling and a sixpence. Seeing that among the *habitués* of Number 6 New Burlington Street were several — notably Lord John Russell and James Smith — who were also regular frequenters of Lady Blessington's drawing-room, long-range hostilities between the two houses could satisfactorily develop. One can imagine that Lady Cork would not mince her words in devising tart reference to the latest society hostess; and the quips of one lady against another, however lightly they be meant, pass rapidly through the *coulisses* of cultivated London, gaining as they go both momentum and asperity.

Such were the three salon holders with whom Lady Blessington was quite ready to compete. So long as rivalry took the form of tempting to her house and away from theirs sufficient persons of the right kind, she was not afraid of the outcome, nor had need to be. Confident in her own power to attract, to interest, and so to hold the sort of men she wished to know, she was careful to provide herself with the setting best calculated to reinforce that power and to display both her beauty and her personality. Hence the lavish adornment of Seamore Place, which became in Jekyll's words "a house of bijoux and a bijou of a house"; hence also the skill with which emphasis was laid, not as usual on the drawing-room, but on a specially created boudoir-library and on the room where meals were taken.

The former — the Countess' particular sanctum — was a long narrow room, with tall windows looking out on to Hyde Park. It was painted in white and gold, and lined with book-cases to within nine feet of the ceiling. On the top of the book-cases stood two superb vases in royal blue Sèvres, mounted in ormolu and carrying five-branched lily candelabra, which had previously belonged to Marie Antoinette; Sèvres bottles of apple green; a pair of Sèvres lidded urns of the same rare colour; a pair of potpourri vases with covers; and a Dresden-china flower basket, also in Sèvres and coloured after nature. Under an elaborately wrought gilt lamp, which hung from the centre of the arched ceiling, stood the Countess' armchair, an immense affair deeply sprung and covered in yellow satin. On a table at her elbow were arranged the newest books and, palely gleaming on some rich morocco cover, a marble or silver model of one of her hands. Other tables and consoles in tortoise-shell or ormolu stood here and there about the room. They were crowded with knick-knacks, among them no doubt the collection of objects once belonging to remarkable men and women, which the Countess had begun at Venice and greatly increased during her first year in Paris. Here lay an *étui* of gold, set with agate and brilliants, and a smelling bottle of rock crystal, both of which

LADY BLESSINGTON
(during the thirties)
After a water colour by Chalon, in the National Portrait Gallery, London

had been the property of Madame de Sevigné; here was Madame de Maintenon's pincushion, heart-shaped, in gold and enamel, and (as Lady Blessington remarked when entering the purchase in her diary) "stuck as full of pins as were the hearts of the French protestants with thorns by the Revocation of the Edict of Nantes." Over there were the same lady's knife, fork and spoon, of old Italian workmanship and set with turquoises; the scissors of Madame du Deffand; the patch box of Ninon de l'Enclos; and the snuffbox, set with diamonds, which once stood on the Marquise's table in the Hôtel Rambouillet. In a glass-topped bric-à-brac table, amid a profusion of costly trifles, lay a watch, painted on the face with a portrait of the Pompadour, on whose forehead an enamelled star flashed on and off at the bidding of some inner mechanism. At its side were two snuff-boxes, one with a lid studded with emeralds, given by Louis XIV to Admiral Tourville, the other in oriental carnelian, mounted in gold and patterned with brilliants and amethysts.

Sofas, ottomans and occasional chairs were scattered about the room; busts and statues occupied niches and corners; and the feet sank silently into a deep, patterned carpet.

To give great originality to her drawing-room Lady Blessington realised was impossible. London made a speciality of drawing-rooms, and the most she could hope to do was to provide it with certain treasures of furnishing and ornament to which no other house could lay claim. The chosen colouring was ruby red and gold, and the walls, not being required for bookcases, were crowded with pictures and miniatures, with mirrors of every size and shape, with shaded candelabra fixed between the panels of silk brocade. Here were the principal cabinets, in black and tortoise-shell buhl; the grand piano; a finely modelled fender, terminating in two superb eagles from Malmaison; and Marie Antoinette's famous clock from the Petit Trianon, with its pedestal of royal blue Sèvres and its case of chased ormolu.

With the dining room, however, she achieved a masterpiece.

The room was octagonal and lined with mirrors, so that the lighted dinner table, with its gleaming plate and glass, was repeatedly and variously reflected. Lady Blessington sat at the head of the table in one of the carved gilt state-chairs ordered by George IV for the reception of Louis XVIII in the early eighteen-twenties. Fully aware of the value of her background of sombre masculinity, she always dined in a richly coloured gown of velvet or satin, cut very low, so that her superb shoulders and arms shone with a sort of dazzling warmth in the candlelight.

To the astonishing loveliness of Lady Blessington at dinner and of the smooth, silent luxury of the meal's organization, many who were privileged to be present have borne witness. The food was exquisite — not ostentatious but very good; the wines were scrupulously chosen; the service, in the hands of footmen in liveries of green and gold, was noiseless and efficient. On the table were bowls of fruit and flowers; and it is said that Lady Blessington was the first to introduce into England the idea that natural colours, as opposed to the glitter of gold or silver plate, are the best central decoration for a dinner table.

Truly Seamore Place made a brave and brilliant début. The installation was perfect, both as a setting for its mistress' beauty and as *décor* for the particular social comedy which she had decided to stage; and from the first moment of its opening, it triumphed. Every evening from eight to twelve, except when she was at opera or theatre, she received visitors. She had made so many friends during her years abroad, was herself such good company and so free alike from coquetry and arrogance that, with a rapidity which was mortification to the rival houses, Seamore Place became the mode among men of talent and distinction. During the first year of her residence, the visitors were not predominantly men of letters. Statesmen, diplomats, soldiers, painters; men of rank and ability from every European land, came to pay their respects to a woman they really liked, and stayed to wander through the brilliant rooms, to examine the treasures of which the house was full, and to enjoy the free and natural conversation of cosmopolitan society at its ease.

Jekyll made a note of one of his evenings there (in January, 1832) and paid tribute to the lavish gaiety of the talk and the hostess' decorative charm:

> George Colman, James Smith, Rogers and Campbell dined with me yesterday at a Parisian repast of much refinement given us by the Countess of Blessington. There was wit, fun, epigram and raillery enough to supply fifty county members for a twelve-month. Miladi has doffed her widow's weeds and was almost in pristine beauty.

A pleasant freedom from the artificial constraints of polite society was the special achievement of Lady Blessington's hospitality. It was not the freedom of license. Indeed, serenity and mutual courtesy were axiomatic, because every one concerned was too much interested in exchanging ideas even to think of rowdier enjoyments. On the other hand, no subjects were taboo; and the scope permitted to conversation, as much as its quality, was the attraction of her home. This enlightened liberty of talk would have been impossible had the guests at Seamore Place included women as well as men; and it is important to realise that the success and popularity of Lady Blessington's parties were largely created by the very ostracism which was meant to destroy them. Respectable British females kept aloof — ostensibly because the Countess was a woman whose present was little less equivocal than her past; secretly, one suspects, because they feared external comparisons and were none too sure of being a match for her mental qualities and her dangerous tongue. But their men-folk had no such prejudice. Lady Blessington had feminine beauty and the quick feminine sympathy which makes a hostess of genius; but her femininity was never a challenge to men, nor imposed that reserve which men instinctively feel in social contacts with the other sex. Also she was as widely read and travelled as most of her guests, could talk to them intelligently on their own subjects, and, being more interested in conversation than in gossip about other people or than in winning admiration for herself, was at once a stimulus and a delightful companion to men seriously concerned with their own activities or with public affairs. So it was that Seamore Place had all the advantages of a congenial club, with the added attractions of a lovely and intelligent hostess, elegant comfort and first-rate catering. To Seamore Place, therefore, men of taste were eager to go.

CHAPTER VII

THE AUTUMN OF 1831

1

BY audacity, combined with a perfect understanding of her own resources and the best way of using them, Lady Blessington had made her coup. The suddenness of her attack had taken her enemies by surprise; and for several months it seemed as though the position carried so gallantly by storm might remain permanently in her occupation.

But counterstrokes were preparing and, more serious still, there came disruption and treachery in her own camp. They worked so quickly and destructively that between July and December, 1831, the whole prospects of her life changed, and whereas in June the frontage of Seamore Place masked not luxury alone but also gay serenity, by the end of the year only the luxury remained.

No period in the life of Lady Blessington is at once so obscure and so vitally important as these last six months of 1831. They are important, because they stand at the watershed of her prosperity and happiness. Previous to them and despite her widowing, she was in a fair way to win just such a victory against the world as she desired; after they had passed, her life — for all its continuing surface bravery — was a *dégringolade* through heartbreak and desperate toil to exile and death. As for their obscurity, it is due, like most other obscurities in the unhappy story of the Blessington succession, to lack of evidence about d'Orsay's marriage to Harriet Gardiner, a lack which can only be due to deliberate suppression. The secret of the disasters which took place during the summer and autumn of 1831 lies in the collapse of the d'Orsay marriage, and the essential details of that collapse have been no less scrupulously forgotten than have those of its planning and its celebration. In consequence, among previous biographers of Lady Blessington is even disagreement as to when Harriet Gardiner and d'Orsay parted, while no one of them recognises in this parting the true crisis in the fortunes of Lady Blessington. And yet it must be so recognised, even though in the process conjecture be used to reinforce fact. Fortunately, certain documentary evidence having now for the first time come to light, the proportion of conjecture can be considerably reduced; but it is only fair to state frankly that what follows is partly inferential and can only claim to be nearer the truth than any interpretation hitherto suggested.

It has been explained that the cost of her ladyship's full-dress invasion of London can only have been met by actually spending (or, at least, by using as collateral) the personal income of the Countess d'Orsay. Lady Harriet was living at Seamore Place, but took little if any part in the continual hospitality of the house. One of Jekyll's letters is apparently the only contemporary document to mention her at all:

"The Countess of Blessington," he writes on July 18, 1831, "gave a dinner on Friday. Lord Wilton, General Phipps, d'Orsay and myself. The pretty melancholy Comtesse glided in for a few minutes and then left us to nurse her influenza."

Madden, while maintaining that her stepmother treated her with civility and kindness, makes clear that Harriet was little less remote from the life of her London home than as a child she had been shut out of things in Italy and France. But there was this difference between then and now — that whereas a shy girl of fifteen in a foreign country could do nothing but submit and nurse her grievances in silence, the now handsome, rather sombre young woman of eighteen was not only herself more assertive, but in London was within reach of sympathisers.

There can be very little doubt that Lady Blessington's enemies recognised in Harriet d'Orsay the joint in the harness of Seamore Place, that they were quick to win her confidence and, having realised her unhappiness, to change it into resentment. Certainly, as 1831 drew on, relations between Harriet d'Orsay, her husband and her stepmother grew rapidly worse. The girl passed from aloofness to ill humour and from ill humour to defiance. It was at this juncture, where he might most signally have helped his benefactress, that d'Orsay failed her. He must have known that the plan to conquer London depended in great part on his wife's money; he must have been privy to that plan and approved it; he must have discerned his wife's growing discontent and have guessed that persons would not be lacking in England ready to work upon that discontent to his and Lady Blessington's discomfiture. Yet instead of grasping the dangers of the situation, instead of exerting himself to counter the influences hostile to Lady Blessington by the personal charm he so abundantly possessed, he went to the other extreme. It is even possible (as will be seen) to suspect him of a villainy which, though it might have been of financial benefit to himself, could only have resulted in complete social ruin for the mistress of Seamore Place.

Nor was this all. At a time when every available pound was required for consolidating the victory so bravely won, he plunged on his own account into insensate extravagance. We learn (from legal correspondence which passed early in 1832) that since reaching London he had raised money to nearly the whole amount of the interest due on the forty thousand pounds which trustees held on his and Harriet's behalf. And that money was not only raised but spent. He ran reckless accounts with numerous London tailors, glove makers, bootmakers, hatters, carriage builders, hairdressers and horse dealers; he played for high stakes at Crockford's; he frequented every haunt of sporting men, aspiring to be as potent an arbiter on the race course and in the boxing ring as he was already of dandy elegance.

These selfish indiscretions on the part of d'Orsay intensified the material misfortunes which, one after another, during the second six months of 1831, befell the hapless Lady Blessington. No doubt those who sought to destroy her would sooner or later have contrived a hostile move; indeed, we can be almost certain that legal action was definitely contemplated. But litigation need not have set all London by the ears, if only d'Orsay had remained loyal to the policy of self-sufficient privacy which was the policy of Seamore Place. Instead, when publicity was least needed, he sought it frenziedly. His levity in company and his ostentatious frequentation of all places where fashion was most spendthrift attracted wide attention. In consequence, what might have remained a domestic quarrel was magnified into a society scandal.

2

The public happenings of these fatal six months which turned Lady Blessington's hopes of social victory into the certainty of defeat, which shattered her prosperity and destroyed her contentment, were in summary the following: First of all, newspaper scandal and ill-natured personal gossip suddenly broke out again. Then Harriet d'Orsay took the extreme step of leaving her husband and seeking the protection of her Gardiner relations. Then, in the name of Blessington's illegitimate son, Charles Gardiner, a suit was filed in dispute of the late Earl's will against both Lady Blessington and Count d'Orsay.

Scandal-sheet scurrility had ceased since the outbreak of 1829–1830, but now it started afresh, voicing apparently a rising murmur of innuendo from certain circles of fashion.

On July 31, the *Satirist* published the following "Riddle by Lord Glengall":

> My first the reverse of a curse,
>   My second a very great weight is,
> My whole neither better nor worse
>   Than a dame from the land of potatoes.

LADY HARRIET GARDINER

After a painting by J. C. Hook, R.A.
By permission of the Reverend A. J. Whyte

Of her daughter-in-law
She makes a cat's-paw
(Ask the fair virgin bride
By Count d'Orsay's side).

There seems no reason to doubt the authorship of this unattractive jingle, which comes convincingly from so second-rate and insolent an intelligence as that of Lord Glengall.[1] Nor need its publication have troubled Lady Blessington, had it not been that Glengall belonged to the small but obtrusive set of titled elegants, who had arrogated to themselves during the eighteen-twenties the right to set the fashion in clubs, clothes and cachet, and found a delightful coincidence between the yellow-press idea of society news and their own idea of self-advertisement. This clique, despite its bad-mannered presumption, stood for *ton*. It could make or mar a social career, for it included persons more important than Glengall, of whom the most dangerous to Lady Blessington was the Countess of Jersey.

Sarah Sophia Fane, daughter of the Earl of Westmoreland, granddaughter and heiress of the banker Child, and wife of the fifth Earl of Jersey, was sister to the same Lord Burghersh who, as minister at Florence, had refused to marry d'Orsay and Harriet Gardiner and had insulted Lady Blessington to her face. Lady Jersey's mind was acute; her social ambitions precise and ruthless; her private fortune very large; and her character that of a carefully emancipated puritan — which type was rarer a century ago than it is nowadays and in consequence less easily neutralised. As president of the committee of patronesses of Almacks, she was a powerful social influence; and because she thought it smart to appear ill-bred but really ill-bred to be immoral, she had established a dominion over the minds of her socially aspiring countrywomen of a kind which any one familiar with the mentality of the British snob will readily appreciate.

Among the preoccupations of Lady Jersey were two no less paradoxical than her nature. In the first place, she was highly conscious of bearing the same name as her predecessor, the fourth

[1] *Cf.* "Edward and Rosina", pp. 156–158, and *note*.

Lady Jersey, who had been notorious as one of George IV's irregularities. So Lady Jersey the fifth determined, by an aggressive parade of personal virtue, to disassociate herself from the too recent past. This naturally caused a breach between her and George IV while he lived, but enabled her puritanism to find congenial expression, and herself common ground with Burghersh — or, at any rate, with Burghersh's wife. It also made her, almost despite herself, an "Exclusive", in that those who did not fear her disliked her. The lofty purity of her attitude was apt to impress non-sycophants as a rather comic superciliousness. "Her bearing," says Gronow, "was that of a theatrical tragedy queen; whilst attempting the sublime, she frequently made herself simply ridiculous, being inconceivably rude and in her manner often ill-bred." Even Greville, who admired her talents and shared her social and political views, admits she was a reckless and contentious talker.

The second of Lady Jersey's ambitions was to be up-to-date. Her enthusiasms, her affectations, her eccentricities, must all be of the very latest, and must be made known as *hers,* to the largest possible number of people. In consequence, she found a place in more than one of the so-called "fashionable novels", which from the mid-twenties to about 1840 were at once the most read and the most abused of contemporary fiction.

In that clever novel "Almacks" (1826) she appears as "Lady Hauton." She rouges heavily; dabbles in political intrigue; is neither young, handsome nor amusing, but well-dressed, ceaselessly and cleverly loquacious, and (above all) *impudent.* "Treat people like fools," she says, "and they will worship you" — which she does and they do. She is rude, capricious, unpunctual, ready to shock but even readier to be shocked. In short, at once intolerant and provocative, she is the ideal despot of a hypocritical society in chaos, and as such dominates the parvenu world of the eighteen-twenties.

As "Lady Tilney" in "The Exclusives" (1829) she cuts an equally coherent and repellent figure. She pretends great scorn of royalty (an echo of the quarrel with the king), is insolent to presumed inferiors, and with the rest of her set (which includes the Princess Lieven, Lady Tankerville and the second and more lurid of the two Ladies Ellenborough), talks in a drawling, cynical manner, speaks of the "baroque fancy of being married in a church", and generally forestalls with commendable accuracy many of the mannered amoralities of another post-war period. She reappears in the more eminent pages of "Coningsby" and "Sybil" as "Lady St. Julians", by this time a mother of marriageable daughters and a matchmaker of ruthless competence.

With such ambitions and affectations, Lady Jersey's hostility to Lady Blessington was instinctive. The story of the d'Orsay marriage would have reached her direct from her brother; doubtless it had been supplemented with comments on Lady Blessington of a highly critical kind. Now there had appeared in London this very woman — a woman whose first matrimonial experiment had been suspiciously obscure and her second no less suspiciously spectacular; of whose life abroad Burghersh, at any rate, took an unfavourable view; whose household in Seamore Place was, to say the least of it, unusual. No self-respecting English lady, with strong and carefully advertised opinions on morals and the sanctity of marriage, could fail to disapprove of the newcomer nor, in the interests of social decency, abstain from active protest against her. And as if this were not enough, Lady Blessington with rapidity and success had won a following of desirable notabilities, by a display of personality as incisive and as unexpected as Lady Jersey's own and a great deal more cordial and unaffected. Clothed, therefore, in the wrathful dignity of outraged virtue, and having exhorted her followers to do their share, Lady Jersey prepared to rid London of a social plague spot and herself (though this more privately) of a vexatious rival.

3

Meantime active hostility of a kind more serious but more respectable was preparing among the relatives of Harriet d'Orsay; and although no connection can be proved between their activities and the ribald chatter of Lady Jersey and her friends, it can hardly be doubted that the one was a reflection of the other.

The fact that at this juncture the Gardiner family were framing an aggressive policy has hitherto been unrecorded. It might have been guessed at, but its details were unknown. Now, however, thanks to the discovery of certain private letters written by the Countess of Charleville (quotation from which their owner has with generous courtesy permitted), important, if sometimes bewildering, light can be thrown on Gardiner aspirations, and also on the extent to which d'Orsay and his wife (to the exclusion of Lady Blessington) were personally and disreputably involved with a rakish set of smart young people.

It will be recalled that Lady Charleville was as much in Irish as in English society, and that she was closely acquainted with relatives of the late Lord Blessington. The Dowager Lady Mountjoy was still resident in Dublin, and presumably Charles Gardiner, the surviving (illegitimate) son of Lord Blessington, who came of age in 1831, was living with or near her. But we now learn for the first time that Lady Mountjoy's stepdaughter (Blessington's elder sister), Miss Harriet Gardiner, had come over to London early in 1831 and there set up house. With her was her niece Emily (Harriet d'Orsay's sister, Blessington's elder and illegitimate daughter). The significance of Charles Gardiner's coming of age in 1831, and of his aunt's and sister's migration to London at the beginning of the same year becomes evident, as the story of what occurred is gradually pieced together.

Now it happens that the proceedings and movements of Lady Charleville's own family, as well as those of the Gardiners, are relevant to the events of the next months. A few words of explanation are therefore necessary. Lady Charleville had two children by her first husband — a son, James Tisdall, and a daughter, Louisa, who in 1828 had married a Colonel George

Marlay and was closely in her mother's confidence. By her second (Charleville) marriage she had another son, Lord Tullamoore, at this time a man of about thirty.

It appears that during the spring and summer of 1831, Lady Charleville was greatly troubled by the reckless extravagance and rumoured insecurity of Tullamoore's establishment. Ten years earlier he had married Miss Beaujolais Campbell, daughter of Lady Charlotte Bury by her first husband, and a young woman both beautiful and spoilt. Of consumptive tendency and made free of society during the hectic eighteen-twenties, Lady Tullamoore had developed into a pleasure-mad neurasthenic typical of a time of post-war carnival. She belonged to a raffish and dissipated set, which included her brother-in-law, Lord Uxbridge (by now a widower), Lord Sefton, and various of the younger Campbells. Tullamoore himself seems to have been easily led, but temperamentally a conscientious young man, who consoled himself for his inability to curb his wife's extravagance and wildness by spending hours at the House of Commons and in the intervals joining in her revels. Lady Charleville strongly disapproved of her daughter-in-law and her friends, but kept on terms with them for her son's sake, whose "social qualities have made him their prey and dupe." Her letters to her daughter, Mrs. Marlay, at present convalescing at Tunbridge Wells, are principally concerned with Tullamoore — his fatigues and his follies and the blatant indiscretions of his wife.

It is in July, 1831, that mention of the inhabitants of Seamore Place is first made in Lady Charleville's letters. Tullamoore has met d'Orsay with Sefton and Uxbridge, while Harriet d'Orsay (who may well in the first instance have been invited to Charleville House) has become quite a regular visitor to Lady Tullamoore. It is important to realise that with Lady Charleville's breeding and good sense was blended a strong element of opportunism — so strong, indeed, that some might call it arrivism. Although she conducted her own life and home with dignity, she was tolerant of society's frailties, except when they led her Tullamoore astray or threatened his domestic peace.

It happened that during July this double menace was clouding her maternal prospect. Gossip was linking Lady Tullamoore's name with that of Lord Uxbridge, and the helpless mother saw her son not only tied to an extravagant hussy but, maybe, cuckolded into the bargain. And as if this were not enough, Tullamoore, already friendly with d'Orsay, was becoming (or so the world said) more than friendly with d'Orsay's wife, Harriet.

It is in some agitation, therefore, that on August 4 Lady Charleville writes to her daughter the first letter from which quotation need be made:

> Tullamoore has been sadly fagged between Committees and the meetings of the House: if it were not for the heat, the business and the excitement wd. suit him. He goes home to dinner only to return, and Ld. Uxbridge dines almost every day.
>
> I do not believe one word of poor Countess d'Orsay [*i.e.*, of her rumoured intrigue with Tullamoore]. Living with Ly. Blessn., suspicion may fall on her; but the fact seems to me that the Ct. d'Orsay is extremely clever and agreeable, exactly in his (Tull's) way, with abundance of demi-connoisances, and the presumption of being the Arbiter Elegantiarum of Dandyism, and so precisely to the taste of my poor conceited dear Child, who has *goût* enough to find his other companions very dull! His career and his wife's must be one of luxury and vanities, and if he had more to support it I dare swear he wd. be less foolish than one half of those he associates with!

From Lady Charleville's next letter transpire several facts of importance, which have been hitherto unrecorded or are of disputable date. The first is that, shortly after August 4, the Dowager Lady Mountjoy appeared in London from Ireland. The second that Harriet d'Orsay had for some weeks (maybe months) been a regular visitor to her aunt's house. The third is that while there, she made no attempt to conceal her unhappiness at Seamore Place. And the fourth that it was some time between August 4 and August 16, 1831, that she took the grave step of leaving Lady Blessington's roof and her husband's side, and of appealing to the protection of Miss Gardiner, who temporarily concealed her whereabouts.

It is impossible not to connect this very serious move on the part of Lady Harriet with her grandmother's presence in London. Wherefore the first sentence of Lady Charleville's letter should be read as merely expressing on Lady Mountjoy's behalf an agreed social pretext.

Lady Charleville to Mrs. Marlay:

August 16, 1831.

Lady MtJoy did not come here with any view to advise or assist Countess d'Orsay. She came to place Richard at East Sheen at a school his father selected, where Greek is first taught, and many other things in the new fangl'd mode. She found her Lady Harriet wretched and only saw her at her Aunt Miss Gardiner's, in a morng. Miss Gardiner brought her up, and the elder sister still resides with her. Miss Gardr. wd. not allow the elder to go to Ly. Blessington's House, and has been here all this spring, and well informed of the whole of Ct. d'Orsay's ménage. Every day the Countess [d'Orsay] went early to see them [the Gardiners]; and Lady MtJoy found her heart-broken, and had certainly very great fears for her health; her mother havg died of decline.

Tullamoore, it is but too true, never was out of the house [d'Orsay's]; and affiche'd, by going on the Dicky with the party to races, parties, park etc. etc., his association with them. Whether the Ct. wished to get him to gamble, or had the views imputed to him [2] by everybody, I cannot be as convinced as others are. The poor young creature [Harriet] was consider'd a wanton by those who cd. not believe in the impressions of early education, and who saw her with Lady Blessington; and your brother [3] so rated her, and withdrew himself instead of warning Tullamre whom I believe as usual sincere and tender-hearted, and [that he] pitied her and admir'd her, which of course Ly.

[2] This refers to the suggestion which was going the round of society, that d'Orsay was trying to involve Tullamoore in an intrigue with Lady Harriet, so as to have grounds for divorce and himself to be free to enjoy Blessington's money in company with his widow. I am afraid that, with slight alteration, this story may not have been wholly unfounded. (See below, p. 158.)

[3] James Tisdall, Mrs. Marlay's blood brother. He flits rather disagreeably in and out of the pages of his mother's correspondence, his chief quest at this period being a complaisant heiress.

Blessn. encouraged. But the young victim no sooner was aware of the dangerous situation she was in, than she withdrew herself from Ly. Blessington's House and is now under the protection of her family; but *where* is a conceal'd thing not to be trusted to paper.

If she loves Tullamoore I do pity her from my heart: but at 19 she will soon get the better of a weakness too natural under such cruel circumstances, — Tullamoore looks fretted, but has not mentioned any of the parties before me.

The next day (August 17) Lady Charleville writes again:

Just as I foresaw, the town will believe La Comtesse to have quarrell'd with her husband, and secreted herself on acct. of her love for Tullamoore. This was what led me to apprise you of the real fact that you might be perfectly at rest on his account.

Apart from the information contained in it, the first of these letters raises an important query. What behaviour on her part gave cause to those who "considered her a wanton"? An attempt to answer this question will be made in due course.

By chance, two of Mrs. Marlay's replies to her mother have been preserved. The first is in direct response to the note of August 17 just quoted:

Poor Tullamoore was not intended for the life he has been led to prefer, and I own I think with indignation that pains are taken to entangle and misrepresent him and excite him. . . . I have not the slightest doubt of the way the whole of this *last* affair will be thought of in the world, and God forgive me if I think too harshly of *her* who ought at least not to heighten treacherously the part poor Tull may have acted in it.

At whom the final dig? Possibly at Lady Tullamoore, between whom and the quiet Mrs. Marlay little love was probably lost; but more likely at Harriet. How then had Harriet "treacherously heightened" the part played by Tullamoore in their too intimate friendship? Once again comment must be deferred.

Mrs. Marlay's second letter reads:

Lady Mountjoy's arrival is then accounted for! and what a disagreeable card she will have to play, but one of great interest and excitement for her. It is very extraordinary the kind of presentiment about Tull, that has haunted me. It is but too evident he (Tull) has got among a bad set, worse than his usual idle companions.

Clearly the writer had no difficulty in seeing through the official explanation of Lady Mountjoy's visit to London. But what was the "disagreeable", though "interesting and exciting", card she had to play? Riddles accumulate, and some of them riddles indeed.

The number is increased by the next letter from Lady Charleville which makes a sensational statement about the d'Orsay marriage and reflects with delightful completeness the credulity, the kindness of heart and the interest in other people's money which constituted the good lady's worldly wisdom.

Lady Charleville to Mrs. Marlay:

August 20 [1831]

I forget if I told you Mrs. Byng inform'd me that Lady Blessington had made it a *sine qua non* that Ct. d'Orsay was not to consummate his nuptials for four years. This promise unluckily he kept for three years only; this last yr. he liv'd with his innocent poor wife which enraged the Lady and led to the last Schemes now frustrated. Had it not been, Lady Harriet might have got back her fortune: as it is, she is to try only for an amicable separation, not a divorce, and to get half her income: poor little soul, she was a victim and an innocent one!

Think what a match for poor Tullamoore £8,000 pr. an. if he had been content to wait a little!

There remain two further letters from Lady Charleville which bear directly on the problem Blessington-d'Orsay, and can conveniently be quoted before we start the work of disentanglement. The first of these, written on August 23, shows that Tullamoore (either himself determined to rebut the charge of having made love to Harriet d'Orsay or urged thereto by his mother) had permitted the latter to visit Lady Mountjoy and convince her that his acquaintanceship with the unfortunate young woman had been wholly that of an older and wiser friend, that indeed he had continually urged — and finally persuaded — her to run away from Seamore Place. It also contains some very hostile comments on the fugitive's husband and stepmother. The second, of a few days later, elaborates the first.

Here is the first (August 23):

Tullamoore seem'd . . . truly happy that Lady MtJoy testified her approbation of his conduct, and really she desir'd I might tell him that she shd. always love him for his proper advice to Ly. Harriet. So far, so good; and that she (Ly. Harriet) is gone is *tant mieux* too, for it is most clear by her favourable representation that she was touched by his attentions.

Ly. MtJoy told me the thing that decided her [Lady Harriet's] going was, that Ly. Blessington. . . .

[*Two lines so erased as to be utterly undecipherable.*]

Now you are to know she (Ly. Harriet) went every day to her Aunt in her Aunt's carriage, and never took the Count's servants or Lady Blessington's, and return'd the same way, and therefore it was impossible they (the d'Orsay servants) cd. have said anything of the sort.

Ly. B. keeps a female Cook who is lying in and has no husband, and when Ly. Harriet sd. they shd. part with her, Ly. B. told her she (the cook) was quite as good as her or her mother before her.

The Count's violence was extreme; he call'd her (Ly. H.) twenty *Catins* and Tullamoore was the mark, because it is evident she preferr'd him to Ld. Forrester and the rest of the pack, but poor thing most innocently. However things cd. scarcely have continued always so, and God Almighty has guarded her lowly head from the misery of self-condemnation, the worst of all sentences.

And secondly, a day or two later:

Tullamoore staid with us all night, and we talked of Ct. d'Orsay, and he seem'd to think very ill of him in every way, and clearly to be affected by her [Lady Harriet's] misfortune. He said she had trusted him and describ'd her as most ill-used by Ly. B. and him [d'Orsay], and that she had left town with Mrs. [*sic*] Gardiner.

Poor Ly. MtJoy is ill of a bilious attack: how she had griev'd to lose the companionship of Richard! he not at all! the hope of playfellows banished care.

Yesterday, Monday, Ly. MtJoy told me all particulars. She is gone (I mean Lady Harriet) to the sea. Ly. H. says Tullamoore behaved like an angel and she will always love him, for it was he counsell'd her to go to her Aunt. She is as innocent as an angel; yet the will of her father is so constructed that, if she divorced this vile man, he may starve her and keep her £8,000 pr. an. when she comes of age!

Here, save for one or two trifling comments at a later date, the Charleville-Marlay papers cease reference to Lady Blessington and her ill-starred household. The Charlevilles, at any rate, were free of the unsavoury business; and the detachment of Lady Charleville herself, once her beloved Tullamoore was safe, was sufficiently complete to allow her, as shortly afterward as September 15, to correspond quite amicably with Alfred d'Orsay on the subject of a picture by Salvator Rosa.

But for Lady Blessington, release came neither now nor ever. The flight of Lady Harriet d'Orsay from Seamore Place was irrevocable; and the final incident of the Gardiner campaign of 1831 — Charles Gardiner's legal challenge to his father's will — was to follow promptly on her disappearance.

4

To what extent is it possible to reconstitute the motives of the various actors in this rather sordid drama and the chronology of the drama itself?

There can, in the first place, be no doubt that the settling of Miss Gardiner and her niece Emily in London at the beginning of 1831 was a direct consequence of Lady Blessington's and the d'Orsays' arrival in that city two or three months earlier. Obviously the Mountjoy interests needed some one on the spot, and it is not hard to guess that Miss Gardiner's duty was to get into touch with Lady Harriet forthwith and see as much of her as possible.

But what actually were the Gardiners hoping to accomplish? No doubt they were sorry for Harriet and wished to see her happy; but it is not extravagant to assume that they were at least equally concerned to prevent Harriet's husband from laying hands on her fortune, which they naturally regarded as Mountjoy money made over (and most suspiciously made over) to a foreign adventurer. By Lord Blessington's will, the daughter of his who married d'Orsay (and that one should do so was formally postulated) would become owner of the Earl's Dublin property and hand it on to her son, if son she ultimately had; the daughter who did *not* marry d'Orsay would receive only a money legacy of much smaller value. If either married him, without having male issue, the Dublin property was to revert to the illegitimate son, Charles Gardiner, after, presumably, the Countess d'Orsay's death.

From this series of possibilities one fact unmistakably emerges. In order that the vital Dublin estates should revert to the Gardiner family, Lady Harriet's marriage must be childless. So far it had remained so. She had been married late in 1827 at an age when, in her father's view, at any rate, she was "marriageable." It was now 1831. Prospects, therefore, from the Gardiner point of view, were comparatively bright, and we may hazard that, ever since they became aware of the terms of Lord Blessington's will (which may have been before his death, but more probably between the date of his death in May, 1829, and the granting of probate in May, 1830) they had kept themselves informed of what was going on. Considering the amount at stake, the girl's grandmother or aunt would certainly have enquired of her, perhaps while she was still abroad, whether an heir was on the way. In reply, in view both of current gossip and of what subsequently occurred, she would almost certainly have confessed that the heir waited on his preliminaries — that, in short, she was still virgin.

The Gardiners may well have been so satisfied with this state of affairs that they forgot discretion and let outsiders guess how matters stood. Whereupon certain cliques of the fashionable world (whom poor Harriet's virginity seemed to have interested more than it concerned) became either ribald or curious. Ribaldry provoked the Glengall riddle; curiosity the strange story told by Mrs. Byng to Lady Charleville.

Now this, at first sight, foolish story may nevertheless have had an original element of truth, even though the truth had been warped by current prejudice into a further falsehood. It was of course generally assumed in society that Lady Blessington was d'Orsay's mistress, and that in view of her general record she could on no occasion be given credit for any motive save the most selfish and contemptible. It follows therefore that her rumoured insistence on the non-consummation for four years of the d'Orsay marriage must be attributed either to jealousy or self-interest, no more respectable impulse being within the bounds of possibility. But, unfortunately, neither jealousy nor self-interest makes sense. If she were jealous, why limit her demand to four years? Was she likely to be less jealous in 1832 than in 1828? As for self-interest, what possible *material* advantage could she derive from having secured to d'Orsay's wife four years of virginity? Her interest was all the other way. She and d'Orsay were as familiar with the terms of Lord Blessington's will as any of their enemies, and would realise that the birth of a son to Harriet was the only certain guarantee that her property would remain perpetually under joint Blessington-d'Orsay control. Is it not obvious that the Lady Blessington of current gossip (a being without scruples, a mere piratical adventuress) would have welcomed the consummation of d'Orsay's marriage as a necessary overture to the so desirable pregnancy?

And yet it is possible so to interpret Mrs. Byng's story as to keep Lady Blessington in character and even help us to guess at events previously obscure. It is very likely that she did in fact insist that Harriet be left alone until, at nineteen, she could more clearly understand what marriage meant. When one recalls

Lady Blessington's own first sexual experience, and that she was virtually the age of Lady Harriet when handed over to Farmer, it seems not only natural but almost inevitable that she would have determined to save her stepdaughter from the shock of even a modified version of her own suffering.

But it is equally likely that her part in the matter ended here. What if Lady Blessington and d'Orsay were not jointly responsible for the whole series of events recorded in contemporary chatter? What if gossip so condensed both motive and happening that accuracy as well as perspective were distorted? Let us suppose that Lady Blessington had stipulated for the four years of abstinence. Let us further suppose that d'Orsay, after a short while in London and in one of the many houses which he but not Lady Blessington frequented, heard that the Gardiners were planning to apply for his marriage to be declared void (there is more than a hint that such had been their intention, in Lady Charleville's letter of August 20: "This last year he lived with his wife . . . Had it not been, Lady Harriet might have got back her fortune.") What would have happened then? Would not d'Orsay's natural impulse have been to try to strengthen his personal position vis-à-vis the Gardiners by getting his wife with child as urgently as may be? But this, according to our previous argument, he could not do. Is it not possible, then, that in his dilemma he saw advantage in encouraging a liaison between her and some one else? He could either claim paternity of an eventual child or, if this seemed wiser, play the injured husband and, having sued for divorce, keep the money?

This is not a pleasant accusation to bring against any man, even in retrospect. But when money and his own material interest were involved, d'Orsay was utterly non-moral. Kindness and code were alike forgotten, and he thought only of saving himself. Wherefore it seems probable that, though he did not of his own initiative work out this disreputable plot, he found himself confronted with a threat of wifely infidelity, and skilfully decided to exploit it to his own advantage.

5

To speak of a "wifely infidelity", even in prospect, is to introduce into the discussion a new element — the personality of Harriet d'Orsay.

It is easy to forget, when debating the confusing incidents of this autumn of 1831, that Harriet was no longer a child. One has grown so accustomed to regard her as a mere cipher that one does not instinctively reckon with her as a possible independent agent, able and willing to affect the course of her own life. And yet, as the vagueness of previous writers on the subject show, to fail to reckon with Harriet is to make nonsense, not only of her flight from Seamore Place, but of all the events which developed from it. Let us remind ourselves, therefore, that Harriet was nineteen years of age. She must have played some part in this unsavoury business. What part did she play?

Concerning the character and actions of Harriet d'Orsay at any stage of her life, the evidence is even more fragmentary than that relating to other protagonists in the baffling drama of the d'Orsay marriage. But evidence there is; and it can be so ordered as to present Harriet as a comprehensible personality and at the same time to explain some of the still outstanding imponderables in the Charleville letters.

From two of the letters (see p. 152) arose the following questions: What cause had Harriet given to outsiders to consider her a wanton? In what way (assuming her to be the person meant) had she "treacherously heightened the part played by Tullamoore" in their joint scandal?

Now obviously neither Lady Charleville nor Mrs. Marlay would thus have referred to Harriet unless she were in some measure food for gossip. The former is so concerned to clear Tullamoore that she must defend Harriet in order to defend him; the latter is less partial, and a temperamental dislike of fast London society makes her readier than her mother to suspect some fire behind the smoke.

And why should there not have been? It is not at all beyond the bounds of credibility that Harriet, since reaching London, had acted with an incautious promiscuity. Indeed, it is even likely, seeing that she had every excuse and considerable opportunity for doing so. Her life, since a meaningless marriage had been forced upon her and until a few months of her return to England, had been the miserable and solitary life of a powerless child. When her father died and the terms of his will were known, she found herself rich. By the time she reached London she was virtually a grown woman. In Lady Blessington's house was no one for whom she felt affection or to whom she owed consideration. She had easy access to the outer world through her aunt's house and, as we know, lost little time in making friends with Lady Tullamoore, whose ideas of amusement were not remarkable for prudery. Who shall blame Harriet if, resentful of her joyless past and warped by her evil upbringing into secretive but obstinate self-sufficiency, she determined to make up such leeway as she could?

If this possibility be realised, if it be accepted as conceivable that throughout 1831 she had indeed made herself conspicuous by too reckless intimacies with this man or that, the reference to her reputation becomes clear. Further, it is not difficult to guess how, in frivolous gossip with her friends, a cynical and loose-living young woman, to whom lovers had become life's choicest seasoning, could "heighten the part acted" by one of them. Nor is this all. In the original of Lady Charleville's letter of August 23 (see p. 154) a passage has been thoroughly erased; but assuming Harriet to have been fallible, and by inference from what immediately follows, the sense of the missing words can fairly certainly be hazarded. Is it not obvious that Lady Blessington accused Harriet either of meeting her lover (or lovers) at Miss Gardiner's house or of going elsewhere to meet them during her daily outings? This fits in perfectly with the remark about the Count's servants not having been in a position to tell tales; with the anecdote of the unfortunate cook; and with Lady Blessington's sharp rejoinder to Harriet's sanctimonious demand that the woman be turned away.

This is not mere reckless blackening of the character of Harriet d'Orsay. Indeed — save for her lack of charity toward the cook — no blame whatsoever is implied. It is a natural deduction from what we know of her independent actions, both before reaching London with her husband and when she went abroad again after leaving him, as well as from a story written by herself.

During the year which elapsed between the death of Lord Blessington and the return of his household to England, Harriet is believed to have made the acquaintance of the young Duc de Chartres, son of the then Duc d'Orléans who was so soon to come to the throne as King Louis Philippe. The acquaintance is said to have developed so rapidly that when in 1830 the Duc de Chartres became in his turn Duc d'Orléans and heir to the throne, authority frowned on what was already an entanglement. The results of this frown were very probably included in the "painful circumstances" to which Madden refers in explaining Lady Blessington's departure from Paris.

The story of this early encounter between Harriet and the Duc d'Orléans has proved unverifiable. M. Flers, in his book about d'Orsay, states it as a fact, but does not give the source of his statement. The next stage in their relationship, however, is undisputed. About 1835, after her sister, Emily Gardiner, had married a Mr. Charles Whyte in Dublin, Harriet returned to Paris once more and settled in the Rue Tronchet. Forthwith she "accepted the protection" of this same Duc d'Orléans, and continued in his eminent custody until in July, 1842, he was accidentally thrown from his carriage at Neuilly and killed. Her liaison seems to have been well known in England. "I fear the unfortunate Countess d'Orsay is a lost character," wrote

Mrs. Hughes to Mrs. Southey in 1842. "I never heard it contradicted that she became mistress to the Duke of Orléans." Nor, to do her justice, did Harriet make any attempt to conceal the fact. Mr. S. M. Ellis, in his book on Ainsworth, remarks acutely that "the Countess d'Orsay had a penchant for converting all her private affairs into sentiment and print for the benefit of the public", and specifies two of her several contributions to *Ainsworth's Magazine,* both of which were unmistakably personal lamentations, one of which almost in so many words was a mourning tribute to her "protector", who had just met his tragic end.

After the death of Duc d'Orléans, if we are to believe the Comte de Vieil Castel, she replaced her royal lover with one of the de Noailles and "a host of lesser stars." She also wrote *feuilletons,* numerous ephemera, and a novel to which, as it bears testimony to its author's earlier life of a kind which can hardly be ignored, attention shall be duly given.

The quiet remainder of her sad career can be quickly told. In September, 1852, and within a month of d'Orsay's death, she married an Englishman, the Honourable Charles Spencer Cowper, and spent her middle age in piety and charity near Sandringham. She died in 1860. Thus ended the pitiful life of Harriet Gardiner, only legitimate daughter of the Earl of Blessington. She was one on whose head the wrongdoing of a father was visited with a wry bitterness beyond the ordinary.

Harriet d'Orsay's novel, of which the autobiographical significance is both suggestive and important, was published in Paris in 1851 and is called "L'Ombre du Bonheur."[4] It was written by her in French and opens with a signed preface, in which she says:

Alone in life since the age of twenty without a home and family, without real interests of my own, I early formed the habit of long

[4] Three vols. Chez Comon. A one-volume English translation, under the title "Clouded Happiness", was published by Vizetelly in 1855. This translation included the preface.

thinking and of writing down what I thought. . . . The written sheets, filled with the inexperience of youth, I burnt; but I kept in mind what was, I suppose, the original idea of this novel.

It is possible that I have failed in my object in composing this work. It is possible that I have over-romanticised the lapse from virtue of the hapless young girl who, the victim of a fatal upbringing, becomes an outcast from society, shunned and despised by all. But God, who reads the heart, who pardons the sincere penitent, has taken into his mercy the woman who sinned. Was I to do otherwise?

Then follows the story — a complex, almost Gothistic, tale of concealed identities, lurid coincidence, agonised death-beds, blatant vice and emphatic virtue — which is staged mainly in Naples in the very early thirties and is full of local colour clearly recovered from the writer's memory. Giuditta, the erring damsel, is the daughter of a courtesan and is supposed to have moral instability in her veins. Nevertheless her only real lapse is to sell herself to a rich debauchee to save her mother's life — the sacrifice (inevitably) coming too late to achieve its purpose. Thereafter, though she lives with a man to whom she is not married, her moral standards are above criticism.

It should be noted that toward the end of the book Giuditta's lover d'Arville (his true patronymic was Darville, and had been "improved" by a parvenu parent) has grown tired of her; he observes that an English lord is inclined to make a bid for her favours and, for his own convenience, encourages the new liaison. As to the rest of the story, it need only be observed that Giuditta's brother is a savage bandit, capable of blackmail, robbery and even murder, but with the face of an angel and a manner of irresistible charm; while Beatrice, the brother's accomplice and mistress, "although lacking in true distinction both of feature and figure, was remarkably beautiful with such beauty as Giorgione and Titian have immortalised. Beatrice's face lacked feminine charm, but she had a certain frankness and her general manner was not at all repellent."

The significance of all this is inescapable. In nearly all first novels it is safe to anticipate a large element of autobiography, more or less disguised, and "L'Ombre du Bonheur" (bearing in mind the author's readiness on other occasions to dramatise her private life) can hardly be suspected an exception to the rule. The preface is admittedly a personal avowal; and if the passage quoted does not mean that Harriet, during her young womanhood, had transgressed the social code of the day and suffered for the transgression, it is difficult to know what it can mean. As for the incidents and characters of the tale above mentioned, these, for all their disguise and adaptation, are surely not difficult to understand. The bandit brother and Beatrice can only be reflections of d'Orsay and Lady Blessington; while other attributes of the former are allotted to d'Arville. This man's deliberate propulsion of Giuditta into the arms of a new lover looks suspiciously like a reminiscence of the very similar procedure which we now have reason to think was attempted by d'Orsay during the dramatic summer of 1831; and the likeness between the name and family history of d'Arville (Darville) and those of Harriet's first husband is too striking to be mere coincidence.

6

And now to return to our attempted interpretation of the tangled events of 1831.

If we assume that Harriet had involved herself with some man (whether with Tullamoore, Forrester or another is immaterial) and that d'Orsay had grasped at the opportunity for self-advantage which her indiscretion offered him, two questions arise.

First, why was d'Orsay at this moment so urgent in his desire to arrange an heir or, conversely, a divorce? Because, as already indicated, the Gardiner faction were on the point of applying for his marriage to be declared void. This application at the period in question could have been made on two grounds, in addition to the obvious one of non-consummation. It is of course possible that the Gardiners proposed to proceed on that basis; but it seems more likely that their scheme followed one of the two other feasible lines. There was precedent in 1811 for the civil suit [5] for the purpose of voiding a marriage, to be brought by persons having a financial interest in the matter. Alternatively there cannot be much doubt that in the early thirties, as to-day, want of consent and duress could be argued as valid ground for decreeing a marriage null; and it would not have been difficult for the Gardiners to put forward a strong case to the effect that Harriet, forcibly betrothed by her father at the age of eleven and fetched to Italy when barely sixteen to be married out of hand to a man she had never seen, had been a victim of duress. Nor can it be doubted that, had a suit been brought on one of these grounds, it would have been successful.

But any plan to void the marriage was ruined by Harriet's impulsive departure from her husband's side. The second question, therefore, arises. Was her flight from Seamore Place in obedience to her relatives' wishes or contrary to them?

Almost certainly the latter. If Lady Mountjoy and Miss Gardiner were indeed playing for annulment, they would wish the unhappy young wife to stick at her post until relief finally came. But suppose that during the early summer of 1831 Harriet had become more and more resentful of her lot, had even threatened, in conversation with her aunt, to take refuge with a lover in order to escape from a house she hated? Would not Miss Gardiner have been so alarmed that she summoned Lady Mountjoy from Ireland, if possible to dissuade the would-be fugitive from running away at all or, if dissuasion were impossible, at least to get her to come to her aunt's house and so make it seem that her desertion had family approval? This theory seems at least to fit the facts. Further, if it may be assumed that Harriet forced her relatives' hand by independent action, Tullamoore's story of having persistently advised her to run away, and finally persuaded her to do so, may have some truth in it. And finally Lady Mountjoy's bilious attack (see Lady

[5] Faremouth *v.* Watson.

Charleville's final letter) can be convincingly attributed, not to her personal and temporary depression at loss of a schoolboy's company, but to chagrin at the collapse of the family scheme to recapture Lady Harriet d'Orsay's fortune.

It was true that the worst had been averted. D'Orsay had at least no grounds for divorce, which would have given him virtually all her wealth. But the young wife's voluntary desertion made judicial separation sooner or later inevitable, with the consequent surrender to d'Orsay of a share at least of her money. And that was bad enough. There remained to the Gardiners only one cumbrous and uncertain method of attack — a legal assault on the general validity of the late Earl's will. This assault was delivered late in 1831. The suit gave rise to weary and complete litigation, which brought success to neither party but merely some sort of order into the legacy of chaos Lord Blessington had left behind. The relevant details of the settlement belong to a later chapter and will there be given.

7

It should now be evident that the worst sufferer from this disreputable and mercenary imbroglio, and on the whole the person least to blame for it, was Lady Blessington herself. Her enemies had been cheated of outright victory; but their discomfiture was only less damaging to her reputation and fortune than would have been their complete success. And in addition to the loss of prestige and money which was evident to the world, she had in secret suffered a spiritual blow which changed her whole nature.

Material misfortune followed directly on the flight of Harriet d'Orsay. Her disappearance and its sequel, the suit brought against Lord Blessington's widow and son-in-law by Charles Gardiner, had an immediate and disturbing effect on the income at the Countess' disposal. Partly because arrangements involving financial adjustments would have to be made for a separation; partly because, to the already heavy claims on Lord

Blessington's estate, costs of litigation were now likely to be added, the trustees became chary of paying out any more money than they could help. Wherefore the balance sheet of Seamore Place leaned suddenly debitwards, and the most immediate of the worries which clouded for Lady Blessington the evening of 1831 and the dawn of 1832 was the worry over money.

But financial cares and even the hostility of those about her, though serious enough, were trifles beside the anguish of heart which some particular aspect of the autumn's events had caused to her. What that aspect was we must try to guess; but no guessing is needed to realise its tragic effect upon her spirit.

They were not money cares or fears of ostracism which prompted her on December 7, 1831, to write to Mrs. Mathews, the only woman to whom she was used to unburden herself: "I confess to you a great part of the milk and honey of nature with which my heart originally overflowed is turned into gall; and though I have still enough goodness left to prevent its bitterness from falling even on those who have caused it, yet have I not power to prevent it corroding my own heart." They were not money cares or fears of ostracism which led her to make these entries in her so-called "Night Book" (a blank book in which she noted down aphorisms from her reading and her own "desultory thoughts and reflections"): "The first heavy affliction that falls on us rends the veil of life and lets us see all its darkness." And again: "We make temples of our hearts, in which we worship an idol, until we discover the object of our love was a false god; and then it is not the idol only that is destroyed — the shrine is ruined." These and other half-stifled cries of pain, wrung from her in the first black moments of a misery which, though she trained herself to control its outward seeming, was never to pass away, came from a wound more terrible than debts or outlawry could ever cause.

There are three sentences in the letter to Mrs. Mathews already quoted, which seem to betray the nature of that wound:

To have a proud spirit with a tender heart is an unfortunate union, and I have not been able to curb the first or steel the second. If an envious or a jealous crowd misjudge or condemn, a proud spirit can bear up against injustice; but if in the most inveterate assailants one finds those whom we believe to be our trusted friends, the blow is incurable.

Cæsar defended himself against his foes, but when he saw his friend Brutus strike at him he gave up the struggle.

The purpose of these words is sadly obvious. The callous frivolity and thoughtless vanity of d'Orsay, which culminated during those evil months of 1831 in the cruel and disloyal plot to ruin his wife and his benefactress for the sake of so many thousand pounds, had suddenly revealed to her the abject, unprincipled thing he really was. And the revelation had broken her heart. From that time forward she was a woman spiritually maimed.

Not for many years did d'Orsay begin to understand the mortal hurt which he had caused. In the first moment of angry desolation, when Harriet had run away and the truth had dawned on her, Lady Blessington drove him from her house and he took up his abode near by in Curzon Street. But in his amiable and impenetrable complacency, he took the banishment for a concession to the *convenances,* and soon was almost as constant an inmate of Seamore Place as though he still lived there. As for Lady Blessington, she had neither the spirit nor the wish utterly to break with him. What good would it have done? Although the deed which had finally closed against them the doors of social toleration was his deed and not hers, she was held to be equally to blame, and if she quarrelled with him would merely make her isolation final and complete. Nor did she feel free on other grounds to cast him off. She had promised Madame Craufurd that she would never desert him, and the promise had been given with all the warmth of the protective love she once had felt for him. This love must still persist. And it did persist, but as protectiveness and as nothing else. He had the claim on her which even the meanest and most selfish of sons has on his mother's help and pity; and she must work and fight for him until the end. So it was that she kept him at her side during her long battle against debt, ostracism and bad health; and her reward — if reward it were — lay in his realisation, after she was dead, of all she had done for him, in his sudden and overwhelming shame at the suffering which, in sheer self-seeking, he had caused her.

The ultimate defeat of Lady Blessington at the hands of a hostile world really dates from this Christmas of 1831. Henceforward she gave up any hope of reëstablishing herself among her kind, almost any hope of real happiness. Her life stretched before her as a prolonged exercise in keeping up appearances. The enjoyment of literature and beauty; the company of congenial friends; the satisfaction of knowing that her house could attract and welcome men who shared her interests and whose talk would reflect the moods and happenings of the outer world — these would in future be her stimulus and consolation. The old life of spontaneous gaiety and unself-conscious merriment was over. In their place must reign graciousness, social tact and, above all, sympathy toward those to whom fate had been unkind.

Without pointing the moral, Madden describes the changes in Lady Blessington which he himself observed between one stage and another of her life. Although these outrun the chronology of the present narrative, they may here be quoted as supporting the statement that from 1832 onward Lady Blessington was acting the character which before that date had been her natural self, that art substituted nature because nature was dead:

> In Naples in 1824 [says Madden], the charm of Lady Blessington's conversation and society was indescribable. There was observable in her animal spirits a flow of hilarity, a natural vivacity such as had belonged to her childhood. The ringing laugh of joyous girlhood was

a reality with her in those merry moods in Naples, which were indeed neither few nor far between.

I next met her in Rome [early in 1826 — just after the d'Orsay marriage] and that vivacity seemed to me to have been considerably impaired. She had become more of a learned lady, a queen regnant in literary circles, but at all times attractive, kindly disposed and faithful in her friendships.

After an interval of nearly five years [1832–1833] I renewed my acquaintance with her in Seamore Place. It was evident that a great change had come over the "spirit of her dream." Cares and troubles of various kinds had befallen her and left, if not visible external traces, at least perceptible internal evidence of their effects.

After a lapse of two or three years my acquaintance with her was renewed at Gore House. There was no happiness in the circles of Gore House comparable to that of the Palazzo Belvedere in Naples. There was manifestly a great intellectual effort made to keep up the charm of that society, and her powers of attraction and of pleasing had lost none of their influence. But the conversation generally was no longer of that peculiarly gay, enlivening and cheerful character, which made the great charm of the Palazzo Belvedere and, in a minor degree, of Seamore Place.

That which Madden leaves unsaid has now been spoken. Through the gilded but unhappy years which were the rest of her life, the soul of Lady Blessington was as though dead. In childhood half of her nature had been paralysed by a man's brutal lust; the other half, late in the year 1831, was killed by the baseness and ingratitude of a mere trousered exquisite.

BOOK THREE

FALSE RELATION

CHAPTER I

Blessington: the Authoress

1

It is a natural consequence of the spiritual catastrophe of 1831 that the life story of Lady Blessington should thereafter, in a narrative sense, be uneventful. Irrevocably debarred from any prospect of mixing on equal terms with her kind, increasingly in need of privacy for the work on which money-making depended, her own zest for life more or less destroyed by private griefs, she shut away her real self from all except one or two of the persons who frequented her house. She hardly went out of doors save to drive in the park or visit a theatre; and though her evening parties continued to be as splendid and as popular as ever, the heart had gone out of them.

No less inevitably had her relations with d'Orsay changed. His outright banishment from her house was brief enough. Although he did not for some years actually live under her roof again, he was soon regularly attending her dinner parties and soirées. His company, the feeling that he was somewhere about the place, had become necessary to her. In his humour and cheerfulness and readiness to perform small services for others, she found a certain recompense for the weight of responsibility she carried. But although she liked him as much as ever, she could not in her heart of hearts trust him any more, could no longer wholly identify herself with him and his doings. In consequence and henceforward, their lives were simultaneous rather than united. In the eyes of the world the pair of them were no less identified than formerly, for they shared an ostracism and their contacts were apparently continuous and intimate. But spiritually they were divided — Lady Blessington having no part in the showy, haphazard career of the dandy gambler and sporting buck, d'Orsay being quite content to leave money troubles and the planning of ways and means to her devoted courage, and himself for a while longer to frolic in the sunshine.

For this reason, the remainder of their life stories can most properly be treated as separate narratives. Although coincident in chronology and ending in a common ruin, they were fundamentally in false relation.

2

When the year 1832 began, the urgent preoccupation of Lady Blessington was to find a new source of revenue. Fortunately the obvious direction for her quest was also the most agreeable. She would turn author; and, like many another embarrassed elegant, exploit her rank in the interest of its maintenance. She did not at first incline to novel writing, feeling (and rightly) that her capacities were better suited to the magazines. These, accordingly, she passed in review. The most promising seemed to be the *New Monthly*, especially so in that the editorship had recently been placed in the radical and enterprising hands of Edward Lytton Bulwer, who in November, 1831, had announced his accession with an "Address to the Public" full of reformist enthusiasm and of hostility to reaction in life, politics and letters.

Edward Bulwer had already made for himself a novelist's name, a dandy's reputation, many enemies and a few friends. Barely twenty-seven years old, he had quarrelled with his rich mother; had married and begotten two children; had published five novels (of which three at least were widely successful[1]); was a Member of Parliament in the Reform interest; and, from his smartly decorated home in Hertford Street, was trying simultaneously to adjust his egotism to that of his wife,

[1] "Falkland" (1827); "Pelham" (1828); "The Disowned" (1828); "Devereux" (1829); "Paul Clifford" (1830).

to earn a livelihood by writing, and to conquer society by whiskers and champagne.

Lady Blessington had not met Bulwer personally when she first thought of writing for his magazine, but she had read his books during 1829 and approved their mental quality. "Read 'Pelham' "; she noted in her Paris journal for that year. "The writer possesses a felicitous fluency of language, profound and just thought, and a knowledge of the world rarely acquired at his age, for I am told he is a very young man. The work combines pointed and pungent satire on the follies of society, a deep vein of elevated sentiment, and a train of philosophical thinking, seldom, if ever, allied to the tenderness which pierces through the sentimental part. The opening reminded me of 'Anastasius',[2] without being in the slightest degree an imitation; and many of the passages recalled Voltaire by their wit and terseness."

"I, who don't like reading novels, heard so much in favour of this one — for all Paris talked of it — that I broke through a resolution. I am glad I did so, for this clever book has greatly interested me."

And a few months later:

"I have been reading 'Devereux' and like it infinitely — even more than 'Pelham.' The novels of this writer produce a totally different effect on me to that exercised by the works of other authors; they amuse less than they make me think."

And later still:

"Read 'The Disowned' and like it exceedingly. The more I read of the works of this highly gifted writer, the more I am delighted with them. The generality of readers pause not to

[2] "Anastasius: or Memoirs of a Greek Written at the Close of the Eighteenth Century", by Thomas Hope. 3 vols. London. John Murray, 1819.

Hope was an amateur of the arts, an antiquary, and an enthusiast for costume and furniture designed to clothe and house the early nineteenth century in the styles of ancient Greece and mediæval Italy. When "Anastasius" appeared it was generally attributed to Byron, who told Lady Blessington at Genoa that he had wept on reading it and for two reasons — one that he had not written it, the other that Hope — "the man of chairs and tables, the gentleman of sofas" — had.

reflect on the truth and beauty of the sentiments to be found in novels. . . . Yet as people who read nothing else will read novels, authors like Mr. Bulwer, whose minds are over-flowing with genius, are compelled to make fiction the vehicle for giving to the public thoughts and opinions that are deserving of a higher grade of literature."

Thus predisposed to admiring sympathy with the editorial mind, she wrote to the *New Monthly* and offered her collaboration.

In response to her letter came a personal visit from Samuel Carter Hall, a picturesque and rather sanctimonious young Irishman, who had succeeded Campbell on the *New Monthly* as stop-gap editor and was now assistant editor to Bulwer. Primly disapproving of the equivocal household to which his duty brought him, Hall was reluctantly impressed by the graciousness of Lady Blessington and the beauty of her drawing-room. Then, lest further weakness endanger his nervous but determined virtue, he became frigidly the editor and frowned at his hostess' suggested contributions. When, however, with her unerring tact she praised to him his wife's recently published "Sketches of Irish Character", he forgot both his profile and his priggishness and became the kindly, deprecating thing he really was. He proposed that she write memories of Byron at Genoa, which the *New Monthly* would be very pleased to publish. The lady gladly consented and the two parted friends. Many years after, recalling this first encounter with one whose life was allegedly at variance with his insistent theories of social purity, Samuel Carter Hall remembered Lady Blessington's praise of his beloved wife, her courtesy and kindness to himself, and contrived with suave humility to reconcile personal liking and objective disapprobation.

> Lady Blessington [he says] may be described as then in her prime, although past forty. She was inclined to embonpoint; her hair abundant and of a lightish brown; her complexion fair and healthily tinged, deriving no aid from art. She must have been very lovely in youth;

she was so indeed when no longer young. Her face was peculiarly Irish — round, soft and smiling, fresh and fair. Her form, rather under than above the middle size, was exquisitely modelled; her voice was low and sweet. There was nothing artificial in aught she said or did; nothing hurried or self-distrustful about her; she seemed perfectly conscious of power but without the slightest assumption or pretence.

He proceeds:

Of the many persons eminent in letters and in art who were her frequent visitors, all, or nearly all, were men. Ladies were seldom seen at her receptions. Mrs. Hall never accompanied me to her evenings, though she was a frequent day caller. We were not of rank high enough to be indifferent to public opinion. Slander was busy with her fame, and Count d'Orsay was so little guided by principle that he could not expect general credit for the purity of his relations with her; yet I think he might honestly have claimed it.

And concludes resoundingly:

It is not enough for a woman to *be* pure; she must *seem* pure. Her conscience may be as white as snow, but if she gives scope to slander and weight to calumny her offence is great. She taints those who are influenced by example, and renders vice excusable in the estimate of those whose dispositions incline to evil.

With this reminiscence of Samuel Carter Hall may be paralleled one of only a few months later, taken from the diary of a man of very different kind. Henry Crabb Robinson — cosmopolitan, widely travelled and as disinclined to judge Lady Blessington for her offences against convention as he was well qualified to appraise her claims to intelligence and beauty — called at Seamore Place at Landor's instigation in September, 1832. His impressions are worthy of remark for their very restraint; and this his first visit evidently pleased him as much as he said, for it was followed by many others.

Sept. 28, 1832

Between nine and ten, I went by Landor's desire to Lady Blessington's, to whom he had named me. She is a charming and very remarkable person; and though I am by no means certain that I have formed a lasting acquaintance, yet my two interviews have left a delightful impression.

Lady Blessington is much more handsome than Countess Egloffstein, but their countenance, manners, and particularly the tone of voice, belong to the same class. Her dress rich, and her library most splendid. Her book about Lord Byron (now publishing by driblets in the *New Monthly Magazine*), and her other writings, give her in addition the character of a *bel esprit*. Landor, too, says, that she was to Lord Blessington the most devoted wife he ever knew. He says also, that she was by far the most beautiful woman he ever saw, and was so deemed at the Court of George IV. She is now, Landor says, about thirty, but I should have thought her older. She is a great talker, but her talk is rather narrative than declamatory, and very pleasant.

"Journal of Conversations with Lord Byron", by the Countess of Blessington, began its serial appearance in the *New Monthly Magazine* for July, 1832, and ran intermittently till December of the following year. The instalments were eagerly read, achieving from the very first a success, part genuine popularity and part scandal. The opening section put into Byron's mouth a description of Lady Holland, which, for all that the names were omitted, was instantly recognised and set the salons buzzing. With such a beginning, what revelations might not be in store? Which of Byron's enemies — which even of his friends — would escape the lashing of that bitter tongue, now so uncomfortably resurrected after ten years of death?

Of all the horrible attacks on Lady Holland [wrote Jekyll on August 1], Lady Blessington's "Memoirs of Byron" in the last *New Monthly Magazine* are the most *sanglans*. He does not spare her son Henry, and deplores Lord Holland's slavery to his rib.

These "Memoirs" will be continued monthly, and Byron's former associates are frightened to death; some, too, who deluded themselves into a belief they were beloved. As Lady Blessington is stout, I hope she will be merciful. The conversations of a dead man cannot be contradicted, so if Miladi is not scrupulous on the score of veracity, she may report Byron as she pleases.

In August it was the turn of Lady Jersey; and once again Jekyll reported a sensation:

[August 27]

My friend, Lady Blessington's "Memoirs of Byron" in the last *New Monthly Magazine* fall desperately foul of the Jerseys, insinuating that Miladi has more talk than brains, and that her lord lives upon horse-flesh at Newmarket, with a clever allusion to Pegasus.

From time to time, as the "Conversations" went their intermittent way, the flurried indignation of fashionable readers was renewed. Late in 1832, Lady Blessington was publicly threatened with a pamphlet to be written by "Dissector", which would expose the scandal of her life with d'Orsay and prove the falsity of her Byronian memories. It does not appear that "Dissector" ever ventured beyond the bounds of menace. The idea that the "Conversations" were a forgery was, however, too attractive to be neglected. Before long Lady Blessington was widely accused of having invented a large part of the material or, alternatively, of having got some one else to do the inventing for her. But as this suggestion was never implemented (or indeed made other than privately by an unprejudiced person), and as the principal modern authorities on Byron's life and character [3] not only accept the "Conversations" for genuine but declare them to contain more sympathetic and convincing evidence of Byron's real mind than can be found anywhere else, the authenticity of Lady Blessington's work need not be seriously doubted.[4]

The sensation caused by this her first serious excursion into letters greatly encouraged Lady Blessington to energetic pursuit of authorship. But it did her a further and more significant service, in that it marked the beginning of her personal friendship with Edward Bulwer, a friendship which rapidly developed

[3] Ethel Colburn Mayne, Harold Nicolson, André Maurois.

[4] It may be added that, unless we are prepared to accept the "Conversations" as basically genuine, we must believe that Lady Blessington, when she prepared her Italian diary for publication in 1839, purposely garbled the text in order to obscure a forgery committed five years earlier. On p. 93 has been quoted her comment on the effect of the news of Byron's death on her household in Naples. "I have been reading over the notes of his conversations with me," she says. Was this remark, purporting to have been written in 1824 and first printed in 1839, a deliberate interpolation? It is hard to suspect her of such chicanery.

into close and sympathetic intimacy and lasted unbroken all her life.

The date of Lady Blessington's first meeting with Bulwer is not recorded. It may have been late in 1831, but more probably took place in January or February, 1832, after the publication of his novel "Eugene Aram." That book was greeted with success more sensational and with critical abuse more scurrilous even than had been "Paul Clifford", and the nature of its reception had a curious effect on its author. A combination of readers' enthusiasm and critics' brutality always worked on Bulwer's peculiar temperament in such a way as to bring out the worst of his many mannerisms. Under the personal insults of his enemies (several of whom he knew to be mere hired bravoes, serving their Tory paymasters by blackguarding a radical opponent in the guise of literary criticism) he would writhe and suffer; in the blaze of popularity he would preen himself. In greater or less degree he thus reacted to the reception given to every one of his books, even to those published in old age; and during the weeks which followed the appearance of "Eugene Aram" in January, 1832, with all a young man's exaggerated sensitiveness and exaggerated vanity, he was in his most miserably vainglorious mood.

Human beings at odds with their kind, provided they were also beings with whose mental quality she could sympathise, were something of a speciality of Lady Blessington. Herself an outlaw, she was instinctively in disagreement with conventional opinion on any subject, and naturally predisposed to like those in similar predicament. Further, the task of putting a shy and nerve-wracked man at his ease challenged her social competence. Wherefore in two ways the problem of liking Edward Bulwer and of making him like her was an attractive one.

So swiftly and successfully did she solve it, that by the autumn of 1832, at any rate, he was among the most regular visitors to Seamore Place, and by the summer of 1833 he was almost the most intimate friend she had. Doubtless the friendship would have developed still more rapidly but for Bulwer's many political engagements during this critical year. The Reform Bill had its third reading in March; and after Lord Grey had resigned and had been recalled (with power to create peers, if by no other means a majority could be produced) the measure passed the House of Lords early in June. During the last three months of the session — May to July — Bulwer was very active in the House of Commons on behalf of the intellectual causes in which he specialised. The reform of the Royal Academy; the reduction of the tax on newspapers; the creation of a dramatic copyright; the suppression of the monopoly rights of Drury Lane and Covent Garden theatres — these were the agitations on which his libertarian enthusiasm spent itself. In November was a general election. The Huntingdonshire constituency which Bulwer represented in the House had been swept away by the Reform Bill; he stood for Lincoln as a radical and won the seat handsomely.

With all this to occupy his time, in addition to the writing of "Godolphin" and "England and the English" and the editing of the *New Monthly*, it was hardly possible for him to frequent Seamore Place save occasionally late at night. Also his wife, who had social ambitions, would have frowned on his too obvious attendance at a house blacklisted by the *ton*. But whenever he could manage it, Bulwer paid his evening call; and took with him, first the young Disraeli, then his own brother Henry, both of whom became special friends of Lady Blessington and constant frequenters of her home.

3

It was probably in the late autumn of 1832 that Lady Blessington first asked Bulwer's advice about novel-writing. The tone of her evenings was not yet so predominantly literary as it afterward became, partly because she had not yet herself become a professional writer and editor, principally because of the overwhelming interest of political events during 1832 —

an interest peculiarly relevant to Seamore Place, which was solid for Reform and the social stronghold of the radicals. But talk of books must have taken place between the hostess and Bulwer, and she had probably confessed to him that the "Conversations with Lord Byron", for all their éclat, were not of themselves sufficient to solve her financial problem.

This problem had been made no easier by the straits to which her Irish relatives had been reduced, and their appeals to her for help. One of the first results of the outbreak of open warfare between the Gardiners and Seamore Place had been the removal of Lady Blessington's brother, Robert Power, from his post as agent for the Tyrone estates. On his salary as agent he had been keeping his old reprobate of a father, his youngest sister Mary Anne, and his own wife and daughters; and with the failure of that salary the position of these dependents became naturally very serious. Equally naturally, they looked to the brilliant Lady Blessington, of whose luxurious house and social prowess they had heard so much, to make good the deficit.

Valiantly she strove to do what was expected of her. Money was sent to Ireland, and Mary Anne Power, who had been with the Blessingtons during their years abroad, was immediately invited to return to London and stay with her sister. She came, and with a precipitancy one would hardly expect from so travelled a young woman, married an elderly French count called Saint Marsault, whom she met in Seamore Place. The story goes that M. Saint Marsault believed he was marrying an heiress; that Mary Anne Power mistook for real the jewelled rings which adorned the long yellow fingers of her decrepit admirer; and that each, with the realisation that the other was as poor as a church mouse, complained bitterly of having been deceived. However this may be, harmony barely outlasted the honeymoon, and the Comtesse Saint Marsault was back at Seamore Place within a few weeks of having left it. She stayed a short while and returned to Dublin, her place in Lady Blessington's household being taken by Robert's two daughters, Marguerite and Ellen Power, who were to remain with their aunt for the rest of her life.

In such a predicament Lady Blessington would certainly have turned to Edward Bulwer and asked his help. Suppose she were to write a novel, could a publisher be found, and what price could be expected for the copyright? Bulwer, although still editing the *New Monthly* for Colburn, had just contracted for three of his own books with Richard Bentley, who had until lately been Colburn's partner, but, owing to a quarrel,[5] was now his successor. It is a fair assumption that Lady Blessington's proposal for a three-volume novel was taken to Bentley by Bulwer, and that Bentley's handsome offer of four hundred pounds for the copyright was in part provoked by a desire to please the very influential and popular writer who was sponsoring the Countess' first attempt at fiction. The offer was promptly accepted; the book little less promptly written (six hundred of its nine hundred and eighty pages were written in four weeks, so that delivery could be made as promised at the end of March); and on June 19, 1833, the three volumes of "The Repealers" made their appearance.

Madden is harsh with "The Repealers." "Her first and worst novel", he calls it, and adds: "From all Irish political novels including 'The Repealers', the English public may pray most earnestly to be delivered." Undeniably, as a novel, the book is bad — written at such speed, it could hardly be anything else. But it is hardly fair to label it outright an "Irish political novel" seeing that quite half of it is satirical description of fashionable jealousies and affectations in English society. Further, although to our present purpose this silver-fork element is the more relevant, it is inherently less interesting than its Irish counterpart. Behind the jejune sentimentality with which are described the adventures of Grace Cassidy and her disaffected husband lies a real sincerity. Lady Blessington knew

[5] *Cf.* "Edward and Rosina", pp. 289–290.

enough of the distresses of the Irish peasantry and had sufficiently shared her husband's progressive ideas, to write of them with sympathy and feeling.

But the main importance of "The Repealers" to students of Lady Blessington's life lies in the fact that, literary quality apart, it offers a definite and dated clue to her real feelings toward the world of which, though not in which, she was. And clues to Lady Blessington's real feelings at any juncture of her life are too rare to be ignored.

"The Repealers" is a *roman à clé* of (for the most part) a particularly transparent kind. The key to the characters (from Lady Blessington's autograph notes) is printed as an Appendix to this book and shows how singularly thin were most of the disguises. Not surprisingly, the persons thus avowedly introduced are described with a facile flattery which precludes characterisation. Even Lady Jersey, Lady Augusta Baring and Lady Tullamoore, toward whom Lady Blessington had no reason to feel kindly, are treated to sugared admiration. But from the list of characters and consequent distribution of compliments, certain personages in the novel are omitted — notably an Irish peer and peeress called "Abberville", who play a much larger part in the story than any of the individuals recorded in the "Key." Now if the Abbervilles were not drawn from life, Lady Blessington had a greater talent for imagining personalities than she ever again displayed; and one is forced to conclude that they were real people. Here (much abbreviated) is their description:

> Lord Abberville owed his title to the Union and a certain, or rather uncertain, portion of his income to a judicious and persevering system of jobbing, only known in Ireland . . . Few persons ever understood the whole arcana of the system of jobbing so perfectly as Lord Abberville and few had derived more advantage from it. Can it, therefore, be wondered at that he was strenuously opposed to every attempt to reform the old state of things? . . . Every change introduced to correct the abuses under which the country had been so long impoverished

BULWER-LYTTON
(in 1837)
After a lithograph by d'Orsay

for the enrichment of the few was resented by him as an act of crying injustice.

Lord Abberville was a representative peer, and had supported every government that had ruled the country since he enjoyed a seat in the House of Lords. Indeed the possibility of opposing Ministers who had anything to give away had never entered his head; though it has been asserted on more than one occasion that he had threatened to vote against them, unless certain sinecures were granted to his near relatives.

Lady Abberville was a woman of fashion in Ireland and a complaisant follower of women of fashion in England. She was indefatigable in her exertions to be useful to the patronesses of the exclusive circle in which her activity had succeeded in getting her tolerated. . . . Was a party to be got up on a short notice? She was despatched to entreat the attendance of the desired guests. Was some unlucky person to be cut? She was appointed to perform the operation. . . . She kept up an extensive correspondence, knew everything that was going on everywhere and possessed a power of ubiquity as extraordinary as her loquacity.

Throughout the story the Abbervilles (and particularly her ladyship) play the part of toadies, arrogants and mischief-makers, and their unpopularity in Ireland leads in the final chapters to the burning of their house by a band of "repealers."

There seems reason to suspect that this piece of vicious portraiture was Lady Blessington's revenge for the part which Lady Charleville was thought to have played in the imbroglio of 1831. The suspicion is the stronger because, if justified, it would largely account for Madden's unusually severe criticism of "The Repealers." In 1833, almost simultaneously with the appearance of Lady Blessington's novel, Madden issued his "Infirmities of Genius" and prefaced the work with a fulsome dedication to Lord Charleville. If, as presumably was the case, Madden at this moment was playing for Charleville patronage, he would naturally resent a novel from the pen of a known acquaintance of his own which ridiculed the influential persons he was anxious to please; and the resentment revived when, twenty years later, he was called upon to write the life of Lady Blessington.

As an actual likeness of Lady Charleville (to judge from her correspondence and such contemporary opinions of her character as survive) "Lady Abberville" is a prejudiced distortion. But this would be only natural — Lady Charleville herself was none too scrupulous in the character she gave to Lady Blessington — and there is at any rate a basic resemblance between the fictional peeress and her likely original. Both were equally active in Irish and English society; both took pleasure in filling their talk and letters with intimate references to persons of importance; both in a social sense were busybodies. As for "Lord Abberville", he is even more arguably Charleville in caricature. The name, to begin with, is suggestively reminiscent and occurs in a novel where most of the names are the merest adaptations. Then Lord Charleville did in fact owe his first peerage (the viscountcy of Tullamoore) to the Union; he was a representative peer, and his opinions were those of a strong Tory and Protestant. But most striking of all is his political record. Obstinate opposition to Catholic Emancipation had been easily reconciled with support of ministers, until in April, 1829, the Lords were confronted with a bill sponsored by Peel and therefore in large part by Government. For the moment Charleville rebelled, voted against the bill and therefore against ministers. But after the bill had become law and as the year drew toward its close, the Earl's indignation against Peel for having betrayed the principles of his party grew suspiciously weaker. The family letters show that both he and his son were preparing to rally to the Wellington-Peel ministry, lest worse befall. On December 23, 1829, Tullamoore writes to his mother: "I hope if he [Lord Charleville] does join the Government, he will sell himself dearly."

The letter goes on to say how high Lord Charleville's credit stands with ministers and that an English peerage might, with luck, be obtained by a renewal of support. Further, that Tullamoore himself wants a job, either at home or abroad. Lady Charleville loses no time. Early in 1830 she writes to the Duke of Wellington, urging her son's claim. But with the fall of the ministry in June and the resignation of the Duke, Charleville hopes are ended.

This little comedy of place-hunting (all of which coincided sufficiently with Lady Blessington's presence in London to have come to her knowledge) makes clear the identity of the "Abbervilles." That Lady Blessington should have felt sufficiently bitterly toward Lady Charleville to publish so insulting a pastiche implies that the part played by the latter in the events of 1831 was certainly no less important than has been suggested; and for this implication, if for no other reason, "The Repealers" deserves to be remembered.

But there is another element in the novel which a biographer of Lady Blessington would do wrong to ignore — and that is the deliberate fulsomeness of compliment showered on the few literary personalities with whom at this early date she had made, or wished to make, contact. In this latter respect the book strongly recalls (and actually mentions) the novel "Romance and Reality", by Miss Landon ["L. E. L."] published two years earlier,[6] not least because, in its desire to please Edward Bulwer, it introduces quite irrelevant flattery of his wife, Rosina.

Here is Rosina, as seen by Lady Blessington's fashionable heroine in her opera box:

"That lady," said Lady Oriel, "is the wife of our most popular writer, and is remarkably beautiful. Features, complexion, expression — all are faultless. Mr. Desmond pointed her out to me the other evening as one of the very few perfect specimens now to be seen of a beauty peculiar to Ireland. Hair like the wing of a raven seen with the sun's rays full on it and skin white as the driven snow with eyes of Heaven's own blue.

"The young lady next the Irish beauty is the authoress of 'Romance and Reality' and of several exquisite poems full of imagery and of a fancy that would not have shamed Hafiz himself. . . . Her novel is exceedingly clever, the dialogue epigrammatic and sparkling."

[6] *Cf.* "Edward and Rosina", pp. 149, 414–415.

A little further on comes Mrs. S. C. Hall:

"In the box to the left is the authoress of 'The Buccaneers', one of the best novels that has appeared for a long time, full of incident and interest, powerfully sustained and clearly developed. . . . This lady's Irish Sketches are portraits from the life and full of truth and beauty."

And further still, a figure who is surely that queen of silver-fork novelists — Disraeli's "full blown rose of a woman" — Mrs. Catherine Grace Gore:

"The lady leaving the box next to Lady Ridley is the authoress of half the popular novels of the day, among which there is not a single failure. Her books give you all the sparkle of fashionable life without any of its inanity, and her fecundity of imagination is as extraordinary as her facility of language. She appears never to tire herself and certainly never tires her readers, for she is always brilliant and often profound."

Cliché apart, there is sounder criticism in this comment than in the praise of L. E. L. But unluckily, if it were intended to win over Mrs. Gore to the writer's party, it failed. With her cosmopolitan and official connections (her husband was for a time in the diplomatic service) Mrs. Gore belonged naturally to the world which disapproved equally of radical *intriguantes* and of equivocal peeresses who had long lived abroad. In one of her novels of fashionable life she makes three disguised, but unmistakable and offensive, references to Lady Blessington; in another she mentions her by name and with amused disparagement; in all the rest (to the limits of my knowledge) she ignores her altogether. It is hard to decide whether to be disregarded by so well-informed and popular a chronicler of society as Mrs. Gore was not more of an insult than to be caricatured.

The two books which recognise Lady Blessington's existence are "Cecil", and its sequel "Cecil: A Peer." The former is perhaps the best known and most popular of all Mrs. Gore's novels. It was published in 1841, with the sub-title "Memoirs of a Coxcomb", and tells in the first person singular the first part of the life-history of a supremely selfish but very entertaining young man of fashion. "Cecil: A Peer" continues the narrative into the hero's old age. A curious feature of "Cecil" is the introduction into the story, and under his real name, of Lord Byron, with whom Cecil is supposed to be very familiar. It is in connection with Byron that all three references to Lady Blessington occur. Here is the first:

"In Byron's life time [Cecil himself is speaking] I often expressed to him my wonder at the total deficiency of elegancy of mind characterising the women who obtained an ascendancy over him. . . . After times will discern the surpassing vulgarity of the Betty Finikin school to which he fell a prey. The Guiccioli — Margarita — Marianna — and others even more lavishly endowed with the 'ogle of the rattlesnake' — successively fascinated the brightest and weakest of mankind."

The "Marianna" here mentioned is a character in the story. The Guiccioli and the Margarita are blandly obvious.

The tale proceeds, and Cecil accompanies Byron to Rome, where the poet spends an impatient fortnight in breathless sightseeing:

"Yet the hurried visit," Cecil says, "enabled Byron to add a brighter leaf to the garland of 'the Niobe of Nations' than the be-laurelling of a whole century of ordinary travellers — bustling Botherbys and maudlin Countesses of Pinchbeck."

The third and rudest slur on Lady Blessington comes nearly at the book's end, and follows on a hearty compliment to the social talents of Lord and Lady Burghersh. Cecil wishes to join Byron at Genoa but "from the tenour of his answering letter, I found that he had again surrounded himself with persons whom I did not affection. The Mereparks, who had spent the preceding winter in Rome, warned me to avoid a clique certain to entail on their associates a disagreeable notoriety; for in a city where there is neither a sovereign pontiffess nor English ambassadress, people sometimes find their way into society whose names are elsewhere spoken in a whisper. . . . I consequently extricated myself from my Genoa engagement and have since lauded my stars therefor — having no mind to figure in anybody's memoirs but my own; or that pennies should be turned by my sayings and doings, even though the purse destined to receive them be emblazoned with a coronet."

In "Cecil: A Peer" occurs Lady Blessington's actual name, and the reference is in consequence rather derisive than venomous. But it is interesting as showing to what an extent by 1841 her activities as editress of "Annuals" (of which more shortly) had identified her with the vapidities of titled scribblers and had caused her to lose caste, even as a "blue":

"Sonnets and *gentil-Bernardisms,*" says Cecil, "I leave to our young Viscounts, a *corps d'élite* called the Countess of Blessington's Voltigeurs, who get amazing credit at Almacks by rhyming for the Annuals."

All this was hardly a handsome return for the pretty compliment paid to Mrs. Gore in "The Repealers", but it undoubtedly represented the attitude of the anti-Blessington section of society and, as such, may claim quotation here.

4

The reception of Lady Blessington's first novel was on the whole good, the principal journals giving it prompt and full notice. It is doubtful whether it had much of a sale; but the author was well satisfied with her four hundred pounds, and something more than satisfied when the publicity given to her story, and the success of her serial reminiscences of Byron's "Conversations", brought her the offer of the editorship of "The Book of Beauty", a recently established annual gift book, financed and conducted by the well-known engraver Charles Heath.

The fashion for "Annuals" — "that epidemic" (as Lady Wilde once wrote) "which raged with considerable flimsiness and platitude" — had established itself in England about 1825. For at least fifteen years elegant volumes, bound in watered silk, in velvet, or in full and elaborately tooled morocco, were so much the mode and sold in such thousands every Christmas season that enormous sums came to be spent on their production and large fees paid to writers of reputation for contributions, which often enough were of a very trivial order.

During the first years of their vogue, the appeal of the Annuals lay partly in the important literary names secured for the contents list, principally in the beauty of their steel engravings which, often quite small in size, attained an extraordinary delicacy of execution. At first famous paintings, then the works of such modern masters as Turner, John Martin, Wilkie and Stanfield, were selected for engraving; but as the twenties went by and the frenzied snobbery of that title-worshipping period took ever firmer hold on the public, the promotors of Annuals began to consider a change of tactics. Instead of a known but minor literary man, such as A. A. Watts or F. M. Reynolds, a lady of fashion should be appointed editor; instead of the skill of engravers being devoted to the reproduction of works of art, it should concentrate on works of nature, and highly idealised portraits of the contemporary nobility should serve at once to illustrate the Annuals and tempt a tuft-hunting public to buy and admire. Finally, even the literary contributions should in large degree be signed with aristocratic names, and the leaven of genuine men of letters correspondingly reduced.

By 1832 the substitution of snob-appeal for a pretence of artistic selection was far advanced, and more than one new Annual began to make an appearance. Of these the most important were the "Drawing-Room Scrap Book", which first appeared at Christmas, 1831, with the date 1832 on its title page, and "The Book of Beauty" which started one year later. Both these Annuals were originally edited by L. E. L., though for different publishers. Possibly Miss Landon found the double activity too great or the conflict of duty too embarrassing; possibly Charles Heath terminated her engagement on "The

Book of Beauty" because he considered a titled editor to be better business. In any event, with the second volume of "The Book of Beauty" (that prepared during the summer of 1833, published in November of that year, but dated 1834) Lady Blessington was established in control.

She threw herself into the work with the energy of one peculiarly suited to her task. Success for a publication of the kind depended on a judicious selection of female portraits, on their accompaniment by verses of a highly flattering but mellifluous kind, written if possible by a member of the fashionable world, and on skilful completion of the volume with tales, sketches and a few picturesque illustrations. Lady Blessington divided her efforts between pleasing her employer and helping her friends; and because among her friends were some genuine writers, the literary standard of her productions was considerably higher than that of their competitors. Her first "Book of Beauty" contains two of Landor's "Imaginary Conversations", verses by John Galt and James Smith, and contributions of some length from both Edward and Henry Bulwer. Much of the incidental letter-press was supplied by Lady Blessington herself, who had a peculiar felicity for writing the smooth trivialities acceptable to the Annual public. No fewer than seven items by her, in verse and prose and all signed in full, were included; while the presence of her portrait as frontispiece, specially drawn by E. T. Parris and engraved "in the highest style", can have left no doubt in the minds of buyers that Heath had gone one better than the "Drawing-Room Scrap Book", and that a real Countess was editress indeed.

The procuring of material for such an Annual as "The Book of Beauty" involved an enormous correspondence; and it is proof how hard Lady Blessington must have worked that, except for one of her nieces who regularly helped her, she had no secretarial assistance. She also supplemented her written requests for contributions with frequent invitations to dinner or to an evening party, and held long conferences with engravers, printers and publishers. She continued to edit "The Book of Beauty" until 1849, and gradually undertook other responsibilities of the same kind. In 1841 she took over from Lady Emmeline Stuart-Wortley the editing of "The Keepsake", and continued the work till so shortly before her death that "The Keepsake" for 1850 is described as "edited by the late Countess of Blessington." She was closely concerned with the compilation of three annual series of "Portraits of the Children of the Nobility"; she supplied long series of verses, in 1835 to an Ackermann publication, "Flowers of Loveliness"; in 1836 and 1837 to a rival venture of Heath's called "Gems of Beauty"; and she regularly contributed verse and prose to other Annuals of the time. For a while the endless and humiliating labour involved in this flimsy form of authorship earned her sufficient money to justify itself. But her private needs outlived the popularity of Annuals, and indeed increased as Annual sales declined. For the last few years of her editorial struggles (that is to say, from about 1845 onward) she was fighting a hopeless battle, with weapons already out of date and for a cause already lost. Her name was losing its power to draw; her employers were every year nearer insolvency; worst of all, she herself was paying a triple and a mounting penalty.

Definitely bad was the effect of this assiduous Annualising alike on her health, her personal associations and her general good name. Physically it tired her out. Compelled to keep her afternoons and evenings free for the social side of her work, she found, as money grew scarcer and the prices at her command fell lower, that she could get through the mass of correspondence and her own prolific writing only by sitting up half the night and starting again early in the day. No longer a young woman, this drudgery was too much for her; it destroyed her constitution more perhaps than she herself realised, certainly far more than any of her friends were allowed to guess.

The amenities of her social life suffered in a different way. Fond though most of them were of the witty and hospitable woman to whose house they gladly flocked, Lady Blessington's visitors began to feel disconcerted by the persistent cadging for contributions which she dared not relax, and which they could not escape. "Wherever a man of note was to be found," says Grantley Berkeley, "the enterprising Irish lady was sure to press him into her service. He was either induced to write verses in her album, or enter into a correspondence with her; when she had materials to find for her Annuals she urged him for contributions, foreign or English, and the higher the rank or greater the celebrity, the better — all were made to furnish literary capital to their charming friend."

It is obvious that, with this undercurrent of editorial importunity, her evenings were no longer quite the occasions for free exchange of talk and merriment which they had formerly been. They had become faintly commercialised; and although Madden does not mention this as part cause of the falling off in the spontaneous pleasure of her parties, it undoubtedly contributed to the gradual malaise which overtook them.

As for her general reputation, it was never sufficiently good to bear continued publicity of any kind, while undesirable publicity could be trusted to make it worse. Probably, if after her defeat in the autumn of 1831, she had been able to lie low and give her enemies time to find some other subject for gossip, she would before long have earned the privilege of being ignored. For herself she would have asked nothing better. But there was d'Orsay to be considered; and d'Orsay had neither intention of sacrificing his own ideas of pleasure, nor capacity to realise that any such sacrifice was desirable. So long, therefore, as he remained in the limelight and showed himself genuinely unabashed by all that had occurred, she must pretend an equal confidence. Nor could she contrive to keep up outward appearances and herself remain in the background, because keeping up appearances cost money; money had to be found; and she could only find it by forfeiting the very obscurity which was necessary to her peace of mind.

And her periodical identification with foolish gift books not only kept alive old gossip, but before long gave the world a chance to colour its moral disapproval with intellectual contempt. As the vogue for Annuals began to fade, the same fashionable triflers who not long before had been eager to get their own insipid verse accepted and had raved over the simpering sweetness of their acquaintances' portraits, began to sneer at Lady Blessington for an activity no more degrading than it had ever been, but now no longer of interest to the *ton.* The same *nouveaux riches* who had lately vied with one another to get their daughters or themselves pictured in this Annual or that, now affected great scorn of such manœuvring and spent their money on snobberies more chic. So Lady Blessington paid penalty a second time for being identified with Annuals, and the very poverty of their literary quality was used in her despite. One example of this process has already been quoted from a novel of Mrs. Gore's; here is another: "Lady Blessington's name is eternally before the public," says Greville. "She provides those gorgeous inanities called 'Books of Beauty' and other trashy things of the same description, to get up which all the fashion and beauty and taste and talent of London are laid under contribution. The most distinguished artists and the best engravers supply the portraits of the prettiest women in London; and these are illustrated with poetical effusions of the smallest possible merit, but exciting interest and curiosity from the notoriety of their authors. And so, by all this puffing and stuffing and untiring industry and practising on the vanity of some and the good nature of others, the end is attained."

From such disparagements and from the atmosphere which produced them, Lady Blessington undoubtedly suffered. But it was a suffering she must have anticipated and one which, for money's sake, had to be endured. She hid her pain, therefore, from those about her and in time achieved a surface serenity which passed for contentment, if for nothing warmer.

By a cruel coincidence, the success of her first year as a

working author was largely offset by a burglary in her house which took place in August, 1833. Jewellery, plate and ornaments to the estimated value of nearly a thousand pounds were taken; the thieves got away; and there was no insurance money to make good the loss. Years afterward one of the culprits, in the meantime taken on some other charge and condemned to the hulks, wrote to her with cynical effrontery that he and his fellow thieves had realised over six hundred pounds on the property stolen. He appeared satisfied with this result. It was characteristic of the poor lady's ill-starred life, indicative of her fundamental lack of status, that even a criminal treated her with a certain wry familiarity.

CHAPTER II

Blessington: the Hostess of Seamore Place

1

Lady Blessington's first "Book of Beauty" was well received, and beat the "Drawing-Room Scrap Book" by two thousand copies. Charles Heath was delighted with his new editress and raised her salary. Then early in 1834 the "Conversations with Lord Byron" appeared in book form, and despite the ill-natured suggestion made in several quarters that the work was not written by her or, alternatively, that the conversations were not genuine, sold rapidly and well. Things seemed promising; a certain tranquillity returned to Seamore Place and to its harassed mistress. Imperceptibly d'Orsay crept back into favour. He still lived apart; still his benefactress' ultimate trust was withheld; but he was in and out of her house with something like his old smiling assurance, and each evening found him at her table or moving from guest to guest in the long library or under the hundred shaded lights of the crimson and golden drawing-room.

Of Lady Blessington at home in Seamore Place by far the most valuable description to survive is one written by the lively American author-journalist, Nathaniel Parker Willis. His account of his visits to Seamore Place has more than once been quoted, but never verbatim as he originally wrote it, and usually with a sneer at its trustworthiness which is not altogether justified. Willis was in some respects an impudent young bounder; but self-satisfaction and intrusiveness did not make him any less competent an observer, and his gossipy narrative of what he saw in Seamore Place, of what was said there, and of his reception by Lady Blessington have all the value of good journalism. He is detailed, indiscreet and, as befitted a visitor from another land, detached from the personal and conventional prejudices of London society. Also, his enthusiastic story of his experiences — though it gave much offence in England — had great influence in the United States and stimulated to an extraordinary degree the popularity in America which the personalities of Lady Blessington and d'Orsay had already begun to acquire.

Willis reached England in May, 1834, after a prolonged European tour. He had been sending home periodical despatches for publication in his paper, the *New York Mirror,* describing the places and persons visited on his travels; and he had no intention of changing his policy while in Great Britain. His pertinacity in contriving the desired encounters and his imprudent levity in writing up the results did credit to American journalism of a century ago, but greatly enraged many of the persons who had shown him hospitality. He was at this time twenty-eight years of age, tall, smiling, fresh-coloured and very much pleased with himself. His bland self-possession impressed even Harriet Martineau, who called him a "buxom young gentleman" with "something engaging in his round face, brisk air and *enjouement.*" Landor had given him a letter of introduction to Lady Blessington, and had written ahead to her, describing him as "the best poet the New World has produced in any part of it." Thus, when Willis presented his introduction, he was forthwith invited to pay an evening call.

It was not one of Lady Blessington's days for entertaining and she was alone. Within a very few minutes hostess and visitor felt themselves in mutual sympathy. The former, with her frank and ready manner, met the latter more than halfway. Naturally without starchiness, and aware that here at least was some one neither criticising nor despising her, she was her friendly, humorous self. As for Willis, he found her natural cordiality irresistible and, being himself a forthcoming young man with no lack either of assurance or conversation, was soon chattering nineteen to the dozen.

He had not been there very long when d'Orsay entered. As always, the Frenchman's charm of manner enslaved the visitor. "Certainly," says Willis, "he was the most splendid specimen of a man and a well-dressed one that I had ever seen." And adds: "Tea was brought in immediately and conversation went swimmingly on."

Lady Blessington asked a lot of questions about America, and was curious as to the reputation enjoyed there by English authors, particularly Bulwer and the two Disraelis, father and son. She also spoke of the letters she was already beginning to receive from America, some praising the "Conversations with Lord Byron", others in naïve but friendly fashion asking all manner of questions about herself, her work and her opinions. She took great pleasure in these warm-hearted enquiries. "A great proportion of the people in England," she said, "are refined down to such heartlessness; criticism, private and public, is so much influenced by politics, that it is really delightful to know there is a more generous tribunal."

By now the trio were all talking at once and completely happy. Lady Blessington spoke of the Americans she had known abroad; Willis of the Countess Guiccioli, whom he had met frequently in Italy and who was now in London; d'Orsay, "who still speaks the language with a very slight accent", contributed anecdotes of Byron "with a choice of words that shows him a man of uncommon tact and elegance of mind."

During the conversation the American's eyes "were busy finishing for memory a portrait of the celebrated and beautiful woman before me"; and he proceeds to compose a detailed description of Lady Blessington, which probably succeeds, as nearly as any word picture could succeed, in capturing a charm three parts expression, voice and manner, and only one part physical beauty:

The portrait of Lady Blessington in the "Book of Beauty" is not unlike her, but it is still an unfavourable likeness. A picture by Sir Thomas Lawrence hung opposite me, taken perhaps, at the age of eighteen, which is more like her, and as captivating a representation of a just matured woman, full of loveliness, and love, the kind of creature with whose divine sweetness the gazer's heart aches, as ever was drawn in the painter's most inspired hour.

The original is now (she confessed it very frankly) forty. She looks something on the sunny side of thirty. Her person is full, but preserves all the fineness of an admirable shape; her foot is not crowded in a satin slipper for which a Cinderella might long be looked in vain; and her complexion (an unusually fair skin, with very dark hair and eyebrows), is of even a girlish delicacy and freshness. Her dress of blue satin was cut low and folded across her bosom, in a way to show to advantage the round and sculpture-like curve and whiteness of a pair of exquisite shoulders, while her hair, dressed close to her head, and parted simply on her forehead with a rich *ferronnière* of turquoise, enveloped in clear outline a head with which it would be difficult to find a fault. Her features are regular, and her mouth, the most expressive of them, has a ripe fulness and freedom of play, peculiar to the Irish physiognomy, and expressive of the most unsuspicious good-humour. Add to all this a voice merry and sad by turns, but always musical, and manners of the most unpretending elegance, yet even more remarkable for their winning kindness, and you have the prominent traits of one of the most lovely and fascinating women I have ever seen.

With this description Willis ended his account of his first and most intimate visit to Lady Blessington. A little later, when he was being generally attacked for making newspaper copy out of private social encounters, it was suggested that both Lady Blessington and d'Orsay were really making fun of his naïve self-satisfaction and leading him on to still more blatant crudities. *Fraser's Magazine* virtually stated that the Countess nicknamed him "Yankee Noodle" and in other ways exploited him for an intrusive fool. But this was gross exaggeration. She may have smiled a little at the young man's bounce and complacency and, as was her mischievous habit, gently played him up; she was certainly annoyed at his subsequent lack of manners; but there can be no doubt that she liked him for his eagerness and

LADY BLESSINGTON
(mid-thirties)
After a painting by Chalon

spirits, relished the freshness of his unspoilt Americanism and regularly treated him with a kindness he never forgot.

On the following evening Willis, in pursuance of Lady Blessington's invitation, came again to Seamore Place. He found her in full dress, seated in the drawing-room "with six or seven gentlemen about her." There was James Smith (brother to Horace Smith, joint-author of the famous "Rejected Addresses", and well-known as a wit), white-haired and handsome, but armed with a crutch and wearing the large India-rubber shoes of a gouty subject. There was Albany Fonblanque, radical publicist and editor of the *Examiner,* whose physical peculiarities Willis described with such offensive emphasis that he was later taken seriously and specifically to task for unpardonable ill-breeding. There was also Henry Bulwer, "a small man, very slight and gentlemanlike, a little pitted with the smallpox and of very winning and persuasive manners." The company was completed by a German prince, a well-known traveller just home from the Near East, and "the splendid person of Count d'Orsay in a careless attitude upon the ottoman."

Conversation soon became general; every subject was discussed, from O'Connell's latest speech to the respective merits of Fenimore Cooper and Washington Irving.

Toward twelve o'clock Mr. Lytton Bulwer was announced, and enter the author of "Pelham." I had made up my mind how he *should* look, but no two things could be more unlike than the ideal Mr. Bulwer in my mind and the real Mr. Bulwer, who followed the announcement. *Imprimis,* the gentleman who entered was not handsome. I beg pardon of the boarding-schools, but he really *was not.* The engraving of him published some time ago in America is as much like any other man living. He is short, very much bent in the back, slightly knock-knee'd and as ill-dressed a man for a gentleman as you will find in London. His figure is slight and very badly put together, and the only commendable point in his person, as far as I could see, was the smallest foot I ever saw a man stand on. His head is phrenologically a fine one. His forehead retreats very much, but is very broad and well-marked, and the whole air is that of decided mental superiority. His nose is aquiline, and far too large for proportion, though he conceals its extreme prominence by an immense pair of red whiskers, which entirely conceal the lower part of his face in profile. His complexion is fair, his hair profuse, curly and of a light auburn, his eye not remarkable, and his mouth contradictory, I should think, of all talent.

Au reste I liked his manners extremely. He ran up to Lady Blessington with the joyous heartiness of a boy let out of school; and the "How d'ye, Bulwer?" went round as he shook hands with everybody, in the style of welcome usually given to the best fellow in the world. A more good-natured, habitually-smiling, nerveless expression could hardly be imagined. He was in the highest spirits, and was not serious the whole evening for a minute.

There followed a conversation which we may be glad that Willis reported, for it was probably typical of the style of talk customary between Lady Blessington and her intimates but, at that date, virtually unknown elsewhere. As from Mathews' record of life in Naples ten years before, so from Willis' description of ten minutes' chatter in Seamore Place, there emerges an atmosphere of rapid and amusing nonsense, so extraordinarily modern that one can hardly believe it existed in fashionable society a century ago. But exist it obviously did; and the contrast it makes with the artificial and simpering tedium, which the fiction of the time shows to have been the normal atmosphere of the fashionable life of the day, is of itself a part explanation of the uneasy dislike with which Lady Blessington and her circle were generally regarded.

It appears that shortly after Bulwer's arrival, the subject of his books' popularity in America was again raised. Lady Blessington, with her gay laugh, offered to take him to the United States and exhibit him at so much a time. Did not Willis think the speculation a good one? Provided she played showman, replied the American, success was certain.

Bulwer said he would rather go in disguise and hear them abuse his books. It would be pleasant, he thought, to hear the opinions of people who judged him neither as a member of parliament nor a dandy—simply a book-maker. Smith asked him if he kept an amanuensis. "No," he said, "I scribble it all out myself, and send it to the press in a most ungentlemanlike hand, half print and half hieroglyphic, with all its imperfections on its head, and correct in the proof — very much to the dissatisfaction of the publisher, who sends me in a bill of sixteen pounds six shillings and fourpence for extra corrections. Then I am free to confess I don't know grammar. Lady Blessington, do you know grammar? I detest grammar. There never was such a thing heard of before Lindley Murray. I wonder what they did for grammar before his day! Oh, the delicious blunders one sees when they are irretrievable! And the best of it is, the critics never get hold of them. Thank heaven for second editions, that one may scratch out his blots, and go down clean and gentlemanlike to posterity."

Smith asked if he had ever reviewed one of his own books. "No. But I *could!* And then how I should like to recriminate and defend myself indignantly! I think I could be preciously severe. Depend upon it, nobody knows a book's defects half so well as its author. I have a great idea of criticising my works for my posthumous memoirs. Shall I, Smith? Shall I, Lady Blessington?"

Willis got home from his party between three and four A.M. He was delighted with himself and with his new friends. As he was remaining in England for some months, he returned to Seamore Place on several occasions, meeting Moore, improving his acquaintance with Disraeli and picking up whatsoever of literary gossip seemed suitable for his paper. In February, 1835, he reported that

Lady Blessington's new book [1] makes a great noise. Living as she does twelve hours out of the twenty-four in the midst of the most brilliant and mind-exhausting circle in London, I only wonder how she found the time. Yet it was written in six weeks. Her novels sell for a hundred pounds more than any other author's except Bulwer's. Bulwer gets fifteen hundred pounds, Lady B. *four* hundred, Honourable Mrs. Norton *two* hundred and fifty, Lady Charlotte Bury *two* hundred, Grattan *three* hundred, and most others below this. D'Israeli cannot sell a book *at all*, I hear.

And he added a sentence which was to get him into serious trouble:

[1] "The Two Friends." See p. 217.

Captain Marryat's gross trash sells immensely about Wapping and Portsmouth, and brings him five or six hundred the book — but that can scarce be called literature.

At some stage of his social peregrinations Willis seems to have taken fright at the possible effect on his more puritanical American readers of frequent references to Lady Blessington. So he prefaced one of his letters with a rather naïve apology. His words are of interest to posterity in that they show the degree to which the hostess of Seamore Place had succeeded in creating that non-political, non-scurrilous society of talent which had always been her aim:

I am obliged [wrote Willis] to "gazette" Lady Blessington rather more than I should wish, and more than may seem delicate to those who do not know the central position she occupies in the circle of talent in London. Her soireés and dinner parties, however, are literally the single and only assemblage of men of genius without reference to party — the only attempt at a republic of letters in the world of this great, envious and gifted metropolis.

Willis' travel letters went their way in the *New York Mirror*, under the title "Pencillings by the Way", until the time came for them to be prepared for issue in book form. At this point, possibly from information received, their cheerful and unimaginative author had sudden qualms as to how his descriptions of certain British personalities and social gatherings would be received in their own country. Accordingly, he took the precaution specially to edit his text for London publication. But an English review had already printed some extracts directly from the original articles with the result that when, late in 1835, "Pencillings by the Way" was published in three volumes by Macrone of St. James's Square, the English critics (some of whom were directly concerned) could in part compare the emasculated text with that actually printed in America. This they did and spoke their minds freely, the lead being taken by J. G. Lockhart, who was editor of the *Quarterly* and himself too cruel a writer to endure with philosophy the counter-cruelty of others. Willis had put certain words into the mouth of Professor Wilson ("Christopher North") in disparagement of Lockhart; and the *Quarterly*, in a savage review of Willis' expurgated edition, had its revenge. Then in the English version of the letters, all reference to Captain Marryat was omitted. But the Captain, who was at this time owner-editor of the *Metropolitan*, had seen the original text; and his retort to Willis was so ferocious that the injured American, after in vain demanding an "explanation", sent a challenge to a duel. The *Edinburgh* and *Fraser's* also treated "Pencillings by the Way" with reproof and mockery.

But even more significant than the printed rejoinders of those offended by Willis' reckless candour was a private letter written to him by Bulwer as early as April, 1835. This letter shows that Willis had himself sent Lady Blessington a copy of the *New York Mirror* containing his account of her party; and in consequence proves how little malicious had been his indiscretion, but how greatly he was himself insensitive to the feelings of others and how ignorant of ordinary good manners. Here is Bulwer's letter, characteristic in its august formality, no less characteristic in its personal forbearance, and unanswerable good sense:

April 28, 1835

SIR,

I delayed replying to your letter until I had read the paper in question, which, agreeably to your request, Lady Blessington permitted me to see. With respect to myself individually, I require no apology; I have been too long inured to publicity to feel annoyed at personal reflections, which, if discourteous, are at least unimportant; and as a public man, I should consider myself a very fair subject for public exhibition however unfavourably minute, except, indeed, from such persons as I have received as guests.

But in exonerating you freely so far as any wound to my feelings is concerned, I think it but fair to add, since you have pointedly invited my frankness, that I look with great reprehension upon the principle of feeding a frivolous and unworthy passion of the public from sources which the privilege of hospitality opens up to us in private life. Such invasions of the inviolable decorums of society impair the confidence which is not more its charm than its foundation, and cannot but render the English (already too exclusive) yet more rigidly on their guard against acquaintances who repay the courtesies of one country by caricatures in another. Your countrymen (and I believe yourself amongst the number) are not unreasonably sensitive as to any stricures on the private society of Americans. But I have certainly never read any work, any newspaper paragraph of which America is the subject, containing personalities so gratuitously detailed as those in which you have indulged.

I allude, in particular, to the unwarrantable remarks upon Mr. Fonblanque, a gentleman who, with so rare a modesty, has ever shrunk even from the public notice of the respectful admiration which in this country is the coldest sentiment he commands; and, I rejoice to add, for the honour of England, that, despite the envy of his fame and the courage of his politics, no Englishman has yet been found to caricature the man whom it is impossible to answer. Your description is not, indeed, recognizable by those who know Mr. Fonblanque, but it is not to be considered so much on account of its inaccuracy, as by the insensibility it appears to evince to the respect due to eminent men and to social regulation. You have courted my opinion, and I have given it explicitly and plainly. I think you have done great disservice to your countrymen in this visit to England, and that in future we shall shrink from many claimants on our hospitality, lest they should become the infringers of its rights.

It is to Willis' credit that he was much moved by this letter, and wrote to Lady Blessington to say so:

A more temperate, just (though severe) and gentlemanly letter I never read. He gives me no quarter; but I like him the better for it, and he makes me tenfold more ashamed of these silly and ill-starred letters.

It would seem that Lady Blessington accepted this undisguised apology in the spirit one would expect, and henceforward regarded the incident as closed. Although the unsuspecting frankness of their earlier relations could never wholly return, they remained friends, and Willis wrote to her intermittently and always with affectionate admiration, until shortly before her death. His last letter in her lifetime from Dublin in January,

1848 — speaks of the impressions made on him by her kindness with a warmth obviously sincere:

> One of the strongest feelings of my life was the friendship you suffered me to cherish for you when I first came to England, and while I have no more treasured leaf in my memory than the brilliant and happy hours passed in Seamore Place, I have, I assure you, no deeper regret than that my indiscretion should have checked the freedom of my approach to you.

As a sort of postscript to the tale of Willis' contacts with the household in Seamore Place may be added a comment on the extraordinary hold which, for a period, both Lady Blessington and Count d'Orsay took on the imagination of the American public. This *Schwärmerei* was largely due to Willis' "special correspondence" and, while it lasted, found expression in curious ways. As early as 1835, Cobden, on his tour through America, met a talkative American "who wore gold spectacles, spat incessantly, talked of taste, and questioned me about Bulwer, Lady Blessington and the Duke of Devonshire."

In 1838, "The Works of Lady Blessington" were published in Philadelphia in two large 8vo volumes. These volumes contained her five novels published to date, the "Conversations with Lord Byron" and various oddments taken from the Annuals. In 1841 Chorley sent her an amusing poem in celebration of her international reputation, of which one verse ran:

> Westward, enchanting stone and stock,
> You hold all Congress fast in fetters;
> And Jonathan in citron frock
> Carves Blessington on every rock
> And for a county sells her letters.

In 1843 there appeared in New York as a volume in "Brother Jonathan's Monthly Library" — "Etiquette: or guide to the Usages of Society, with a glance at Bad Habits", by Count Alfred d'Orsay. In the same year, both in Philadelphia and New York, was published "The Ladies' Science of Etiquette and Handbook of the Toilet", one edition described as "by an English Lady of Rank", with an indirect suggestion of Lady Blessington, the other as by the "Countess de Calabrella." To these catchpenny ingenuities can probably be attributed the curious legend which still survives that Lady Blessington and the Baroness de Calabrella were one and the same person. Finally, as late as 1861, an American publisher issued the Countess of Blessington's "True Interpreter of Dreams", and the book also appeared in England.

Willis may have outraged the *convenances*, but he played press agent to perfection.

2

Ever more closely interwoven with her social life were the literary activities of Lady Blessington. Throughout the first six months of 1834 she was busy collecting material for her next "Book of Beauty" (the make-up had to be complete by early summer, so that the books could be produced and shipped to America, India and the colonies, where large sales were made) and learning to adjust her own tastes to those of her public.

From this and later years much of her correspondence with contributors and would-be contributors has been preserved. Its general effect is naturally monotonous, its details unimportant. It is, however, worth remarking that she showed unfailing civility to every one, replied punctually to all letters, and was more than usually considerate toward those whose manuscripts she must reject. In this she markedly differed from some of the other fine ladies, whom a passing fashion had raised to editorial dignity. One such had the reputation of neither advising authors of rejection nor troubling to return their manuscripts. When a suppliant called in despair to ask for his story or poem to be given back, she would send a servant down to the hall with a drawer full of manuscripts and a message that the caller could take his choice.

Now and again in her letters Lady Blessington revealed something of the difficulties against which she had to contend. On

ALFRED D'ORSAY
(mid-thirties)
After a lithograph by Lane

one occasion she writes, rather pathetically, to Charles Mathews that his verses are "a *leetle* too warm for the false prudery of public taste" and continues: "I have been so long the mark for the arrows of slander and attack, that I must be more particular than anyone else; and your verses, which in any of the Annuals could not fail to be admired, would in a book edited *by me* draw down attacks."

A later letter on the same theme is addressed to Captain Marryat. Here she is more defiantly indignant with the spirit of the age, knowing that Marryat — himself a frequent sufferer from the refinement of the period — would sympathise:

> I have seldom been more annoyed than on receiving the enclosed [doubtless a letter from Heath or his publishers] half an hour ago. I had thought that with the omission of the objectionable word, the story would have been a real treasure for the book. But the ridiculous prudery of a pack of fools compels me to abandon it.

This extreme (if reluctant) delicacy in editorial policy was also maintained in her novel-writing, and so scrupulously that it deprived her stories of the character they might have had. Passion and fervour were beyond her reach, but if only she would have let her people talk as she herself must have talked, there might have emerged not only some amusing books but a crystallization of her own vivid charm. As things are, the novels are stilted, colourless and terribly genteel; and posterity is constrained, with the help of a few reminiscences and the half dozen of her actual remarks which have survived, to imagine as best it can her fascination and her wit.[2]

And the irony of her deliberate literary propriety is the greater, in that it did not even save her from the very malevolence it was designed to forestall. Her raciness of talk had always been an offence to persons whose conception of deportment was carefully in the mode of the day. The conventional fine lady

[2] Rather than interrupt the narrative of her life with too many quotations from persons who had known her, I have collected in Appendix V a few of the more convincing descriptions, both friendly and hostile, of her appearance and manner.

of the twenties and thirties was rude when she dared to be, ill-natured when opportunity offered, and witty when she could think of witty things to say; but she was seldom merrily free-spoken and was careful to blend censure with any anecdote at all full-flavoured. Lady Blessington, on the other hand, gave free play to her native boldness both of speech and humour, combining piquancy of language with thoughtful courtesy toward every one and a complete absence of arrogance and pose. She was, in short, nearly a century before her time in her idea of feminine good manners, and paid the inevitable penalty of being so. The correct members of the English colony in Naples called her "The Countess of Cursington"; Greville described her as "ignorant, vulgar and commonplace"; while Grantley Berkeley, whose loutish coarseness is the more intolerable for his blatant pride of pedigree, devoted a chapter of his recollections to similar denigration of a woman whose hospitality he had never scrupled to exploit.

Presumably those critics of Lady Blessington who were shocked by her freedom of manner into general condemnation of her mind and morals, never troubled to read her books, but assumed that they must outrage polite convention as thoroughly as did their author. Greville is naïvely candid on the point:

"While it is very difficult to write good books," he says, "it is not easy to compose even bad ones, and volumes have come forth under her name for which hundreds of pounds have been paid. . . . In America this trash goes down because it is written by a Countess." Then adds: "I never met with any individual who had read any of her books except the 'Conversations with Byron'."

And how, save on the assumption that any stick is good enough to use against a dog, can be explained the following criticism, published within ten years of her death, by a man with some pretension to literary knowledge:

Lady Blessington [says John Cordy Jeaffreson in "Novels and Novelists from Elizabeth to Victoria"] might have gone down to posterity with a fair and distinguished literary reputation, if she had never published her works. . . . But with such evidences of flippancy of thought, superficiality of observation, feebleness of expression and commonness — we do not like to say *coarseness* — of taste as abound in her novels, it is impossible for us to romance about her. . . . They really possess no merit whatever, being weak imitations of the Hook School, the best being just readable repetitions of the semi-satirical and entirely abusive descriptions of vulgar people; they are loosely and ungrammatically worded and are throughout pervaded by bad taste and disreputable morals. . . . Lady Blessington never took her pen in hand to write a story that she did not immediately proceed to describe, in terms calculated to raise a blush on a modest girl's cheek, intrigues that would shock the morality of a greenroom and the delicacy of a kitchen. . . . And yet this lady was rewarded for her flimsy nastiness with £2,000 a year!

One is tempted to wonder whether Jeaffreson had ever opened one of the novels he thus grotesquely travesties, particularly as his list of Lady Blessington's works is chronologically in confusion, catalogues a short story as a novel and introduces one book she did not write at all. But the very publication of such an essay so soon after her death, and its gleeful quotation in her despite by Grantley Berkeley a few years later, prove to what little purpose she imposed on her natural self a literary personality of desolating delicacy. The pity is the greater in that she had a shrewd and skilful adviser in Edward Bulwer, who from the first urged her to write what she wished to write and to think less of her audience. But even he could not convince her.

3

It was during 1834 that her affectionate friendship with Bulwer was finally sealed. They had advanced rapidly in mutual sympathy and trust during the previous summer. In June, 1833, had appeared Bulwer's novel "Godolphin", as to whose authorship the strictest secrecy was observed, and for long enough with success. But it may be taken for certain that Lady Blessington was in the book's secret, partly because, when in 1840 authorship was avowed, the story was given a dedication to d'Orsay beginning: "When the parentage of 'Godolphin' was still unconfessed and unknown, you were pleased to encourage his first struggles with the world"; mainly because the theories of social behaviour voiced throughout that part of the novel which deals with fashionable life are unmistakably those of Lady Blessington.

Three months later had been published "England and the English", a book in which Bulwer analysed the characteristics of his countrymen. In this book he made a public attack on the editor of the *Age,* under the transparent nickname "Sneak." He did not mince his words. "Is a lie to be told of any man?" he asked. "Sneak tells it. Is a Countess to be slandered? Sneak slanders her. Sneak would declare his own mother a drab and his father a hangman for sixpenny halfpenny."

The second of these rhetorical questions was of course a reference to Lady Blessington, the campaign against whom had been opened, as already recorded, in the columns of the *Age.* Thus on two occasions during 1833 Bulwer had shown the community of ideas and the personal loyalty which already bound him to Seamore Place.

Lady Blessington, for her part, had gone to great pains to bring Bulwer into contact with that inspired radical leader, the Earl of Durham. She felt, and rightly, that here was the man to give direction and discipline to Bulwer's sincere but florid reformism; that as a disciple of Durham he might go any distance and take the freedom and happiness of England along with him. Her letter bidding Bulwer to his first meeting with Durham, written some time in 1833, was in itself a revelation of her understanding of the former's difficult, self-thwarting character. "You are going to meet Durham," she wrote, "and he is prepared to admire and like you. Pray do not be supercilious to him as you are to most people."

Thus adjured, Bulwer was on his best behaviour; and in the drawing-room of Seamore Place the foundations were laid of a political alliance which, had Durham only survived, might have changed the face of mid-Victorian England. How nearly that alliance led to great things, how crushing was the effect on Bulwer's political ambition of his leader's untimely collapse and death, has been indicated elsewhere.[3] Lady Blessington foretold mutual sympathy (and therefore harmonious collaboration) between two men notoriously "difficult", successfully brought them together and, had fate permitted, might have seen Bulwer launched on a great political career. Fate forbade; but there remained Lady Blessington's will to serve her friend.

Almost simultaneously, this same will found another and a more intimate outlet. The tragic development of Bulwer's private life caused him to turn to Lady Blessington — not for help with his ambition — but for sympathy in the most personal of griefs.

In October, 1833, he had gone to Italy with his wife, taking letters of introduction from Lady Blessington to Sir William Gell, Landor and others of her old friends. Although he progressed with his work (collecting material for "Rienzi" and "The Last Days of Pompeii" and even writing a portion of the former), although both he and Rosina made a large number of new acquaintances, the journey ended in catastrophe. Husband and wife had a bitter quarrel and reached home on March, 1834, exhausted by savage resentment one against the other.[4]

In July 1834, "The Last Days of Pompeii" was published and Bulwer had another terrible quarrel with his wife. Both events served to bring him into intimate correspondence with Lady Blessington, who wrote to him in Ireland (whither he had fled to recover some measure of serenity after his domestic brawl), praising the book, reporting its immediate success, and at the same time soothing his jangled nerves with words of sympathy. He replied:

October 23, 1834

I cannot tell you what pleasure I felt in my solitude, first at the sight of your hand-writing, next at the praises; and above all at the

[3] "Edward and Rosina", pp. 375–382.
[4] For the story of this unhappy tour see "Edward and Rosina", pp. 168–171.

sympathy of a friend. That I feel at times thoroughly overpowered, not by any ordinary melancholy, but by a profound dejection which leaves me literally crushed and helpless, will not seem strange hereafter, when I am dead, if all I have suffered and struggled against is ever known.

When you say that you also have lately been suffering from depression, I will not reply to you by the commonplace compliments addressed to common minds. Anyone can remind you of admiration, adulation and so forth. But those who seem to have most cause of happiness are often the least happy; and I can so far enter into your heart as to feel that it may be susceptible to a thousand wounds. . . . Yet I implore you not to give way to the indulgence of sadness, however reasonable the causes of it may be. . . . I entreat you not to let depression become a habit. Resist it, at its outset.

. . . This letter, my dear friend, is for your eyes only. That is a grand and true saying of yours, "There are so few before whom one would condescend to appear otherwise than happy." Bright heroism of a woman! It echoes all my wish, but exceeds all my power.

As a result of this correspondence (from which the merest extracts have been quoted) Bulwer wrote his essay "On the Want of Sympathy", which was published in 1835 in a miscellaneous volume called "The Student." He must have avowed to Lady Blessington that she had been in his mind when he wrote the essay, for in a note sent to him just after "The Student" appeared, she "glories in being the person you describe in 'The Want of Sympathy', who, incapable of any effort of genius can yet sympathise in the feelings and sufferings of genius in another."

In December, 1835, she gave him a snuffbox, and his letter of thanks has an unself-conscious warmth rare in his correspondence:

December 29 [1835]

I have to thank you for the most beautiful snuff-box I ever saw. I shall bequeath it to my boy as a token of the pride and affection his father has felt in one of the few friendships he ever permitted himself to form; and one of the few out of that few, of which he has none but pleasureable and grateful recollections, unbroken by a single shade of insincerity or wrong. . . . Kindness does more than please, it conquers me.

Finally, and while on the subject of the instinctive friendship of these two lonely souls, quotation may be made from a letter Lady Blessington wrote to Bulwer just after his separation from his wife in April, 1836, and at a time when he was even more than usually subject to public calumny.

I do assure you that I never permit myself to question the motives or feelings of those for whom I entertain affection and esteem. The duty of a friend is to defend and adhere to a friend through evil report. Happy it is for those who, like me in the present case, find their reason completely satisfied, and know that the persons who censure you are prompted by envy and jealousy. . . . Even had you been faulty I should, whilst lamenting it in soul, have espoused your interests in public no less fearlessly and warmly. A sort of silent respect for myself and contempt for the world has induced me to set its laws at defiance whenever I found them based on hypocrisy. I am now an old woman, and I have never for a moment repented the independent line of conduct I have adopted. . . .

You will forgive me this egotism, and not like me the less because I dare to be honest in avowing opinions that few of my sex have the moral courage to acknowledge. Count on me, therefore, to the death. For as I have no battle to fight for myself, I am at liberty to fight without any *arrière pensée* in the cause of those I love and honour. You will smile at this rhapsody. *N'importe!* so long as you never doubt the true regard of your affectionate and faithful friend.

This gallant avowal of support through thick and thin may well have gladdened Bulwer's heart. His immediate reply has not survived. But in October of the same year, in response to some appeal from her for help in her drudgery of potboiling, he wrote to her from Knebworth:

Oct. 20, 1836

I shall be most delighted to save you any trouble in looking over the proofs of the novel, which will besides be a great luxury to me. If in any other book I could be of use in filling up in outline, or in any work for Heath, contributing any assistance by contributions, no matter how much or how little, believe me I should be most unfeignedly happy.

My dearest Lady Blessington, there is hardly any person in the world

I esteem and regard so much as yourself, or for whom I feel so grateful and warm an interest, and to prove this, however humbly, would be a delightful vent to my sentiments.

From a desperately busy man, from a writer whose reputation all over the world had at this time reached a height nowadays difficult to realise, these offers are striking indeed. Taken in conjunction with the second paragraph of the letter, they prove that toward Lady Blessington he felt such gratitude and affection that he could forget his position, his dignity and his troubles, could even control his demons of shyness and self-pity, in a desire to do her service.

And serve her he did, continually and with willing industry. To any one familiar with the sense of his own literary integrity (and, to be just, of the integrity of a writer's calling) which at once possessed and thwarted Bulwer all his life, the regularity with which he contributed to Lady Blessington's Annuals is of itself remarkable. He hated Annuals and despised alike those who wrote and those who read them. But for her sake, to help her to earn more money and therefore to suffer less anxiety, he sent her contributions freely and frequently.

Nor did his help stop there. In the course of the summer of 1834 she was engaged on her second novel, "The Two Friends", and during the autumn arranged for its publication by Saunders and Otley. It is likely that once again Bulwer's influence with publishers was put at her service. Already in March, 1834, he had succeeded in selling Sir William Gell's "Roman Topography" to this ambitious firm, who were busy building a list to rival that of Bentley and, in consequence, reckless in author-payments. The negotiations had a natural sequel, for Saunders and Otley seized the opportunity to secure some future work from Bulwer himself. They bought for issue as a Christmas gift book his rhetorical story "The Pilgrims of the Rhine" and contracted for more than one work yet unwritten. Wherefore it was probably at Bulwer's suggestion that Lady Blessington, after Colburn had turned down a new manuscript

"BLESS-'N-TON"

Lady Blessington and d'Orsay at the King's Theatre, after a caricature of the thirties

of Landor's which she was handling on the author's behalf, summoned Otley to Seamore Place and persuaded him that Landor should be added to his list. The personal connection thus made would easily have led to a sale of her own new novel.

"The Two Friends" appeared in January, 1835. A few days before it was out, Bulwer wrote to her, hoping that she had not repeated the mistake of "The Repealers" and, for fear of shocking her public, watered down her real feelings into ladylike gentility:

Jan. 7, 1835

I am rejoiced that you like "Ormond."[5] It is full of true pathos but exaggerated and unreal in the midst of some veins of simplicity and nature. You have only to write passions instead of thoughts to excel fifty Ormonds. You fear too much. You have the prudes before you. You do not like to paint the passion of love; you prefer painting its sentiment. But perhaps I am wrong and in "The Two Friends" I shall find you giving us another "Corinne" or a better "Admiral's Daughter,"[6] both being works that depend solely on passion for their charm. In writing we should see nothing before us but our own wild hearts; our own experience. Not till we correct proofs should we remember that we are to have readers.

Admirable advice! But Lady Blessington was never to follow it. Nor was her failure to write passion instead of thought due mainly to policy. She had no passion; and her heart, though kind and brave and patient, was not wild.

In response to this letter she sent Bulwer a copy of the book, with a letter expressing her dissatisfaction and her dread of his verdict. Before reading it, he replied:

[5] By Maria Edgeworth, first published in 1817.

[6] The second story in "Two Old Men's Tales" [by Anne Marsh]. 2 vols. 1834. This book was the literary sensation of its year and the talk of all the coteries. Willis spoke of it in one of his letters to America and said: "The authoress — an old Unitarian lady — declared she would never write another book, but that this one was glorious." Mrs. Marsh was forty-three when this her first novel was published, but so far from ceasing to write, she produced nearly twenty novels before her death in 1874, of which one at least, "Emilia Wyndham", belongs to the small class of best-sellers whose popularity lasted for a generation.

Jan. 23, 1835

I do not believe a word you say about "The Two Friends." If it have no passion, it may be an admirable novel nevertheless. Miss Edgeworth has no passion and who in her line excels her? I want you to write so as to command and arrest the passions, because I think you would succeed. As to your own doubts, they foretell your success. One is never so successful as when one is the least sanguine. I felt in the deepest despondency about "Pompeii" and "Eugene Aram," and most presumptuous about "Devereux," which is the least generally popular of my writings.

Shortly afterward his verdict reached her:

[not dated]

I have just finished "The Two Friends." I congratulate you on a most charming publication which cannot fail to please universally. It is written in a thoroughly good tone and spirit: very elegant and sustained. . . . The happiest and newest character is the Comte de Bethune . . . Lord Scamper is very humorous though in one part his verisimilitude is a little injured by your making him talk sense about the Revolution. Your politics there, by the by, are shockingly Tory, and will please Lord Abinger. . . . Lady Walmer is a very harsh but a very true portrait.

You have improved prodigiously since "The Repealers." This is more systematic and artful. . . . The printers have made some verbal mistakes which I should notice in an errata or a preface. I do not know that they much signify, but it is well to show that they are not yours. I preach against my own practice as I am a wretched corrector for the press and my first editions are generally full of such errors, which I rarely refer to, but I should have escaped some malice if I had.

The only fault I see in your book is that it is a little too prudent, but perhaps you are right and a man does not allow for the fears of a woman; at all events such prudence will make you more popular.

Bulwer was right about Lord Abinger (Sir James Scarlett, Lord Chief Baron of the Exchequer) who wrote to the authoress:

I have made acquaintance with "The Two Friends" and like them very much. The characters are well drawn, the incidents well imagined, the interest well kept up, the sentiments of high moral cast and the composition always marked by correct feeling, well expressed.

The novel may well seem to modern taste undeserving of this praise. By any standards the actual tale is violent and absurd; there is a surfeit of French phrases (not all of them correct); and, as the reviewer in *Fraser's Magazine* shrewdly remarked, the book is essentially a "she-novel" — impulsive, rather disordered, a little feline. All the same it has a quality, and to the student of period manners, a definite value. The money worship of the twenties; the scandal-cum-prudery mentality of the upper class; life in Paris up to and during the Revolution of 1830 (which is described in much detail and with an anti-French bias highly grateful to insular prejudice); the complacent masculine conviction that women are inclined to love when really they are only being polite — these and other elements in the book have an application both dated and permanent. Doubtless, also, the manifest portraiture in the novel appealed to contemporary readers. No key to "The Two Friends" survives. One critic claimed to identify Lady Walmer (whose portrait Bulwer had recognised) with Lady Ellenborough; Desbrow (the idealist, whose lofty moral fervour was the joke of the more Philistine clubs) with Bulwer himself; and Lord Arlington (the fashionable young buck with a soul for higher things, who responds gradually to the influence of the serious-minded Desbrow) with the enlightened aristocrat T. S. Duncombe, radical member for Finsbury, admiring follower of Lord Durham, and known intimate of Lady Blessington.[7]

But beyond these three, the riddle of "The Two Friends" remains unread. Are Lord and Lady Arden the Hollands? Who is Lord Scamper — "famous at Melton and nowhere else . . . his language only fit for the stable and with lavender water on his

[7] Duncombe's son, in his biography of his father, states categorically that the hero of "The Repealers" (a "Colonel Forrester", who does not appear in Lady Blessington's manuscript key) was drawn from Duncombe, senior. If this were so, Lady Blessington would hardly have used him again in her next novel. On the other hand, the biographer may have confused "The Repealers" with "The Two Friends", an event which seems more than possible, partly because Duncombe was not among the earliest frequenters of Seamore Place and it is doubtful whether Lady Blessington knew him at all well until after "The Repealers" had been published; partly because he was much more like "Arlington" than "Forrester."

handkerchief"? Who is old Lady Bronze, "a demon at écarté and as eager to help her friends into adultery as to cut them once they are found out." And the Comte de Bethune? And half a dozen more? Even to-day a reader closely familiar with the personalities of Anglo-French society between 1820 and 1830 might well be able to identify some of these lively and unsparing pastiches. It is to be hoped that one such may be found, for "The Two Friends", remote though it be from any genre of literature, has a vigour and a tartness of detail which could only have come from actual observation.

Lady Blessington virtually admitted that she was describing things seen. Sending Landor both "The Two Friends" and "The Repealers", she apologises for their triviality. "They are written on the everyday business of life without once entering the region of imagination. I wrote because I wanted money, and was obliged to select subjects that would command it."

By December, 1835, after the work of preparing her Annual was over and she had taken a holiday in Hampshire in search of health, she selected another subject of the same kind, and for the same reason. She decided to write "The Confessions of an Elderly Gentleman" and to fill them with the melancholy of dead but cherished love affairs. Jekyll offered to stand as model. He was an old gentleman, he said, who could laugh as heartily as any youngster. But Lady Blessington smilingly declined. Not laughter, she explained, would sell her ancient's memories, but tears. He must look back upon the lovely women he had loved and lost, and shake his head and bless them for their very fickleness. Thus would the vanity of every female reader preen itself; and publishers would smile — and pay.

This settled, she turned to the more serious business of moving house.

CHAPTER III

Blessington: the Queen of Gore House

1

Early in 1836 Lady Blessington's five years' lease of Seamore Place was due to lapse; and for more than one reason she decided against renewal. Chosen at a time when she hoped, by facing up to social disapproval and using all her skill in entertaining, to impose herself on the only London which she aspired to dominate, the house had qualities which time had turned from good to bad. Its situation in the heart of the fashionable neighbourhood was ideal for a woman who wished to keep open house from six P.M. to three A.M., and at other times of day — or on evenings when entertaining palled — herself to be within convenient reach of the Park, the shops, the theatres and other people's homes. In other words, if Seamore Place were to be so exploited as to justify its cost, the door must open outwards as well as inwards.

But the events of the last four years had deprived Lady Blessington alike of the time and the inclination to go about London. She was still glad that people should visit her; there was no one whom she herself was free to visit. Instead of the lady of leisure whose preoccupation it was to create a social circle and maintain it, she had been forced to become a working author; and as the pressure of her writing and editorial work increased, the hours which would normally have been spent here and there about the town were passed at her desk. Further, the absence of noise, necessary for the endless scribbling of letters and manuscripts, was not to be had in Seamore Place. Finally, the realisation of her utter defeat at the hands of respectable society inclined her more and more to withdraw herself from chance encounters. Though she still visited the opera or the theatre, she did so with increasing reluctance; her famous green chariot — with its white wheels picked out in green and crimson, its driver and footman perched high above the normal level of their kind — was seen ever less frequently in Hyde Park; indeed the days multiplied when she never left the house at all. It was a natural consequence of all this that her health, always threatened with the effects of insufficient air and exercise and now further harassed by the nervous strain of working in continuous, if muted, noise, began seriously to suffer.

At the end of 1835, therefore, she concluded negotiations for a lease of Gore House, Kensington, which stood a mile beyond Hyde Park Corner and was, in comparison with her present home, wholly countrified. Built (so far as can be ascertained) about the beginning of the century, it had been from 1808 to 1821 the residence of Wilberforce. Standing back from the road, with a high wall and double entrance gates to protect its privacy, it was a place of large and airy rooms, of which the principal ones faced south on three acres of beautiful garden. The site of Gore House was that now occupied by the Albert Hall; and although all trace of it vanished when it was pulled down in 1857 and its materials were sold for building, its general appearance can be imagined even to-day by any one passing the beautiful but melancholy façade of Kingston House — now the only survivor of the series of dignified homes which once stood between Hyde Park Corner and Palace Gate.

Although Lady Blessington spoke cheerfully of the economies which her change of residence would make possible, she did not unduly restrain her love of interior decoration. Gore House was most elaborately prepared for its new mistress; and when early in March, 1836, she moved in, the place had been refurbished from cellar to attic. As befitted a country house, the spaciousness of the new home was very noticeable in contrast to Seamore Place, and the number of rooms greater. Once again the library was designed to be the house's social centre, and except when its mistress was actually at work, was her favourite sitting room. Through a masked door and down three steps, one passed from the library into the drawing-room, whence through a vestibule one reached a small boudoir. Other rooms were a large dining room; two studies, one large and the other small; a long gallery; and ten bed and dressing rooms, in addition to the Countess' private suite, the attic bedrooms and the rooms over the stables. In a half basement on the garden side, a big room was fitted up as a studio for d'Orsay. He, however, actually lived in a small house facing on to Kensington Gore. A door in the wall of the grounds of Gore House gave access to his own little garden.

Of the interior of Lady Blessington's new home the only detailed description extant is one of the library, included in her reminiscences by Camilla Toulmin, afterward Mrs. Newton Crosland. According to her, the walls of this room, which ran right through the house from north to south with windows at each end, were lined with bookshelves. The edges of the shelves were painted ivory white and enamelled, a startling innovation in those days and one of the several fashions in decoration, dress and interior furnishing of which Lady Blessington was the precursor. The interstices of the shelving were faced with looking-glass, the panels of the doors being also mirrored. The room, which had originally been two, had supporting columns part way across its centre, and two fireplaces. Only one doorway was retained — that opening directly to the right of the front door as one entered the house, so that the southerly end of the room, looking on to the garden and flooded with sunlight, was secured from draughts and disturbance. At that end, beside the fireplace, stood Lady Blessington's great chair, with the table at its side littered with the usual books and bibelots. The china, statues, clocks and other treasures were disposed very much as at Seamore Place. The furniture was entirely re-covered in apple-green silk damask, and the chair backs were protected by antimacassars of muslin and lace. The curtains were of green figured damask, with fringes. A single small-patterned carpet, specially made and of a shade of green rather darker than the upholstery, covered the entire floor.

The furnishings and colour schemes of the other principal rooms in Gore House have to be reconstructed from scattered evidence. It seems that, as in Seamore Place, the drawing-room was crimson and gold, the vestibule and boudoir being decorated to match. The dining room was a much simpler affair than its predecessor, because Lady Blessington intended her dinner parties to suit her country house and be therefore occasions more informal and less splendid than in the heart of the West End. The long gallery was as green as the library, but the carpet was of more ordinary quality, the curtains of cloth instead of damask, and the whole room designed less for comfortable living than to display certain works of art and fine furniture. Lady Blessington's bedroom was blue and gold, with blue carpet, blue curtains, blue hangings to the great white and gold Malmaison bed, and blue covers on the gilt cabriole chairs and the gilt-framed ottomans. Her dressing room was also blue, but relieved with threads of silver and a single circular table-cover in crimson velvet. Her upstairs study-workroom had a red and gold carpet, old-gold silk curtains and red and gold chair covers. She wrote at a pedestal table with a green leather top, by the side of which stood a six-foot cabinet in white and gold, fitted for filing papers.

Satisfied as she was with the amenities and fittings of her new home, Lady Blessington came to take even more pleasure in the garden of Gore House than in the house itself. Here at last were peace and greenery; here at last was space for the various pets which she for long wished to keep. Old red brick walls enclosed the garden, over which grew pear and fig trees. Roses were massed in the flower beds; the terrace along the southern

GORE HOUSE

After a water colour by Shepherd. By permission of the Print Room, British Museum

front was banked with lilac. Many fine old trees grew in the grounds, and there were sheltered paths winding between bushes or under grassy slopes where she could walk, and forget that London was anywhere near.

Her pets were diverse. A large white poodle had been a popular inmate of Seamore Place. He was now partnered by an Italian greyhound and by a talking crow, who lived in the house and shrieked "Up boys and at 'em", with his head on one side, to the great delight of the Duke of Wellington, who would roar with laughter at the bird's absurd gravity. In the grounds lived pigeons and several gold and silver pheasants, the latter so tame that they would eat from their mistress' hand. Finally, with d'Orsay's help, she returned to her old hobby of keeping an aviary, and the one built at Gore House was soon stocked with birds many and various.

2

Lady Blessington's house-move provoked characteristic comment. Grantley Berkeley, putting on paper long after the event what doubtless he said aloud at the time, was insulting:

> In the year 1836 Gore House, previously the residence of the pious William Wilberforce, became the headquarters of the demi-monde, with the Countess of Blessington as their queen.

He adds, lest his readers mistake for sour grapes what were only unripe manners:

> I contributed to her "Book of Beauty," which literary association naturally brought me often to Gore House and I had plenty of opportunities for witnessing the queen of a certain male society lauded and toadied by her admirers.

James Smith was neatly humorous:

> Mild Wilberforce, by all beloved,
> once owned this brilliant spot,
> whose zealous eloquence improved
> the fetter'd negro's lot.

Yet here still slavery attacks
when Blessington invites.
The chains from which he freed the blacks
she rivets on the whites.

Bulwer, in a letter to Lord Durham, allowed himself a moment of cheerful flippancy, and sandwiched these paragraphs between two chunks of political discussion:

Lady Blessington has moved into Wilberforce's old house at Knightsbridge. I consider that a sign of the times, and a sure pledge of carrying the Irish Church Appropriation Clause. She has got Gore House for ten years. It costs her a thousand pounds in repairs, about another thousand in new furniture, entails two gardeners, two cows, and another housemaid; but she declares with the gravest of all possible faces she only does it for — economy!

D'Orsay is installed in a cottage *ornée* next door, and has set up an aviary of the best-dressed birds in all Ornithology. He could not turn naturalist in anything else but Dandies. The very pigeons have trousers down to their claws and have the habit of looking over their left shoulder.

Bulwer was naturally among the first guests invited to Gore House, and in a further letter to Durham, written very shortly after that just quoted, he described dinner at the "newly completed palace." Lady Blessington, he stated, had engaged Lord Chesterfield's cook "from motives of economy", and her salon was more crowded than ever. Fonblanque and himself were placed opposite the forensic eloquence of Abinger and Lyndhurst, whilst Barnes and Strangford sat "cheek by jowl in the middle of the table, and Disraeli amphibious and alone." Bulwer supposes Dizzy was placed there "to keep peace between the company", and adds: "Lady Blessington, ever a consummate hostess, managed the incompatibles with singular dexterity, and we neither bit nor scratched each other."

Lady Blessington had hardly settled into Gore House when she wrote and begged a visit from Landor, who late in 1835 had broken finally with his wife and, leaving her and his children in Florence, had settled, miserable but determined, in Bath. He replied: "If you should not have left London in the beginning of May, do not be shocked at hearing that a cab is come to your door with a fierce-looking old man in it." The cab arrived; and Lady Blessington took instant and characteristic pains to pay her old friend the compliment of a little special hospitality. On May 4 she wrote to T. N. Talfourd:

> Mr. Walter Savage Landor, a rare sojourner in England, is come to stay a few days with me, and as I wish to procure him as much enjoyment as I can, I venture at this short notice, to request you will come and dine with me on Sunday next at half past 7 o'clock to meet him. He is one of the warmest admirers of "Ion", and is most anxious to become acquainted with its author. I have this evening sent some invitations to several of my friends, who I know honour the Genius and character of Mr. Landor, to meet him on Sunday, and I hope you will not fail me.

Landor was delighted with Gore House, and his visit of May, 1836, was the first of a long series. His letters to his sister are full of his fondness for the house, the garden, and above all for Lady Blessington, "whose unaffectedness and warmth of heart presided over us all." He soon had a favourite seat on the terrace between two lilac trees (trees which he remembered when he wrote a farewell poem after his friend was dead), and there he would sit in the sun, and talk or write or read or listen to his hostess and d'Orsay joking and laughing, "with Disraeli silently watching their conversation as if it were a display of fireworks."

But even at Gore House, Landor was sometimes contentious and difficult, and then Lady Blessington, with her gentle tartness, would not hesitate to call him to account. One evening at dinner he was particularly petulant, and in conversation with a devout Catholic who was the author of a well-known book on Christian art, began extravagantly to depreciate the beauty and significance of the Psalms. The unfortunate visitor became very uncomfortable. Lady Blessington, with her brilliant smile, intervened: "Do write something better, Mr. Landor!" she begged.

3

The months slipped away. So regular and so detached from current happenings had the life of Lady Blessington now become, that new faces among her visitors and the periodical sight of old friends were the only breaks in a daily round of strenuous monotony.

During the next six months several additions were made to the Gore House circle. The bulkiest was John Varley, a huge man with a face like a shattered rock and wistful eyes. More than fifteen years ago, he had been used to frequent Lord Blessington's house in St. James's Square, but now reappeared almost as a stranger to his hostess. Famous as a painter in water colour, he was at this time more absorbed in astrology and magic than in art. Vividly and sincerely he would discourse on his beliefs and experiences to the party assembled in Lady Blessington's library. A craze for occultism seized on the company. Headed by Bulwer and Disraeli, they plunged into discussion and experiment. They listened entranced to Varley's stories of his extraordinary friend, William Blake; they debated the pros and cons of witchcraft and spiritualism; they even tried their hands at crystal-gazing with the help of a famous crystal given to their hostess by Nazim Pasha.

Strangely precise and literal by the side of Varley must have seemed the young John Forster, at that time twenty-four years of age and writing literary and dramatic criticism for the *Examiner*. Forster was a serious, rather pedantic young man, whose force of character and remarkable practical abilities were destined so to impose themselves on more than one talented friend that he became in time a sort of organiser of literary genius, and a dominant factor in the lives of Dickens, Bulwer and Ainsworth. At this date, however, he was still an earnest junior, a little bruised by his recent implication in the affairs of the hapless Miss Landon [1], and still shyly assenting to those extravagances

[1] *Cf.* "Edward and Rosina", pp. 249, 422–426.

of Bulwer's which in a very few years he was respectfully but firmly to chide and to control. No doubt Fonblanque, the *Examiner's* editor and Forster's chief, brought him to Gore House, where any one so recommended was sure of a welcome.

Lady Blessington had both fondness and admiration for Fonblanque. She had been more annoyed with Willis for his ill manners toward the sensitive editor than for any other of his indiscretions; she had done everything possible to bring together Lord Durham and his principal journalistic supporter, and it seemed during 1836 that her efforts and theirs were within sight of success. Her letters both to Edward and Henry Bulwer are full of praises of Fonblanque. "Lay this man to your heart," she wrote to the latter. "He is one of those extraordinary men too good for the age in which they are born, too clever not to be feared, instead of loved, and too sensitive and affectionate not to be grieved that it is so."

At this juncture the prospects of the liberal cause were at their brightest, and the influence of the *Examiner* at its most powerful. A rival newspaper admitted that "an epigram in the *Examiner* went off like a great gun"; and with Durham still expected to emerge as leader of a great radical movement, Fonblanque's paper and Fonblanque himself were powers in the land. Forster, therefore, came to Gore House under the right auspices and at the best moment for his own acceptability; and Forster, once accepted, knew how to maintain himself.

He was responsible some three years later for introducing Charles Dickens, if not to Lady Blessington's circle, at any rate to Lady Blessington herself, her nieces and d'Orsay. The novelist was not then thirty years of age, and naturally his attitude toward his hostess was, and remained, that of a rising young man toward an important lady in early middle age. Nevertheless their relations soon became sufficiently cordial, and they corresponded throughout the forties with the gay friendliness of persons sharing private jokes and private ways of speech. The more real intimacy of contemporaries came to exist between Dickens and the Misses Power. Toward one of them — Marguerite — he showed great kindness after her aunt's death, accepting her work for his magazines, helping her with her writing, and sending her letters full of an easy affection to which, vis-à-vis Lady Blessington, he would never have thought to aspire.

In January, 1837, Macready dined at Gore House for the first time. He had just produced Bulwer's play "The Duchesse de la Vallière", and talk was entirely of things theatrical. He complained that the supper was too rich. Not long afterward came the Guiccioli who, although she had seen Lady Blessington on her several visits to England since 1830, had always maintained a guarded aloofness surviving from those Genoa days. It seems that her sojourn at Gore House brought the two women as near to cordiality as they could hope to get. In any event Lady Blessington wrote to her after her departure:

> I have missed you continually and thought of you often. Were you less amiable by many degrees than you are, it would be difficult, after having enjoyed your society for a few weeks, to resign it without regret. I hope you will come to me next year again, when we shall renew our sober conversations by the fireside, like two philosophers who have acquired wisdom by suffering.

Of the regular habitués, Landor continued to come and go; and Durham, until his departure late in 1837 on the mission to Canada which was the last labour of his life, was as frequent a visitor as his already failing health allowed. Marryat, who had returned from a forced absence in Belgium in 1836, resumed his intimacy with Lady Blessington and d'Orsay, helping the former with her Annuals, driving out with the latter in his private cab.[2]

[2] In addition to a few comments on Marryat's association with Lady Blessington and d'Orsay, an interesting letter from him to his rather censorious wife, excusing himself for frequenting a society of which she disapproved, is printed in the introduction to the illustrated edition of "Peter Simple." London. 2 vols. 1929.

Disraeli, in February, 1837, paid Lady Blessington a visit of several weeks, in order to revise the text of his novel "Venetia." On March 21, after leaving her house, he wrote a letter of thanks, saying: "The fair Venetia has grown under my paternal care, and as much in grace I hope as in stature, or rather dimensions. I hope she will prove a source of consolation to her parent, and also to her godmother, for I consider you to stand in that relation to her. I do not think you will find any golden hint of our musing strolls has been thrown away upon me; and I should not be surprised if, in six weeks, she may ring the bell at your hall door."

There remained, of Lady Blessington's close friends, the brothers Bulwer. Henry, the elder, had been too much abroad on diplomatic work to be constant in personal attendance, although he wrote to her regularly. But in his diary for Christmas Eve, 1837, he notes: "Dined with Lady Blessington, whom I had not seen for some time. Her powers of conversation seem much increased, but her beauty is now on the wane. D'Orsay told her after dinner that she was the only author of the present time who read as well as wrote." And the evening passed in attempts to cheer Disraeli, who was downcast by the failure of his recent speech, and in anecdotes of the "egregious vanity" of G. P. R. James.

As for Edward Bulwer, he also, though for different reasons, was away from London during the late autumn of 1836 and for a large part of 1837. Work and worry haunted him. He was correcting the proofs of "Athens", finishing "Maltravers", and planning another play. His wife had by no means gone out of his life, and though their quarrelling was now at long range rather than face to face, it was even more bitter and nerve-wracking than before. Then "La Vallière" (full of hope for which he had come to town in the new year) was a failure and withdrawn after a few performances. For this reason and that, he sought health and distraction in Devonshire and at Margate. From both retreats he wrote to Lady Blessington, with the lightheartedness which she more frequently than any one else seemed able to evoke:

There is a cottage eight miles hence which I longed for you and d'Orsay to see. It belongs to a Mr. Fish. . . . He must have a vast deal of life to spare, for he beats you and the Count hollow in his animals. What think you of half a dozen Kangaroos, or fifty parrots or two buffaloes or two Cape sheep or a South American camel or a pelican or two emews? They give me a temporary consumption only to look at them pumping away all the oxygen into their exhausted lungs.

And later from Margate:

Here runs a gaiety that is quite Continental. People walk about in white shoes and enjoy themselves as much as if they were not Englishmen. I lodge over a library and hear a harp nightly, by which the fashionable world is summoned to raffle for card racks and work boxes. It commences at 9 o'c. and twangs on till 11 o'c. If Margate itself be not exactly for you to illumine, I cannot help thinking that some proud solitary villa on this cheerful coast would brace and invigorate you.

How is *le beau roi* Alfred? I can fancy him on the Margate pier, but he would be nothing without white shoes.

I am now going to stroll along the sands and tease shrimps, which abound in little streamlets and are singularly playful, considering they are born to be boiled.

To this last letter she replied with a cheerfulness so clearly forced that Bulwer feared a return of the depression which, it was hoped, the peace of Gore House had served to dispel. He wrote privately to Fonblanque, expressing his uneasiness: "It seems to me as if d'Orsay's blague were too much for her," he said. "People who live with those too high-spirited always get the life sucked out of them."

The diagnosis was skilful. Once the excitement of the change of home had passed and despite the soothing calm of her lovely garden, the old worries came crowding back. Her health, though improved by fresher air, still caused her anxiety. Her need for money was little less urgent than before, and she could not afford to relax her writing and her editing, even during the turmoil of a house-move. D'Orsay, on the other hand, was in bounding spirits. To him, as to a child, the selection, the preparation and the occupation of Gore House had been pure diversion. He had been able to indulge his genuine talent for decoration and invention, and console himself by thinking that prodigality was sane and necessary. He was satisfied that Lady Blessington's anger against him had quite passed away, that they were on their old footing of gay and sympathetic intimacy. And so, to all intents and purposes, they were. It was always a pleasure to her to see him happy; and by now she was so busy and so tired as to wish to avoid whatsoever unpleasantness might be avoided. Wherefore, if resentment lingered, she shut her mind against it; smiled fondly at his hilarity; gave him laugh for laugh; and only in privacy sat and stared hopelessly across her desk into the future or, lying awake in the early morning, wearily wondered how it was all to end.

About the beginning of April, 1837, was published her novel, "The Victims of Society." This book merits the attention of students because, to judge from four closely written pages of criticism of the manuscript, Bulwer was definitely responsible for some parts of the finished work. It is the bitterest of all Lady Blessington's novels, and the terrible story it tells of an innocent young wife driven to death by the malicious slanders of heartless fashionables must surely have been founded on fact.

Crabb Robinson declared that the book expressed Lady Blessington's anger with the women who had cold-shouldered her; but it seems more likely that, on this occasion at least, she was writing of some other tragedy than her own. That the characters were in fact recognisable is certainly suggested by Bulwer's letter to the author, written on April 13, after he had finished reading the novel in printed form:

> You are indeed very severe in the second volume, more so than I had anticipated, but it is sane truth finely conceived, ably attempted and consummately executed. . . . I cannot conceive that you have any-

thing to dread. . . . You have attacked only the persons whom the general world like to hear attacked, the few who wince will pretend not to understand the application.

Being written throughout in letter form, "The Victims of Society" seems more than ordinarily stilted and old-fashioned; but, as usual with Lady Blessington's work, there is shrewd observation and sincerity of feeling beneath the feeble style.

Anxious, as always, to serve her interests, Bulwer with some difficulty persuaded Macvey Napier to let him write for the *Edinburgh Review* a short article on Lady Blessington's novels. It appeared in the number for July, 1838, and dealt specially with "The Victims of Society" and her two gift books — "The Confessions of an Elderly Gentleman" and "The Confessions of an Elderly Lady." The writer was very careful not to praise extravagantly, and two thirds of the essay are devoted to general discussion of various types of the English novel. He wrote to her after the article appeared, excusing himself for his apparent aloofness. "You little know how much I was hampered," he said. "Fortunately the modicum of praise which the Scotch dictator assigns to all works is well known, and looking over the volumes of the *Review*, you would be surprised to see how rare and how stinted is anything in the shape of eulogium awarded to any living writer." But one suspects that in fact he praised to the limits of his literary conscience, and certainly what he said was sensible and true. "The novels of Lady Blessington," he wrote, "are strongly characterised by the social phenomena of the times. They are peculiarly the *Romans de Société*. The characters that move and breathe throughout them are the actual persons of the great world, and the reflections with which they abound belong to the philosophy of one who has well examined the existing manners."

He proceeds to summarise the plot of "The Victims of Society" and concludes: "The story is conducted by the medium, once so much in vogue, of correspondence. Though this mode of consummating the plot is now to the distaste of the public and foregoes many opportunities of dramatic effect, it is favourable to the easy introduction of acute reflections upon society and manners, and of much subtle and elegant criticism upon men and books. In fact, the work will well repay perusal, as the observation of a calm observer of the world."

4

From now onward the years so merge one into another that to trace their course in any detail would merely be to reproduce their melancholy monotony. Let us therefore record their few outstanding incidents.

In February, 1838, d'Orsay was formally separated from his wife, and his interest in the Blessington fortune was compounded by payments distributed over several years. This certainty of considerable sums to come might have been expected to secure for Lady Blessington at least an interval of rest. But in fact it did little if anything to ease her problem. Most, if not all, of the money due was mortgaged in advance to the Count's many creditors; and the mere knowledge that cash in large quantities would sometime pass through his hands set him spending as merrily as though it stood already to his credit in a bank.

Simultaneously, with the illogicality characteristic of a spendthrift, d'Orsay determined to turn working artist. The studio in the basement of Gore House, hitherto in rather desultory use, became a scene of fierce activity. Alfred set up as society portraitist and soon became the rage. The *ton* flocked to the studio (the ladies, in the interests of their reputation, going through the garden) and paid their guineas for tinted drawing or for bust. For several years, while the fashion lasted, the artist made a considerable sum of money from this exercise of his charming, if rather limited, talent. It was even rumoured that he kept himself in gloves.

Before the end of 1838 an important new visitor made his appearance at Gore House. In October of that year Louis Napoleon Bonaparte, son of the King of Holland and, since the death of the great Napoleon's only son in 1832, Bonapartist claimant to the throne of Louis Philippe, settled in London. He had made an attempt two years earlier to assert his claim to kingship, had ignominiously failed and been banished to America. Thence he had sailed under a borrowed American passport to England on his way to Switzerland, where his mother, Queen Hortense, was dying. He spent a year in Switzerland, his importance as Pretender growing despite itself, thanks to the exaggerated nervousness with which Bonapartism was regarded at the court of the bourgeois monarch. The French Government requested his expulsion from Swiss territory; the Swiss refused. The more that France betrayed her alarm at his continued presence beyond the frontier, the more were the Swiss pleased to honour him. At last, when an army corps was actually mobilised at Lyons to operate against a possible Bonapartist invasion, the Prince felt that his time of obscurity was over. He was now an international figure; almost a menace to the peace of Europe. Skilfully he chose this moment himself to yield to the wishes of French officialdom. He declared with some unction that he would leave Switzerland of his own free will and for his country's sake. In this mood of self-immolation he came to England.

His arrival was doubly of interest to Gore House. Lady Blessington had met the Prince's mother many years before in Rome and had been received with favour. Her youthful admiration for the great Napoleon had been kept alive by this encounter, and she was now eager to welcome the exiled Prince to London. On d'Orsay the Bonapartist tradition worked at once more strongly and more legitimately. To whom should a Napoleon turn for support, if not to a d'Orsay? And he lost no time in presenting his credentials at the Prince's house in Carlton House Terrace and assuring him of his loyalty and desire to be of use.

Thus it was that Louis Napoleon, when in London and not touring the industrial centres or sheltering from that never-to-be-forgotten rain which turned the Eglinton Tournament into a scurry of bedraggled mummers, became something of a habitué of Gore House, where he was remarked by other visitors with respect or with dislike, but always with curiosity. He was a silent man, of rather distrait appearance, and to Greville "short, thickish and vulgar-looking, without the slightest resemblance to his Imperial uncle or any intelligence in his countenance." Toward Disraeli, however, whom the Prince — an amateur at sculling — had run aground on a mud bank in the Thames, "nothing could be more good-natured", and the character of "Prince Florestan" in Lord Beaconfield's "Endymion" represents the impression made by the Pretender, softened by forty years of retrospect. Bulwer was civil and invited the Prince to Craven Cottage, his riverside retreat in Fulham. But an instinctive caution in political enthusiasm checked him from expressing too extravagant a belief in the prospects of his visitor's success.

One more witness may be quoted, if only for the sake of his final sentence. Archer Shee met the Prince at Gore House in 1839. "He was quiet and inoffensive," he noted, "but does not impress one with the idea that he has inherited his uncle's talents any more than his fortunes," adding that, after Louis Napoleon had gone, the company began pulling him to pieces "until d'Orsay came in and stood up manfully for his friend, which was pleasant to see."

Those final words of Archer Shee's seem to confirm what one wishes to believe — namely, that in his enthusiasm for the cause of Louis Napoleon (an enthusiasm which led him over the next nine years into untiring efforts to win sympathy both in England and France for the claimant Bonaparte) d'Orsay was for once taken out of himself by an idea. He had found a cause which for its own sake he was proud to serve.

It would appear that from Lady Blessington also, the Prince received the treatment suitable to a Man of Destiny, although she may well have made fun of his remote solemnity, as in her moments of gaiety she made fun of most people. In her case the impulse to Bonapartism was partly a revived romanticism, partly delight at seeing d'Orsay so eager and so interested. But for all its lack of political faith, the unaccustomed exercise in partisanship had a welcome, if transient, effect upon her mind. The presence of Louis Napoleon in her house seemed to rejuvenate her, to cause her to behave as though once more she were in touch with public affairs. She regained something of what a friend called her "eager languor" of manner; also the resilience of mind which enabled her to be up-to-date about everything and even when caught unawares over some topic of the hour, to improvise, until she could once again play the part of one to whom all the latest and most private information was well known. Haydon noted early in 1835 that "Lady Blessington has the first news of everything, and everybody seems delighted to tell her"; and there can be no doubt that, so long as possible, the pose of omniscience was studiously preserved. But from 1836 onward it could hardly be maintained, and its revival in connection with Louis Napoleon was generally noticeable.

The events of August, 1840, provided an example of the old power of recovery after an initial slip. In that month, after he had spent two years in England, Louis Napoleon made his second attempt on the throne of France — an attempt which failed even more ignominiously than the first, and landed him for six years in the fortress of Ham near St. Quentin. On the very day when the Pretender crossed secretly to Boulogne, the rumour of his departure and subsequent intentions reached the ears of Chorley and Henry Reeve, who lodged together and were that evening to dine at Gore House. They repeated the rumour, and both Lady Blessington and d'Orsay laughed at the absurd gossip which servants would sometimes spread about their masters. It was true that only a day or two previously the Prince had dined at Gore House, wearing an unusual ornament — "a large spread eagle in diamonds, clutching a thunderbolt of rubies"; it was true that he had invited every one present to dine with him at the Tuileries that day twelvemonth. But it was inconceivable that he could have contemplated action so immediate as that now reported. And again they laughed. Two days later the news of the Prince's arrest in Boulogne reached London, and was told to Lady Blessington. Without a moment's hesitation, she turned her earlier misjudgment to account. "Oh, yes," she said, with casual omniscience, "to be sure, I know all about that! Chorley told me on Saturday."

But this return of her liveliness and dexterity could only be maintained by effort. In company she could still force herself to sparkle and excel, but she knew that her vitality was increasingly artificial, and occasionally to Bulwer or to his friend John Forster would admit as much. "I have been a sad invalid of late," she wrote to the latter in one of her rare moments of self-avowal, "and my literary labours, slight as the subjects to which they have been directed are, have fatigued me. I now discern that light works may prove as heavy to the writer as they too frequently do to the reader."

Nevertheless there could be no respite. The pot must be kept for ever on the boil. "The Confessions of an Elderly Lady" had appeared in April, 1838; an illustrated poem, "The Belle of a Season", was announced for November (but was in fact postponed for twelve months); she had put together some "Desultory Thoughts and Reflections", a little volume of aphorisms selected from her "Night Books", which came out early in 1839; she was finishing a novel, which had been on the stocks since 1836 and was published late in 1839 under the title "The Governess"; and all the time the "Book of Beauty" and its kind went their relentless way.

"The Governess" is the last of Lady Blessington's novels to which the modern reader need be specially directed. Landor declared it the best of them all, and he may have been right. It is a simpler, more unified work than its fellows, and inasmuch as its purpose was to fight the battle of a class at that time peculiarly helpless and peculiarly oppressed, it can be read to-day with a sympathy which Lady Blessington's usual theme — the selfish vapidities of fashionable life — fails to provoke. That the author wrote it in a crusading mood and, had she been permitted, would have painted her picture in still darker colours, is shown by a letter to her niece, Mrs. Fairlie, dated November 30, 1839:

I am very much gratified by what you tell me of Miss Lane's approbation of "The Governess." It was my anxious wish to point attention and excite sympathy towards a class from which [more is] expected and to whom less is accorded, than to any other. It has always struck me that no situation is so painful as that of a Gentlewoman constantly occupied in the difficult task of forming the youthful minds, and instilling not only all the rudiments of education, but what is of infinitely more importance, those principles on which the [? happiness] here and hereafter, of her pupils must depend; and exposed to the neglect, rudeness or jealousies of those who confide to her the most sacred of all trusts, the minds of their children.

I felt this so much that I wished to make my book a much more grave one; but the publisher, thinking only of the sale, bargained for its being interspersed with lively sketches, which in my opinion interfere sadly with the original intention.

Bulwer from Craven Cottage wrote her his usual letter of comment, regretting the parts which border on caricature, but praising the sustained interest of the story, and especially commending the sketch of an unhappy, broken-spirited little girl whose very life is finally sacrificed to the vanity of a repulsive gorgon.

This portion of the governess' adventures is certainly the most striking, and in a novel by Lady Blessington very unusual. The heroine is engaged by a Mrs. Vincent Robinson, ostensibly to take charge of an orphan child, actually to minister to the monstrous conceit of an ageing "blue." The young governess finds the child crushed into pale submission, forced to address as "beautiful mamma" the bedizened old creature who rules her life, liable to be bitten by a spoilt and peevish lapdog, and cruelly punished for any attempt at self-defence. The evil old woman responsible for this childish misery must surely have had an original. She is drawn with an angry certainty and in such detail that one can hardly believe her to be imaginary. The climax of the governess' adventures in her house presents a scene of macabre power. At an evening party of her toadies, Mrs. Vincent Robinson, dressed for half her age and heavily painted, has to be discovered by her guests bending over a child's cot in an attitude of maternal adoration. Two hours before the time, the luckless little girl, who has been badly bitten by the dog and is already sickening with fever, is brought to the drawing-room and placed in a cot draped with curtains and decorated with bows of ribbon. The harridan rehearses her part. The candles are lighted, the fire grows hotter, the room is arranged and rearranged. Still the child must lie motionless and play the cherished baby. At last the party begins. Mrs. Robinson droops affectedly over the little bed. The guests gush admiration. When the grisly masquerade is over, the governess can see that the child is seriously ill and insists on her removal from the hot and noisy room. Mrs. Robinson is very angry and declares that the little girl is perfectly well and malingering to spite her "beautiful mamma." Ten days later the child is dead. This gruesome episode, which is told with an unusual lack of periphrase, gives to "The Governess" a distinction almost impressive among its author's work.

As soon as this story was off her hands and before it actually appeared, Lady Blessington busied herself with preparing for public issue her private journals of the tour taken with her husband through France to Italy, and of those lotus-eating years in Naples, when she and Blessington and Mary Anne Power and d'Orsay lived in the sunshine and were happy. The work appeared with Colburn as "The Idler in Italy" in two volumes in March, 1839; a second edition followed in 1840, to which a third volume of wholly new material was added.

The book's success was considerable and, in view of its genesis and history, deserved. To turn those leaves of memory must have been a bitter experience, and it would have been easy for her, by supplying a substratum of reproachful melancholy, to underline the difference between then and now, to appeal for pity, to become herself the central figure of a drama of unmerited misfortune. Instead, such alterations as she made were designed to convert a personal record into a bright narrative of foreign travel, with a deal of general feminine interest and as little individual application as possible. It has already been made plain that her editing damaged the book's appeal to posterity, because posterity is more interested in her and in her party than in observations of Continental life or in descriptions of works of art. But in 1839 she was out for immediate popularity; and there is no denying that, with this in view, she used her diary skilfully and well.

Colburn was pleased with the sale of "The Idler in Italy" and gladly agreed to follow it with a companion work entitled "The Idler in France." This book embodied the journals of her two eventful years in Paris and appeared in March, 1841. It proved as acceptable as its predecessor.

"The Idler in France" was the last of Lady Blessington's books to make more than a transient mark on public favour. She published five more novels during her lifetime, and left a sixth complete in manuscript which appeared after her death.[3] But no one of those was a success. With "The Governess" she had exhausted her meagre vein of fictional originality; in her two diaries of travel she had had recourse to such documents as remained from her gay and vigorous past. Thereafter remained only fatigue, and listless rehandling of material already used.

5

In 1840, for the sake of some extra hundreds of pounds, she had undertaken to edit "The Keepsake" as well as "The Book of Beauty." The money was hardly earned, for the additional correspondence weighed heavily on her already burdened time,

[3] See Appendix III.

and between the rival claims of her two Annuals she was often hard put to it so to apportion the work of her contributors that they were not offended nor the publishers displeased.

But although the number and worry of her literary tasks increased, she still kept herself free to entertain her friends, to help by letter or by spoken word any one who asked her influence in likely quarters.

It would be impossible at this distance of time to compile a complete list of the persons, deserving and undeserving, whom Lady Blessington put herself out to assist. Even those cases known would make a catalogue more instructive than amusing. But the will to help others was so much a part of her nature that her benefactions cannot go wholly unrecorded. To her relatives she was uniformly generous. After her father died in 1837 (he was seventy years old, "unable to make the slightest movement without screeching with agony", yet to the last night of his life draining the four tumblers of punch to which he had grown accustomed) she continued to support her youngest sister (the Countess Saint Marsault) and for a while her brother Robert also. Owing to her influence with Lord Durham, Robert Power was at last given a post in Canada, and presumably her budget was thereafter relieved of the cost of keeping his family. She was very active in trying to get a pension from Sir Robert Peel for Lady Canterbury, after Lord Canterbury's death; she tried to sell a Lawrence portrait on the same lady's behalf; she solicited (and successfully) from the Duke of Wellington a brigade-majorship for Captain Home Purves, a son of Lady Canterbury's by her first marriage. These are specimens of the importunities which, for her relations' sake, she was continually addressing to men of influence. That there were others of the same kind is shown by the correspondence printed in Madden's biography and in the "Blessington Papers."

Those who benefited by her efforts were not always grateful, but for the kindness she showed to Lady Canterbury's daughter, Louisa Fairlie, she was rewarded by true affection and congenial company. Mrs. Fairlie collaborated with her aunt in Annual editing and was continually at Gore House, whither she would bring her little daughter Isabella, whom Disraeli once called "the beautiful mute." Deaf and dumb from birth, the child's affliction, even more than her loveliness and strange gifts of mind, endeared her to Lady Blessington. She spent a large part of her short life at Gore House, playing in the garden while her great-aunt sat under the trees, greeting the various visitors, to all of whom she was well known.

In addition to her relatives, numerous literary folk and their dependents came to rely on Lady Blessington's willingness to help, and seldom appealed to her in vain. She besought Sir Robert Peel for a government appointment for her old friend Captain Marryat; she used her friendship with Sir Francis Freeling to secure a place in the post office for a young friend of S. C. Hall's and tried to repeat the experiment on behalf of Thackeray, but this time unsuccessfully. She offered to bear the cost of a tombstone for poor L. E. L., who had died tragically in West Africa soon after her marriage in 1838, and contributed generously to the fund raised for the dead woman's mother. As a result of this last kindness, she was bombarded with begging letters by L. E. L.'s parson-brother, a man for whom she had already obtained one living, who now thought himself due for preferment and in some place other than London. She canvassed for Disraeli's election to the Carlton Club. She succeeded in getting the Royal Literary Fund to grant a pension to Mrs. Charles Mathews. Verily, as a distinguished neighbour wrote to her, if half the happiness she dispensed to others were returned to herself, she would have been amongst the happiest of the human race.

6

It was during 1841 that the first crack made public appearance in the jerry-built solvency of Gore House. Lady Blessington had for long enough been only too aware of her dangers and difficulties; but until the day in 1841 when d'Orsay, to escape arrest by his creditors, deliberately became a "shy cock" and remained behind the garden walls save on Sundays and after sundown, she had contrived to hide the seriousness of the position from all save her few real intimates. Now, however, d'Orsay's insolvency was publicly realised, and the many tradesmen to whom he owed money took alarm and jostled one another in their demands for settlement. In consequence, Lady Blessington's own credit was inevitably, though indirectly, damaged, and the menace of the future weighed ever more heavily on her spirits.

Then came a series of personal sorrows. In January, 1843, the child Isabella Fairlie died after a long and painful illness. Madden prints the touching letter which the dying child wrote to her great-aunt, three days before the end. The note was endorsed by Lady Blessington, "Written by my blessed grandniece on Saturday night, the 28th of January, 1843. She expired on the 31st, at twenty minutes before eight in the evening, resigning her pure spirit without a groan or struggle." It reads:

MY DEAR AUNT

I am so pain in my breast and cough a deal. I thank you for a barley sugar and large cake. Papa gave me a flower paper. I am writing in bed, at night. How kind you are to bring what I want. Mamma send me large round barley sugar, not like you give me. Give my love to Alfred, Margery, Ellen, from

I. L. F.

Hardly had Lady Blessington forced herself back to work, and so dulled her grief at the loss of this beloved little friend, when Mrs. Fairlie — worn out with the anxiety and toil of her child's long illness — herself collapsed, and about two months after Isabella's death, died also.

"This blow," Lady Blessington wrote to Henry Bulwer, "has fallen heavily on me. . . . This has indeed been a melancholy year for me, Alfred's position, as you may well imagine, filling me with chagrin, and the protracted illness of two beings so dear to me, closed by their deaths, adding the last blow to my troubles."

But there were other torments in store. The death of Mrs. Fairlie deprived her family of its breadwinner, for John Fairlie, though a worthy man, seems to have been ill-equipped for earning a living. Normally, and inasmuch as Mrs. Fairlie had been Lady Canterbury's daughter, her widower and surviving children would have looked to the Canterburys for help in their distress. But when this crisis of 1843 arose, there was no such help to be had. Wherefore they turned to Lady Blessington, and she, for the sake of Louisa and the little Isabella, assumed the embarrassing burden of their maintenance.

Why, precisely, the task of caring for the Fairlie family should have devolved on a great-aunt rather than on a grandmother, has never been explained. Of all Lady Blessington's relations, the only one who seemed on solid ground was her sister Ellen, who first as Mrs. Manners Sutton and then as Lady Canterbury, lived ostensibly in easy and assured circumstances. When Manners Sutton failed to secure reëlection to the Speakership of the House of Commons in 1835, he was given not only a peerage but also a pension of four thousand pounds a year. Surely, less than ten years later, something might have been spared from so considerable an income for a needy son-in-law and grandchildren? But for causes unknown, Lord Canterbury's pension had proved wholly insufficient for his needs, and he and his wife, from the late thirties onward, had been struggling with increasing difficulties.

There is some obscurity as to the relations between the Canterburys and Lady Blessington during the whole period of their joint residence in London. Jekyll reported to his sister in July, 1831, that "the Speaker and his wife have thrown my Blessington overboard." But his information was either incorrect or shortly became so. Quite early in the thirties Mrs. Manners Sutton joined with her sister in contributing to the support of their father; her husband (by then Lord Canterbury) dined with Lady Blessington during 1837; in 1840 Archer Shee specifically mentions Lady Canterbury as one of the few ladies regularly at Gore House; and when the ex-Speaker fell into the financial troubles which clouded the last years of his life, Lady Blessington exerted herself to get him a pension and was rewarded, even in failure, by her sister's affectionate gratitude.

In July, 1845, Lord Canterbury died suddenly. His widow, to whom the shock of her husband's death had been very severe, went abroad for a while, but feeling her health failing, returned to England and visited her sister at Gore House. There she was seriously ill; recovered sufficiently to go to her own home in Clifton; fell ill once more, and died in November, four months after her husband.

One by one the few persons to whom Lady Blessington could turn for sympathy were dropping out. To the pressure of money cares, to the slow failure of her own health, were added a growing isolation and the secret panic caused by the loss of friends.

But the worst was yet to come. In 1846, and as though tiring of the slow torture applied indirectly through d'Orsay's irresponsible gaiety and the death of those she loved, fate turned savagely on Lady Blessington and with a quick succession of blows beat her to the ground.

The assault was cruelly prefaced with a momentary good fortune. In January, 1846, under the editorship of Charles Dickens, the *Daily News* had started its still prosperous career. Through her friendship with the editor, Lady Blessington was engaged as "Society Correspondent" at a provisional (and very welcome) salary of two hundred and fifty pounds for a trial six months. But it would seem that this piece of luck was only vouchsafed to her in order the more grimly to prove that her days of sunshine were over. She had hardly started on her new job than the foundations on which it rested began to crumble. Dickens threw up his editorship after three weeks. His place was taken by Forster, but only reluctantly and pending the appointment of a new editor. In due course the appointment was made, and the newcomer declined to renew Lady Blessington's contract. Thus, through no fault of her own, there vanished a piece of badly needed income and work both congenial and easily performed. Wearily she turned back to novel-writing and to Annuals. The earning power of both was clearly on the wane; but they were her only hope, and the two yearly thousands of her jointure must be in some way supplemented if they were to meet the expenses of her daily life.

That the jointure itself might fail had not seriously occurred to her. Yet this crushing blow her evil fate still had in store. The winter of 1845 had brought, first potato blight and then famine in Ireland. To the misery caused among the Irish poor throughout the years 1846 and 1847, many books bear witness; but it does not seem that the effects of the calamity were immediately felt among those residents in England whose income came from Irish sources. Early in 1847, however, they made disastrous appearance, and among the victims were those who drew their money from the Blessington estates. Lady Blessington was blandly informed by the trustees that her jointure would not be paid. In the utmost panic she sought the advice of Edward Bulwer-Lytton. He sent her a reassuring letter, bidding her insist through her lawyer that her jointure have the absolute priority to which it was legally entitled. Apparently she succeeded by this means in extorting at least a portion of her annual income; but it was only a portion, and the balance was made up by pledging her jewellery in return for loans.

In the late autumn of this same year befell another disaster — and one nearly as grave. Charles Heath, impresario and financier of "The Book of Beauty", "The Keepsake" and a host of other illustrated works, was declared bankrupt. Among his liabilities was a sum of seven hundred pounds owing to Lady Blessington for work performed.

The poor lady had no reserves either of money or spirit with

LADY BLESSINGTON
(early forties)
After a lithograph of a drawing by d'Orsay

which to meet these misadventures, and the year 1848 found her at the end of her resources. Publishers would not accept her novels unless she paid for them; and one experiment of the kind had left her with a deficit too large to be repeated. The bankruptcy of Heath, and the administration of his properties in the interests of creditors, meant that payments to the editor of his two chief Annuals were on a new and harsher scale. Of her personal valuables a large proportion were already pledged. Discreet attempts to sell some of the remainder met with failure, because it was now evident to every one that a crash was coming, and tradesmen, who hoped before long to buy at a sale of bankrupt stock, were naturally unwilling to purchase in advance and at a pre-bankruptcy valuation.

She had nowhere else to turn. Credit might hold a little longer; something might turn up. But when credit failed and unless a miracle happened, she was finished.

The doors of Gore House were now shut against every one during the hours between sunrise and sundown. The year dragged by, and the place remained virtually in a state of siege. Outside the bailiffs prowled, watching an opportunity to force an entrance; within, amid splendours which had always been a sham and were now a savage mockery, two ruined gamblers waited for the end.

For there was no longer question but that the end had come. Sooner or later vigilance would nod; sooner or later would yield the frail barrier, which legality and locked gates could for a while interpose between creditors and their prey. And now that downfall was at hand, Lady Blessington felt as much relief as dismay. We know from a letter of d'Orsay's that she had wished to make an end early in 1848. She accepted the fact that control had finally slipped from her hands; she realised, with the relief of exhaustion, that there was now nothing to do but wait — and while waiting, to smile as bravely as she might. If Gore House were indeed dying, it should die game.

It is strange to picture the evening parties which, even during this year of humiliation and suspense, were still occasionally held. It is strange to imagine Louis Napoleon (who had come straight to Gore House after his escape from Ham two years earlier, and had been a constant visitor ever since) starting back to France in February, 1848, standing at last on the threshold of his destiny, while behind him the house which had for so long been to him a kindly refuge was now poised on the edge of dissolution.

Yet the contradictoriness of those final scenes was wholly in character. Irrational from its first moment, the bizarre drama of the Blessington inheritance had now been played to within a few months of its end. For thirty years act had followed on topsy-turvy act, and to the moment of the curtain's fall the air of fantasy must be maintained. Only behind the masks was now tragedy — Marguerite Blessington with her broken heart; d'Orsay, with his tarnished beauty and his wasted life.

CHAPTER IV

D'ORSAYS THE MAN UPON TOWN

1

"HIS wasted life. . . ."

In the record of this career so fair in promise, in fulfilment so futile, lies perhaps a tragedy even more melancholy than that of Lady Blessington. She had known misery; then excited happiness and the admiration of her world; then the joy of pitting her wits against her kind; then, after a shock of sudden grief, a time of bitter disillusion and the thrill of fighting for survival; last of all the grim exhaustion of defeat. She at least had lived; and in the living had grown in wisdom and in tolerance. But to d'Orsay life had taught nothing — not because he was unable or even unwilling to learn, but because he was incapable of regarding it as a lesson at all. To him life was a plaything provided by others for his amusement and, when damaged, to be repaired at their expense. Being a good-tempered person with ready sympathy for the difficulties of his friends, he did not unreasonably complain at the occasional breakdown of his toy; but that he himself should take steps to put it right never occurred to him. Some one else always had seen to it, and some one else would see to it now. So he just waited, smiling amiably, until his game could be resumed.

The story of d'Orsay's personal existence from 1832 to the end of his sojourn in London cannot be understood without a realisation of his utter irresponsibility toward the actualities of life. Up to a certain point he could (and did) calculate the result of his own actions; beyond that point he never attempted to do so. He regarded the mechanics of existence much as a small boy in a happy home regards the meals provided by his parents — as something beyond his province and to be taken gratefully for granted. For d'Orsay was always ready to be grateful. His attitude toward Lady Blessington was exactly that of cheerful but thoughtless boyhood toward a devoted and widowed mother. He shared her existence, abused her trust, but — within the limits set by his egoism — he loved her better than any one else. He loved her because he knew her very well, because she shared his jokes, because she was interested in his amusements, his painting, his aviary, his manifold little activities. If he fell down and hurt himself, she consoled and doctored him; if he brought home a prize from school or got his first-eleven colours, she was happy in his success and glad to see him happy. When, as now and again she would, she spoke seriously to him of the difficulties of their joint existence, he would become at once tender, sympathetic and even comically protective. On such occasions a small boy will throw his arms about his mother, beg her to cheer up and — playing the little man — undertake by doing this and that to make things easier. But when he has left her and run out of doors, he forgets everything save that the trees are golden in the sunshine, that the dog is leaping at his side, and that the world as he sees it is no less gay and healthy than himself. Precisely in this way, when periodically her troubles became too heavy for Lady Blessington to bear alone and she called him to her room to hear and share them, d'Orsay would be full of plans and hopefulness and valiant promises. But when he had coaxed her back from melancholy to smiles, and returned to his studio to find Chesterfield or Anson waiting for him with plans for a trotting race or a cheerful day at Newmarket, all his grave resolutions were forgotten, and he was on with the new as though the old had never been.

Everything conspired to keep d'Orsay in this mood of happy but disastrous instability. He had all the qualities which enchant a new acquaintance — good looks, great charm of manner, a quick sense of social atmosphere, a talent for saying amusing things, an interest and some skill in manly sports, considerable proficiency in the arts. Practically every one who came into contact with him liked him. With his equals he was frank, well-informed but never dogmatic, eager to share their interests and not over-insistent on his own, generous alike with help and praise. Toward social inferiors he was invariably courteous and considerate, so that they liked to serve him and greeted him with smiles.

He grew so accustomed to popularity that he could hardly conceive it possible for unfavourable criticism to be seriously meant. Of course, as time went on and the reality of his ostracism in certain quarters could no longer be ignored, he accepted the fact that there were folk too stupid or too prejudiced to like him as he was. Then his social sense came to his aid and enabled him most deftly to avoid those places and persons where snubs and other awkwardness might possibly occur. But even with this realisation of not being universally welcome, came no attempt to relate effect to cause. It was an odd thing that some people did not want him. Presumably their attitude was due to a misunderstanding, for he had not harmed them nor did he wish to do so. But it did not become a d'Orsay to seek recognition where recognition was denied; and with all his other friends and occupations, he could afford to leave the starchy to their starchiness. As for pausing to think whether, by standards of social conduct, his critics might possibly be justified, any such reflection was utterly beyond the scope of his mind. Not conceiving himself answerable for anything save the need to do justice to his own innate distinction and to express his natural good will to those about him, he had neither social standards of his own nor any sense of their importance to other people. So, serene as ever, he put his enemies out of his mind, hardly troubled to enquire the reason for their enmity, and pursued his happy way along the path of pleasure.

Simply to describe d'Orsay as selfish and vain would be at once an under and an over-statement. Judged by his actions, and their effect on others, he was super-selfish and super-vain; but personally he was sublimely unconscious of being either. A selfish man is one who indulges his own inclinations with calm disregard for those of others, and a vain man is one who compares himself with others to his own advantage. D'Orsay did neither of these things. He was most sensitively aware of the wishes of those about him and (it was one of his most charming traits) often forestalled them by ingenious generosity. Acts of kindness were his hobby, and he spared himself no pains in contriving and performing them. If challenged, he would have declared (and genuinely) that a desire to help others was the dominant motive of his life. But if he had then been told the simple truth — that his consideration for others did not begin to operate until after his own convenience had been reasonably secured, he would have failed to understand what was meant. Similarly with vanity. How should he in the ordinary sense be vain, when it never occurred to him to be other than he was, or that any one could wish him to be so? He did not think himself more important or better than his fellows; he merely started with the assumption that he was on a different plane from them — not a higher plane or a lower one, but a unique d'Orsayite plane, with which no other had any relationship whatsoever.

He presented, therefore, the paradox of an egoism so sublime that it transcended itself and became the equivalent of a divine condescension. D'Orsay was wholly unaware that he played the divinity or condescended; but he was equally unaware of his egoism, which, inasmuch as it functioned in a void where were no other egos, was implicit and never explicit. For this reason his impulses and his actions were perpetually dislocated. When the latter proved disastrous, he could console himself with the integrity of the former; but he never understood what was wrong, and lived his twenty years of London life in a gentle crescendo of suave bewilderment.

2

D'Orsay dropped out of our narrative of Lady Blessington's career with the public breakdown of his marriage in the autumn of 1831. The part he played in that still mysterious drama was, by ordinary standards, a discreditable one. But d'Orsay's standards were not ordinary; and it is now easy to see that his behaviour was in character and his motives consistent. He had married Harriet Gardiner in order to secure the money which her father had promised him — the money without which he could not live as he was meant to live. So long as Harriet fulfilled her purpose, and nothing occurred to disturb the tranquillity of his self-indulgence, he was prepared to admit her claim to enjoy the pleasure of his company. But when the validity of his marriage was threatened by jealous outsiders, when into the bargain his wife showed so little sense of her privileges as to get herself involved with another man, his attitude was immediately transformed. It underwent the equivalent of a reversion to savagery. Quite suddenly he realised that he — d'Orsay — was in serious danger of social and economic destruction; and from the moment of that realisation nothing existed for him save the necessity of self-preservation. Toward Harriet, who had publicly humiliated him, he felt fully entitled to be ruthless. If he could turn the consequences of her actions to his advantage, he would naturally do so; but they would remain her responsibility and the blame for them would be hers. Of Lady Blessington he probably never thought at all. Even afterwards, when to his surprise she bitterly reproached him for the ruin of her hopes and ambitions, he only realised that she was angry with him. He did not really understand that he had done anything to which she could reasonably take exception. He had only saved himself from an unpleasant predicament. What could be more natural?

The fact remained, however, that she was angry; and because he was very fond of her and did not like to see her other than fond of him, he did not answer her back, but submitted with graceful humility to her reproaches and determined, for a while at least, to keep out of her way. Her anger would pass, and before long everything would be as pleasant as before. Pleasanter, indeed; for already that tiresome Harriet had gone, and Harriet had never really fitted in. . . . So, philosophically enough and pending a reconciliation with his charming protectress, d'Orsay set out in search of entertainment on his own account.

The years from 1832 to 1841 were his years of London splendour. He went almost everywhere, knew almost every one, and imposed himself on the imagination of masculine society with a completeness at which one can only marvel. Not his equivocal domestic life, or the unsavoury stories which survived from 1831, or the denigration of the Gardiners and their friends, or even the murmuring of his creditors, served to cast more than an evanescent shadow on this gleaming glass of fashion. He became the beau ideal of all save the most censorious among the young bucks of the day. His horsemanship was a virtuosity, his clothes an intoxication; his sangfroid at the gaming table, his wit and unfailing good temper in dining room, smoking room or paddock were irresistible. Never has a man established a more complete supremacy over the minds of gilded youth than did d'Orsay during his nine years of social despotism.

Of the events of those glittering years was the d'Orsay legend born — a legend compounded of whole-hearted liking and admiration, of jealous detraction, of anecdotes, of *mots*, of triumphant experiments in courtesy, sport and tailoring. And the chorus of praise is virtually unanimous. Only here and there sounds a dissentient voice, among them that of Creevey, who in October, 1834, wrote from Stoke Farm to his stepdaughter:

> Our party here have been the little Russian ambassador; d'Orsay, the ultra Dandy of Paris and London, and as ultra a villain as either city can produce — you know he married Lord Blessington's daughter, a beautiful young woman, whom he has turned upon the wide world

D'ORSAY DRIVING IN HYDE PARK
(late thirties)
After an illustration by "Standfast," in "D'Horsay or the Follies of the Day"

and he lives openly and entirely with her mother, Lady Blessington. *His* mother, Madame Craufurd, aware of his profligacy, has left the best part of her property to her sister's — Madame de Guiche's — children.

Then, according to J. H. Jesse (in a letter written after d'Orsay's death, to an enquirer),[1] he had to be withdrawn as a candidate for White's, owing to a group who had sworn to keep him out. No date is given for this incident, but it almost certainly occurred during the thirties. A decade later, his own ambition would not have soared so high.

A third episode can now, thanks to the discovery of the Marlay-Charleville papers, be recorded with comparative completeness. In the diary of the Duchesse de Dino is a story that early in 1834 Sir Willoughby Cotton posted two letters in the wrong envelopes, one to d'Orsay, the other to Lady Fitzroy Somerset. D'Orsay, on opening his letter, found that Cotton was retailing to his woman correspondent gossip about an intrigue between Lady Tullamoore and some man, and incidentally making an offensive observation about d'Orsay himself (probably with reference to the old scandal involving Tullamoore and Harriet). He went down to the club, read the letter aloud to a group of men, and then, putting it in another envelope, posted it to Tullamoore. There was, as can be imagined, a scene.

Here the Duchesse de Dino stops, merely saying that the affair was hushed up. But among the Marlay papers is this letter from Tullamoore to his mother, written in January, 1834, which takes the matter further:

I was obliged to come here as my friend Willoughby Cotton felt it necessary to call out Count d'Orsay. We have fortunately arranged the business and got an ample apology. The Count's conduct was unjustifiable and he could not have found an English gentleman to go out with him. He was therefore compelled to make an apology, but he has lost the little hold he has in society, as the Seftons, Worcester and ourselves were at most the only houses open to him, and these can be so no longer. He is so agreeable and clever one regrets his conduct.

[1] "Blessington Papers", p. 88.

Now it is obvious that d'Orsay's action in this matter was, by masculine code, unforgiveable; yet he contrived — and before very long — to charm away all memory of his misdeed. Sir Willoughby Cotton was among the fashionable folk whose portraits he subsequently drew and published; the two men were regarded throughout the thirties as in the same set at Crockford's; and d'Orsay was welcome in many other houses besides those of Sefton and Worcester for years after this incident occurred.

What did d'Orsay look like, and what sort of life, while freedom and credit were still his, did he choose to live?

In the matter of personal appearance two contemporary witnesses shall be heard — one hostile and the other friendly. Mrs. Newton Crosland, to whom reference has already been made, did not like d'Orsay and her testimony, coming from a woman, is significant. She saw him several times at Gore House and once he took her in to dinner. The following is the impression she afterward recorded:

> He was tall and with a good figure and carriage and had fine hazel eyes; but he had one great defect which made me wonder he was so much admired. His teeth had gaps between them, which caused his smile to degenerate into something approaching a sneer; and his hands, large and white and apparently soft, had not the physiognomy which pleases the critical student of hands. I thought his conversation commonplace; but perhaps, though he spoke English fluently enough, his vocabulary was somewhat limited. He struck me as being mannish rather than manly, and yet with a touch of effeminacy quite different from that woman-like tenderness which adds to the excellence of a man.

She adds that between Lady Blessington and d'Orsay the manner was very much that of mother and son.

These comments certainly harmonise with the portrait of d'Orsay by Aubry, reproduced in the present volume, the only portrait I can find which makes the Count look like a human being and not a mere evocation of period elegance.

Gronow, on the other hand, writes from a point of view

very friendly to d'Orsay. His indication that the Count's vanity and foppishness were on a par with his good looks corroborates Byron's statement of many years earlier that Cupid-at-Large was well aware of his beauty. His description of d'Orsay's mouth and teeth strikingly forecasts what Mrs. Newton Crosland was to write many years later.

D'Orsay was rather above six feet in height [says Gronow], and when I first knew him, he might have served as a model for a statuary. His neck was long, his shoulders broad, and his waist narrow, and though he was, perhaps, somewhat under-limbed, nothing could surpass the beauty of his feet and ankles. His dark chestnut hair hung naturally in long waving curls; his forehead was high and wide, his features regular, and his complexion glowed with radiant health. His eyes were large and of a light hazel colour, he had full lips and very white teeth, but a little apart; which sometimes gave to the generally amiable expression of his countenance a rather cruel and sneering look, such as one sees in the heads of some of the old Roman emperors.

I remember on one occasion, when about to fight a duel, he said to his second, Monsieur D——, who was making the preliminary arrangements, "You know, my dear friend, I am not on a par with my antagonist; he is a very ugly fellow, and if I wound him in the face, he won't look much the worse for it; but on my side it ought to be agreed that he should not aim higher than my chest, for if my face should be spoiled *'ce serait vraiment dommage!"* He said this with such a beaming smile, and looked so handsome and happy, that his friend, Monsieur D——, fully agreed with him.

Though his tastes, pursuits, and habits were thoroughly manly, yet he took as much care of his beauty as a woman might have done. He was in the habit of taking perfumed baths, and his friends remember the enormous gold dressing case, which it required two men to carry, and which used to be the companion of all his excursions.

As for the life which d'Orsay led, it was the typical life of the man of fashion of the day — but with a difference. There was a side to his nature unusual in a man about town — the side shown in his visits to Benjamin Haydon and the Carlyles, the side which won him inclusion in Maclise's caricature of the "Fraserians." His interest in things of the mind — in decoration, in painting, and in the theatre — was shared by few of his regular companions nor, one may be sure, did he thrust it upon them. Nevertheless, this duality of temperament existed, and gave him the distinction which, even in self-indulgence, he never lost. It did not, however, check his enjoyment of the conventional delights of fashionable idleness, as the thirties knew it. This idleness was a round of strenuous and spendthrift trifling. In town it involved visits to tailors, hatters and boot-makers; attendance at Tattersall's; race-going; rides in the Park; excursions on the box of a private hansom or with a four-in-hand; whitebait dinners at Greenwich or Blackwall; visits to opera or theatre; nightly (often all-night) sessions at the gaming table. In the country it meant hunting, shooting and the eternal gambling. In London there were interludes for social occasions with feminine respectables; in the country the ladies were more at hand and escape was more difficult.

D'Orsay, essentially an urban type, shone more brilliantly in town than in the provinces. Also his complete freedom from domestic responsibility, which might elsewhere have provoked comment, was an asset in London; for the London life of a gentleman of leisure was in those days the gayer if it were free from the embarrassment of women-folk. Indeed — except for occasional frolics with members of the ballet and other lights of love, a man had — and desired — little enough of feminine society. In consequence, his club was his favourite resort. In the club he spent his days from afternoon till the dawn following; at the club, save when a formal dinner party took him elsewhere, he dined; to the club, after the opera or a boxing match or a cock fight or a spell of social duty at Almack's, he returned to sup; from the club, and in company with a party of friends, he made his outings to Richmond or Greenwich or Blackwall, to Epsom or Newmarket.

D'Orsay's club was Crockford's, established in St. James's Street in a fine house built in 1827, and during the thirties at the height of its fashionable notoriety. The aristocracy of club-men naturally denied to Crockford's the status of a club at all.

They declared it (and rightly) a gambling hell, and not all the gilding and luxury of its magnificent saloons could make it other. Nevertheless it was the haunt par excellence of masculine fashion. It had *ton;* its cellar was above reproach; its cuisine, presided over by Ude, was incomparable, and its famous suppers — served from midnight until five o'clock in the morning — were unique. For these suppers no one was ever asked to pay, because all who partook of them were expected to gamble at the tables, and unfailingly did.

The gaming room was, of course, the nerve centre of Crockford's and the prime justification of the club's existence. Likely enough it ruined one visitor for every thousand pounds it earned, for its proprietor. When "Crocky" died in 1844, it was reckoned that he had made £1,200,000 out of the reckless folly of his age. Whether indeed twelve hundred bankrupt fools were milestones on this road to fortune has never been computed; but whatever their number d'Orsay was one of them. He had other extravagances no less crazy than a taste for hazard bank; but none so fantastic or so desperately costly. In Crockford's temple of prodigality, he rapidly became a leading figure. Even at a time when readiness to play high, combined with complete impassivity in the face of fortune, was considered the hall-mark of a gentleman, he was notable for the recklessness of his gambling and the serenity of his demeanour. He sometimes played at the Cocoa Tree or at the Kildare in Bennett Street (once winning at the former thirty-five thousand pounds in two nights off a luckless challenger) but it was at Crockford's that he was regularly seen. Lord William Pitt Lennox records that his mere arrival at the table sent the stakes rocketing. Bernal Osborne wrote in "The Chaunt of Achilles":

> O'er play, o'er dress, extends his wide domain
> And Crockford trembles when he calls a main.

A contemporary print of the club gaming-room actually showed him as central figure, calling this maximum stake.

One story (vouched for by Molloy [2]) helps to an appreciation of the mixture of impudence and impulsive generosity which must have been very characteristic of him. He found one of his acquaintances in despair at having to sell his commission in order to pay his debts. There was no alternative. Either he must turn his officer-status into cash or be forever dishonoured. D'Orsay immediately asked for a loan of ten pounds, explaining blandly that if money were to be raised on the commission and immediately distributed, he would like his share. Almost despite himself, the other complied.

Next morning d'Orsay called at his friend's lodgings and pulled notes and gold from all his pockets to the total of seven hundred and fifty pounds. "*Voilà,*" he said. "Here is your money. I won it with your ten pounds at Crockford's last night. It is yours by right. For you know, if I had lost, you would never have seen your ten pounds again."

In sport d'Orsay became, as his social renown increased, less prominent as a practitioner than as a patron, an organiser and, of course, a maker of bets. He hunted fairly regularly, and we hear of him at Melton on more than one occasion, but there only by invitation. He was an actual member of the Royal Hunt (the pack was known as "His Majesty's Staghounds"), of which his friend Lord Chesterfield was master. They hunted round London and often in the Vale of Aylesbury. The sporting folk of the district came to call d'Orsay the "King of the French", and stories of his lavish generosity became part of local legend. He was placed in a prominent position in the, at one time, famous picture of a meet of the Royal Staghounds on Ascot Heath, painted by Francis Grant.[3] This picture was afterward engraved and sold largely in the late thirties

[2] *Cf.* Appendix VI.

[3] Afterward Sir Francis Grant, P.R.A. He also painted an impressive equestrian portrait of d'Orsay, which is well reproduced in Teignmouth Shore's book (see Appendix VI), and is used to-day as a sort of trade-mark by the makers of the "Parfums d'Orsay."

at three guineas a copy. "One of the first works of the kind extant," declared "Nimrod" in the *New Sporting Magazine* in June, 1838.[4] "A sportsman's picture every inch of it, and he must indeed want taste who does not add it to his choicest collection."

The article proceeded to make the following references to d'Orsay, which prove that his horsemanship was always of the dashing, rather than of the technically perfect, order:

> D'Orsay, the "observed of all observers", appears in the picture in all the glory of French-polish; satin neckcloth; the inside of his coat lined with white kerseymere; leathers and boots to perfection.
>
> I never saw the Count d'Orsay in the field, but I have heard of his doings there, and especially on a horse called Shamrock, which he purchased at the stiff price of £400 from Mr. Anderson. On him, I am told, he would ride a burst in right good form; and when missing, it was not to be attributed to want of pluck. In fact, he is said to have looked upon hunting — I speak now in the past tense, having reason to believe, he has nearly given it up [March, 1838] — chiefly as an arena in which adventures were to be sought, inasmuch as he would go out of his way to charge a large fence or a wide brook, after the manner of Don Quixote with the windmill, and not unfrequently meeting with a similarly disastrous fate.
>
> Characteristic of the tact and generosity of the Count, I must be allowed to mention one circumstance. On the day of the great steeple chase in the Alyesbury country, a deer was to be turned out, but the number of horsemen present — about two thousand — was so great that the farmers demurred. As they were on their road home despairing of further sport, a liberal occupier of land rode up to Lord Errol, and said, if his lordship would order the deer to be sent to his house it should be turned out on his farm; and it was done accordingly. The next day the Count wrote to his wine merchant to send the said farmer four dozen of his best port wine, with his compliments.

One wonders whether the words "tact and generosity" are used ironically. Dozens of port are easier to give away than to pay for; and the *New Sporting Magazine*, at the time Nimrod's article appeared, had evidently no illusion as to d'Orsay's

[4] Vol. XIV, p. 174, *et seq.*

solvency. Two months later (in the number for August, 1838) was printed a satirical poem describing the Devil on a visit to London. One verse runs:

From d'O——y, Nick stole his leathers and boots,
  And rode to the Woolwich review;
He found in his pockets, a *draft on Coutts,*
  Thought the devil, *can this be true?*

On the race course d'Orsay was more in his element than on the hunting field. There he had scope for arbitrating between good and bad manners; for fixing the rules of the sport, the programme and the personnel; above all for dressing the part of the race-going exquisite. He became a member of the Coventry Club, where the rules of racing and boxing were virtually determined in unofficial committee by the leading patrons of race course and ring. He and Chesterfield were joint stewards of the grand opening meeting at the Hippodrome, Notting Hill, that short-lived and almost forgotten race course which was laid out on the site now occupied by St. John's Church, Ladbroke Grove, and was expected to rival Auteuil as a place of sporting pilgrimage for metropolitan fashion. This opening meeting took place on June 3, 1837, and d'Orsay reappeared on handbills as steward on a number of later occasions. Significantly enough, however, in 1841 his name suddenly vanished and never reappeared. That is evidence, if more be needed, for the date and abruptness of his compulsory withdrawal from daylight society.

Of the d'Orsay of legend — the public d'Orsay who rode the streets of London, dazzled provincials in the Park, served as part model for Ainsworth's "Crichton" and was at once the scandal and the admiration of the clubs — three elements still require examination. This given, we can follow him into retirement behind the ramparts of Gore House, and from the testimony of a few intimate friends, as well as from private letters of his own, gather what clues we can to the last phase of the mysterious reality which lay behind his mask of impudence and elegance and charm.

First, his reputation for wit. M. Flers, who has not a good word to say for him, denies that he had any humour and avers that even his talent for smart sayings was that of a mere punster. Without going to the other extreme and endorsing the claim of numerous contemporary apologists that d'Orsay was a wit of the calibre of Luttrell or Sydney Smith, it is permissible to suspect M. Flers of over-disparagement. Many of the jokes preserved by tradition are admittedly mere *jeux de mots,* and some of them of an elementary kind. But at their best they have the quality of readiness, and the fact that Theodore Hook "loathed" d'Orsay is in itself a tribute to his verbal felicity. Also it must not be forgotten that the manner of his jokes' utterance was probably half their charm. D'Orsay had a pleasant voice and a twinkling eye; he spoke a mixture of French and English, and throughout his life talked the latter with a marked accent, which he was suspected (probably rightly) of having carefully cultivated.

One evening in Crockford's, Lord Allen, who was apt to be quarrelsome, was chaffing d'Orsay rather offensively. The Count's temper was wearing thin, when a fellow member, John Bush, entered the room and saluted him. Instantly d'Orsay flashed his famous smile: "*Voilà,*" he cried, "*la différence entre une bonne bouche et une mauvaise haleine!*"

Other sallies of his were quaint conceits rather than puns, but evidence all the same of a ready and resourceful wit. When Henry Bulwer was sent on a diplomatic mission to Constantinople d'Orsay said: "*Quelle bêtise,* to send a little grey man like zat among ze big Turks wiz zeir bears and zeir shawls! Zey might as well have sent one whitebait down ze Dardanelles to give ze Turks an idea of English fish." His drawing of Chesterfield was criticised by some one, on the ground that the subject's ear was grossly out of proportion. "Pardon," replied d'Orsay, "it is ze picture of ze 'e-ear."

Once at Gore House, he interviewed a member of the publishing firm of Saunders and Otley, taking the man very severely to task for some incident in connection with Lady Blessington's books. The publisher was offended, drew himself up and declared he would rather lose Lady Blessington's patronage than submit to such abuse.

"My dear Sir!" cried d'Orsay warmly, who knew too well the value of the firm's good will, "nozzing personal is meant, I assure you. If you are Saunders, zen damn Otley; if by chance you are Otley, zen damn Saunders."

Of the anecdotes, which he is said to have related endlessly and well, one sent by him at Fonblanque's request for use in the *Examiner* has a demure humor which is very engaging.

"*Mehemet Ali demanda à un Français de lui expliquer ce que c'était qu'une république. 'Si l'Egypte était une république,' lui dit-il, 'vous seriez le peuple et le peuple serait le Pacha.' Mehemet lui répondit qu'il ne se trouvait aucun goût, aucune sympathie, pour une république.*"

Something of this quality of quaint absurdity is in many of his letters. Amusing descriptions of their life in Naples, written to young Mathews after he had returned to England, are printed in the biography of Mathews, and the same good-tempered raillery of himself and others persists in d'Orsay's correspondence of a much later date. Henry Bulwer notes in his diary that d'Orsay invited him to a Friday dinner with Louis Blanc: "*Venez,*" the Count wrote, "*vous aurez le plus petit homme et le plus grand poisson que vous avez jamais vu.*" Louis Blanc was only four feet six inches in height.

On another occasion he begged Henry Bulwer to intervene with Mrs. Fonblanque: "*Je vous accable de commissions. Faites moi le plaisir de prier la Fonblanque de ne pas baptiser son gilet rouge de dessous 'gilet à la d'Orsay.' Je viens de recevoir la nouvelle qu'elle me calomnioit de la sorte. Si je suis innocent, c'est certainement d'avoir porté un tel oriflamme.*"

To Mrs. Maberly, silver-fork novelist and wife of the post-office official with whom Trollope came into youthful conflict, he wrote a letter regretting that he could not find pupils for one of the lady's protégées who wished to teach German. "I have more applications from teachers than pupils," he said. "It looks as though all these people have come to England in the expectation that Prince Albert will change the language of the country."

It is obvious that in the classical sense d'Orsay was no wit. But to deny him the infectious humour of high spirits, an ingenious turn of phrase, and a mind quick to note absurdity and enjoy it, is impossible.

The second element of the d'Orsay legend — his outstanding achievements in dress and personal luxury — is nowhere disputed. This delight in clothes was, of course, on one side an expression of the personal vanity which the man so abundantly possessed; on another it was a naïve delight in rather florid beauty. D'Orsay's taste was ornate in everything and to everything he applied his taste. He deliberately created in Seamore Place and in Gore House glowing interiors for the better display of hostess, host and other less animate *objets d'art.* He delighted to have a hand in designing scenery for plays and spectacles, devising settings for Bulwer's "Money" which enchanted theatre-goers of 1840. And in just the same way he rejoiced to be able to use his own handsome person as a basis for experiments in ostentatious dress. Numerous comments on his clothes, his horses, his harness, his carriages and his other accoutrements occur in memoirs of the time, but they are for the most part too trivial to merit quotation. Of the more important extracts, four, and from very different sources, will suffice.

D'Orsay's artistic taste was undeniable [says Gronow]. It might have been objected that this taste was somewhat too gaudy; but the brilliant tints with which he liked to surround himself suited his style of beauty, his dress, and manner. When I used to see him driving in his tilbury I fancied that he looked like some gorgeous dragon-fly skimming through the air; and though all was dazzling and showy, yet there was a kind of harmony which precluded any idea or accusation of bad taste.

Next comes Edmund Yates, who provides a recollection of Hyde Park from the days of his youth:

There in a hooded cabriolet, with an enormous champing horse and the trimmest of tiny grooms — tigers as they were called — half standing or the footboard behind, half swinging in the air clinging on to the straps, would be Count d'Orsay, the greatest "swell" of the day. He always drove in faultless white kid gloves, with his shirt wrist bands turned back over his coat-cuffs.

The third contribution is from Benjamin Haydon, and is not a reminiscence but a vivid entry in his diary. In July, 1839, he was busy on his equestrian portrait of the Duke of Wellington. On the 10th:

D'Orsay called and pointed out several things to correct in the horse. I did them, and he took my brush in his dandy gloves and lowered the hindquarters by bringing over a bit of the sky. Such a dress! White great coat, blue satin cravat, hair oiled and curling, hat of the primest curve and purest water, gloves scented with eau de Cologne or eau de jasmin, primrose in tint, skin in tightness. In this prime of dandyism he took up a nasty, oily, dirty hog-tool and immortalised Copenhagen [the Duke's horse] by touching the sky.

I thought, after he had gone, this won't do — a Frenchman touch Copenhagen. So out I rubbed all he had touched and modified his hints myself.

Finally, and a little unexpectedly, the correspondence of Mr. and Mrs. Thomas Carlyle testifies that not only could d'Orsay carry off the extravagances of costume by exactly suiting them to his own physique and carriage, but he did not make the mistake of dressing out of his age. In March, 1839, d'Orsay came to Cheyne Row "in an equipage [as Mrs. Carlyle noted] all resplendent in sky blue and silver."

This Phœbus Apollo of dandyism, [wrote Carlyle two or three weeks later to his brother] escorted by poor little Chorley, came whirling hither in a chariot that struck all Chelsea into mute amazement with splendour. Chorley's under-jaw went like the hopper or under-riddle of a pair of fanners, such was his terror on bringing such a splendour into actual contact with such grimness. Nevertheless, we did amazingly well, the Count and I. He is a tall fellow of six foot three, built like a tower, with floods of dark auburn hair, with a beauty, with an adornment unsurpassable on this planet; withal a rather substantial fellow at bottom, by no means without insight, without fun, and a sort of sarcasm rather striking out of such a porcelain figure. He said, looking at Shelley's bust, in his French accent: "Ah, it is one of zose faces who weesh to swallow zeir chin."

Mrs. Carlyle, in a letter to her cousin, was rather more explicit in the matter of costume:

"Sky-blue satin cravat, yards of gold chain, white French gloves, light drab great-coat lined with velvet of the same colour, invisible inexpressibles, skin-coloured, and fitting like a glove etc. etc." She enjoyed the contrast of "Carlyle in his grey plaid suit and his tub chair, looking blandly at the Prince of Dandies; and the Prince of Dandies on an opposite chair, "all resplendent as a diamond beetle, looking blandly at him." Six years later, in April, 1845, d'Orsay paid the Carlyles another visit; and Mrs. Carlyle's description of the occasion in her notebook is perhaps the most comprehensive and convincing account extant of how he looked and the manner of man he seemed.

Today, oddly enough, while I was engaged in re-reading Carlyle's "Philosophy of Clothes", Count d'Orsay walked in. I had not seen him for four or five years. Last time he was as gay in his colours as a humming bird. Today in compliment to his five more years, he was all in black and brown — a black satin cravat, a brown velvet waistcoat, a brown coat, some shades darker than the waistcoat, lined with velvet of its own shade, and almost black trousers, one breast-pin, a large pear-shaped pearl set into a little cup of diamonds, and only one fold of gold chain round his neck, tucked together right on the centre of his spacious breast with one magnificent turquoise.

Well! that man understood his trade; if it be but that of dandy, nobody can deny that he is a perfect master of it, that he dresses himself with consummate skill! A bungler would have made no allowance for five more years at his time of life; but he had the fine sense to perceive how much better his dress of today sets off his slightly enlarged figure and slightly worn complexion, than the humming bird colours of five years back would have done.

Poor d'Orsay! He was born to have been something better than the king of dandies. He did not say nearly so many clever things this time as on the last occasion. His wit, I suppose, is of the sort that belongs more to animal spirits than to real genius, and his animal spirits seem to have fallen many degrees. The only thing that fell from him today worth remembering was his account of a mask he had seen of Charles Fox "all punched and flattened as if he had slept in a book."

Lord Jeffrey came, unexpected, while the Count was here. What a difference! The prince of critics and the prince of dandies. How washed out the beautiful dandiacal face looked beside that little clever old man's. The large blue dandiacal eyes, you would have said, had never contemplated anything more interesting than the reflection of the handsome personage they pertained to in a looking glass; while the dark penetrating ones of the other had been taking note of most things in God's universe.

The influence of d'Orsay's dandyism on his young admirers was unbounded. Sometimes he prescribed for them. He decided for example that Chesterfield ought to dress in blue; and the docile Earl found himself ordering blue ties, blue coats, blue waistcoats, and forbidden to wear anything else. Others, in default of instructions, copied the oracle's every innovation. But as often as not they lacked his instinctive knowledge of the border line between challenging eccentricity and vulgar ostentation; and few of them possessed even a part of his natural advantages. Wherefore, the inevitable consequence of their imitative exuberance was to bring the whole mode for highly coloured masculine fashions into disrepute, so that when the leader vanished a reaction set in, and men have tended to sombre colours ever since.

It is a part of the d'Orsay legend that he contrived to secure personal luxury without paying for it, by persuading tradespeople that his very adoption of their goods was an advertisement worth more than the goods themselves. Undoubtedly this was his method for so long as it could be made to work. For example, he wrote as follows to Feist, a banker at Frankfurt:

> Would you please send me a dozen pairs of gloves of a dead leaf colour which can be bought from the Tyrolean glove sellers? Have them so that they will fit your hand (this is a compliment) and I will send you the cost (this is a lie).

Feist countered the request by engaging d'Orsay to boom a Rhine wine in London, in the sale of which the banker was interested, and d'Orsay replied:

> I have got your famous wine and have given some to Prince Napoleon, to Soliman Pacha and to Ouvrard, the Napoleon of financiers. All these people and others have found it perfect. Here are two letters to Eugene Sue and the Comte de la Tour-du-Pin at Paris, who will recommend your wine to real connoisseurs.

It may even be true that, at the height of his fame, he only gave patronage to tailors who slipped bank notes into the pockets of new clothes when they were delivered. It is said that once, when a garment was sent home without this endowment, d'Orsay returned it, with the message that the lining of the pockets was unsatisfactory. But when John Mills, in his satirical novel "D'Horsay or the Follies of the Day", implies that the keeper of a gambling hell would offer to forgive the Count a debt of five thousand pounds if his "flashy cab" were left at the curb outside the gaming-house door for two hours one Saturday night, we begin to suspect the embellishment of malice. The d'Orsay legend was quickly susceptible to the exaggeration of word-of-mouth report, even of developments into the realm of the impossible, as the following examples show.

Riding out one day, the Count stopped a boy who was passing and asked for a light for his cigar. The lad was well-mannered and attractive, and d'Orsay, with his ready interest in any one and every one, asked him whence he came and what he hoped to become. The boy said he was from Wales and would like to return there to his own people, but that he had no money and must find work in London. "Come to Hyde Park to-morrow when the promenade is full," said d'Orsay. "Bring a tray of matches, and when you see me in a crowd of men, come up and offer me a box." The lad did as he was bid, and at a suitable moment began to cry his wares. D'Orsay turned and saw him. "At last!" he cried. "Quick, give me a box!" and threw the boy a guinea. Then, to his circle of admiring friends: "You know, I came across this boy the ozzer day and can now only taste a ceegarr lit with the kind of matches he sells. Zey are ze only possible matches, and I do not know any one else who sells zem." Instantly the whole crowd of disciples were throwing guineas to the match-seller, taking their boxes and ordering more.

This story, whether true or not, developed strangely with time. A French paper, *Le Globe,* published an article during 1843, in the course of which it stated that Count d'Orsay, the famous English dandy, regularly every day gave a beggar at the corner of Regent Street a guinea for lighting his cigar!

But the limits of absurdity to which malevolence could go, and the extent to which ill-disposed persons were willing to believe evil of a man they never saw, are best illustrated by the solemn assertion that, among other deeds of heartless money-grubbing, d'Orsay gambled away his wife Harriet to her second husband, the Honourable Spencer Cowper. Not only is it doubtful whether d'Orsay ever set eyes on Harriet after 1838, but it is certain that she was not with Spencer Cowper until she married him late in 1852, and by that time d'Orsay was dead.

And finally, in our survey of the d'Orsay tradition, must come his reputation for promiscuous gallantry, a subject of some importance in view of the theory of his sexlessness, on which the present attempt to interpret his baffling personality has been partly based. The material on which this particular reputation is founded impresses itself as at once flimsy and profuse. Its contemporary sources are strangely few, being limited to Mills' novel "D'Horsay" and to scandal sheets of the type of Renton Nicholson's weekly paper the *Town*. The former of these is lavish of information both general and particular. The latter, which made a speciality of the intrigues of men of fashion (even down to the addresses and competence of their lady friends), are queerly mechanical in their numerous references to d'Orsay. They resemble Mills in picturing Lady Blessington as an ageing and neglected mistress, and include the Count, apparently automatically, among the clients of the various courtesans whose activities they chronicle.

Of subsequent commentators on d'Orsay's life, M. Flers is alone in making deliberate play with his subject's amourettes. He implies that d'Orsay was the favoured lover of every prima ballerina and light comedy actress who won the heart of London in the thirties — of Taglioni, Grisi, Fanny Ellesler, Fanny Cerrito, Albino; he speaks airily of four native danseuses imported by the Count from Paris and installed in London. But as he gives no specific references to the source of these statements, and as two at least of the theatrical ladies are also identifications by Joseph Grego of characters in John Mills' novel, one is inclined to suspect that d'Orsay's most destructive biographer has followed his inclinations rather than the evidence.

There is no alternative but to turn back to our two contemporary authorities, and decide the extent to which we may accept the d'Orsay of Mills' novel and that of the underworld press as equivalents of the original.

"D'Horsay or the Follies of the Day" appeared in 1844 as by "A Man of Fashion", and was republished in 1902, with an introduction and a "Key to the characters" by Joseph Grego. The editor of this reissue states that the book was instantly suppressed, and one is less surprised that it should have been withdrawn than that in 1844 it should ever have been published. Many of the disguises are impudently thin. We meet the Earl of Chesterlane, the Marquis of Riverford, Lords Nedstone, Muffield, Huntingcastle and Bitchfield, the Earl of Raspberry Hill, Lord

George Bedtick — and other characters no further removed from their originals. Lady Blessington appears as "Lady Rivington" and is presented rather sympathetically as a cast-off mistress of D'Horsay, sitting at home and weeping while he paints the town red. The bulk of the novel describes in detail the riotous living of the hero and his buckish friends; and although d'Orsay himself may have been regarded by 1844 as so déclassé as to be fair game for satirists, it is astonishing that a book should have been put on public sale describing Chesterfield as lover and financier of Fanny Ellesler; picturing Waterford and Waldegrave in a brothel in St. Giles; representing the well-known auctioneer George Robins as surreptitiously introducing extraneous and worthless material into the great sale of Horace Walpole's collection at Strawberry Hill; and depicting several easily recognisable persons as the victims of horse-copers and fraudulent billiard saloons.

Yet the book was published; and Mills (better known as the author of "The Old English Gentleman" and "The Life of a Foxhound" than as the author of "D'Horsay") was certainly a member of the very world whose antics he therein describes. Undoubtedly, therefore, his story was founded on fact, and we may assume it to have reflected current gossip if nothing more substantial.

The *Town* and its kind are less reputable witnesses. They lived by muckraking and, inasmuch as they raked with skill and humour, lived successfully. But Nicholson and his rival editors were always concerned to get for their papers the maximum of effect with the minimum of risk, and therefore concentrated for their most suggestive libels on those least likely to defend themselves. One such was certainly d'Orsay, who even as early as 1837 (in which year the *Town* started publishing) was sufficiently insecure financially and socially to be very careful in seeking legal redress for injuries to himself. For this reason his persistent appearance in the lists of *coureurs de filles* cannot be taken very seriously. He was a notorious gambler and man about town; the irregularity of his relationship with Lady Blessington was taken for granted; he was known to owe money right and left. In other words, he was fair game; and if an extra dissipation were laid to his account, no one would be any the worse.

As with so many other elements in this obscure story, so with this problem of d'Orsay's promiscuity. It is only possible to argue its likelihood or otherwise in the light of what we know of his general character. Let us even leave out of account altogether the theory of his impotence; it is (and must remain) a theory, and has no sanction save that of a probability more comprehensive than any alternative. Let us assume him to have been a normal man, with a normal man's capacity for elegant incontinence. Was he the sort of person to lavish money on fashionable demi-mondaines? Was his vanity of the kind to find satisfaction in winning the favours of the actress of the day?

Unless he is to be denied every essential quality of dandyism, both these questions must be answered in the negative. To waste money on ladies of the town is of all expenditures the least spectacular, and is unproductive of anything save a pleasure both transient and unostentatious. To pay court to stage stars in their dressing rooms, to bear with their caprices, to flatter their conceit, involves self-humiliation of a kind so repellent to a dandy's egoism as to be intolerable. Further, d'Orsay's personal vanity was in large degree a vanity of health, of brilliance of eye and complexion. Would he have risked sapping his energies and losing the bloom of his beauty for the sake of a trivial traffic in sex? Finally, if he were the debauchee Mills and M. Flers imply, and if, as the same authorities are careful to explain, Lady Blessington were aware of his many gallantries, is it conceivable that she should still have written to her friends about him as she did throughout the forties; and that Forster and Fonblanque and Macready and Dickens and Tennyson and Landor and Bulwer-Lytton (all of whom, whatsoever the occasional failings of some of them, were persons anxious to maintain in public an attitude of disapproval toward sexual irregularities) should have gloried in his friendship and, after his death, have paid him the tributes which they so generously expressed?

On the ground, therefore, that a wenching d'Orsay does not, any more than a drunken one, make sense, it is suggested that these lurid stories of amorous adventure are part imagination, part deliberate misunderstanding of appearances. For this much is possible — is indeed probable — that d'Orsay countenanced and even encouraged the excesses of his friends. He would not wish, by untimely disapprobation or by admitting his own inability to share their tastes, to weaken his hold on their loyalty. So he would go with Chesterfield to see the Ellesler in her dressing room, would accompany Duncombe or Lichfield to the discreet dwellings of the demi-monde. It would not have been difficult at the right time to slip away, untouched in pocket and with his abnormality unbetrayed.

CHAPTER V

D'ORSAY: THE "SHY COCK"

1

THE *Town* on November 9, 1839, published a paragraph to the effect that Count d'Orsay had let his house and "gone to live with his mother, the Countess of Blessington, next door", elaborating the same theme in more than one of its December issues for the same year. The paper's main purpose in each case was, of course, to reiterate its favourite gibe, and to present Lady Blessington as the ageing mistress of an unfaithful libertine; but the scurrilities have, quite unintentionally, this much of historical importance — that they fix the date of d'Orsay's relinquishment of his own little house two years earlier than has hitherto been stated. It has been assumed that his change of residence took place in 1841, that it was the result of a sudden threat of arrest, and that from the moment of his migration to Gore House, he became a daytime prisoner, and so remained. But if in fact he moved house in 1839, some re-interpretation of motive and event becomes necessary, because there is evidence that until 1841 his freedom was unimpaired.

We know from Lady Blessington's correspondence that he was sufficiently a free agent to be at Doncaster in September, 1840; and from the programmes of race meetings, that up to 1841 he appeared as steward at the Notting Hill Hippodrome. What then provoked him to move house in 1839 and what happened two years later to turn the gardens of Gore House into a prison?

The answer to the first question is probably twofold. His formal separation from Harriet in 1838 would have removed any scruples Lady Blessington may have had as to his openly sharing her home. In addition, the change of residence would (as he himself indicates in a letter to Henry Bulwer, quoted below) be a simple economy.

The answer to the second question is more complicated. That a single arrest for debt could permanently have transformed d'Orsay the man-about-town into d'Orsay the "shy cock" is difficult to believe. Something more inescapable, something from which recovery was obviously impossible, must surely have occurred to bring about so lasting an alteration in his way of life. I suggest that only in the outcome of the litigation over the Blessington estates can that something be found. It therefore becomes necessary to reconstruct so far as possible the history of the liquidation of Lord Blessington's disastrous will.

The details of the history are obscure and confusing. Madden had all the documents and summarised them in his book. But his habitual inaccuracy and lack of arrangement make their later interpretation hazardous, so that only on very general lines can the sequence of affairs be stated.

Between Lord Blessington's accession in 1798 and his death in 1829, the estimated income from his vast estates had fallen, as a result of capital expenditure, from about thirty thousand pounds per annum to about twenty-two thousand pounds. On the most conservative basis, this means that he had reduced the capital value of his property by twenty-five thousand pounds. After his death, it was found that he had raised mortgages to the amount of forty-eight thousand pounds and incurred various debts to the amount of a further forty thousand pounds. When to these sums were added the d'Orsays' marriage settlement of forty thousand pounds and other legacies to the amount of twenty-three thousand pounds, the trustees found themselves in the necessity of raising over one hundred and fifty thousand pounds.

They had not yet tackled this considerable task, when

in 1831 Charles Gardiner filed his suit against his father's widow and son-in-law. The case was now thrown into Chancery, and after an interval of (apparently) three years, the Court of Chancery declared the will valid, so that on this head the Gardiners' suit was rejected. But in view of the shrinkage of assets and the doubtful method of raising the huge sum of money required, the Court determined to keep the administration of the estate in their hands; Luke Norman should continue to act as sole agent, but under receivers appointed by the Court.

Almost simultaneously with the filing of her brother's suit, Lady Harriet d'Orsay had left her husband. In consequence, to the conflict of interest between Charles Gardiner and Blessington-d'Orsay was added a further conflict between Harriet d'Orsay and her husband and, by inference, yet a third one between her and her brother. Legal correspondence published in the "Blessington Papers"[1] shows that letters passed in 1832 between a business friend of Lady Harriet's, d'Orsay's solicitor and Luke Norman as to the disposal of the income of the forty thousand pound marriage settlement and with a view to arranging a final division of proceeds, if and when the surplus value of the whole estate had been determined. These negotiations came to nothing, because the Court of Chancery held that the claims of Lady Harriet, d'Orsay and Charles Gardiner to receive support were all worthy of consideration, and that, pending a final settlement, the Court could not do more than allow to each claimant a modest annual income. It seems that in July, 1834, the Court ordered the payment of about four hundred and fifty pounds per annum to Lady Harriet and about five hundred pounds per annum to d'Orsay. What, if anything, they allowed to Charles Gardiner is not known; but according to a letter of d'Orsay's solicitor written in 1832, he (Charles Gardiner) was at that date receiving one thousand pounds per annum, and this sum, though it seems disproportionately large, may have been continued.

[1] Pp. 44–47.

In February, 1838, Lady Harriet and d'Orsay were formally separated by deed; and at the same time the former's advisers brought to a head a proposal by which she should buy out both the other claimants to her father's residue. Once again the settlement, so far as Charles Gardiner was concerned, is not known; but the price of d'Orsay's interest in the Blessington estate was finally agreed upon. A period over which this price should be paid by instalments was also fixed, because it was impossible to close the negotiation by a cash payment, money for this and other purposes being obtainable only by a gradual sale of the various properties. The actual sum decided as payable to d'Orsay is given quite differently by Madden in two different chapters of his book; but the most convincing estimate is that, between 1838 and the final sale of the Blessington lands in 1851, d'Orsay (or rather his creditors) received something over one hundred thousand pounds, which sum included annuities given by him to various persons during the previous twenty years and redeemable for about twenty-five thousand pounds.

The negotiations over this settlement between the Count and Lady Harriet must have lasted for about two years from the time of their formal separation in 1838. In December, 1841, Lady Blessington wrote to Henry Bulwer in Paris: "Alfred's embarrassments have been greatly exaggerated, and when the sale of the northern estate in Ireland is effected — which must be within a year, as Lady H. and her brother are now in Ireland for the purpose of urging it forward — he will be relieved from all his difficulties." But she was over-optimistic. The sale of the Blessington estates did not begin until 1846 or 1847, and was not concluded until 1851. Also the true extent of d'Orsay's debts was probably unknown to her. What can, however, be fairly certainly assumed is that *during 1841 the Count was made finally aware of the extent of his expectations from his father-in-law's estate.*

For nearly ten years he had been living at a rate of expenditure which can only be estimated as fabulous. During the first four or five of these years (roughly from 1830 to 1834) he had received the income from his marriage settlement of forty thousand pounds — at four per cent sixteen hundred pounds, at six per cent twenty-four hundred pounds per annum. For the remaining years (roughly from 1835 to 1840) he had enjoyed an additional five hundred pounds per annum. How meaningless this income was in relation to his actual expenditure is shown by his having, as early as 1832, found it necessary to raise money recklessly on the security of the forty thousand pounds given him by Lord Blessington on his marriage.[2] Between 1832 and the date of his separation in 1838, as he himself admitted to Henry Bulwer,[3] he existed by gambling and by continuing to raise money on his expectations. It is obvious that by 1838 his debts to tradespeople and to money lenders must have amounted to a very large figure.

And then suddenly he is presented with Lady Harriet's proposal, as with an ultimatum. He tries to show fight, but is at length convinced by his own lawyers that even prolonged litigation (which he could not afford) would not secure him better terms. If he refuses this offer, he may even get nothing. So some time in 1840 or 1841 he resigns himself to the inevitable, accepts, and for the first time becomes familiar with absolute finality in his future expectations.

Unluckily for him, others share that familiarity. Formal separations cannot be kept private. His creditors suspect a financial settlement behind the matrimonial one. Either they find out its terms, or are sufficiently sure one has been made to decide that their claims shall ruthlessly be pressed. Like a hunt in full cry, they are after him. He is not in danger of one arrest but of fifty; also he now knows that he can never buy his freedom, because the limit of his resources has been fixed, and beyond that limit there is no more money to come, at any time or from

[2] "Blessington Papers", p. 45.
[3] *Cf.* letter, p. 286.

any source. So he goes to ground in Gore House; and the next eight years are spent by his pursuers in slowly but inexorably digging him out.

From this survey of d'Orsay's financial adventures emerge not only the reason why in 1841 he decided on voluntary incarceration in the gardens of Gore House, but also two other facts which, to judge by what has been written of the matter since, have never been properly realised. In the first place, during the ten years following the Earl's death, it was not Lady Blessington but d'Orsay who held the key to the financial situation. In the second place, Lady Blessington's share of her husband's money, in comparison with that enjoyed by d'Orsay, had never been other than negligible.

It has been generally assumed that she had captured a large fortune at Blessington's death; had squandered it on herself and on a penniless d'Orsay, and had then been forced to work in order to keep her household going. In actual fact, the case was very different. While her husband was alive, Lady Blessington had certainly spent freely and often foolishly; but she was encouraged to do so by him, and naturally concluded from his own lavishness that there was money and to spare. From the moment of her widowing, however, she trained herself to be a careful and efficient manager; and it is a not unreasonable supposition that her determination to earn money by writing followed promptly on the breakdown of the d'Orsay marriage, because she did not wish to rely any more than was necessary on the financial help of two people who had basely treated her. Throughout the thirties, although she maintained an expensive establishment, she spent very little on herself and almost certainly (apart from the large debt to Howell and James for her installation in Gore House, which debt was finally to destroy her) paid her way with her annual two thousand pounds and her, at that time, considerable literary earnings. D'Orsay, meantime, was rioting about London, contributing little, if anything, to the upkeep of Lady Blessington's home, but living on his own prospects and exploiting his own credit to the utmost limit of its endurance.

As from the end of 1841, however, the whole position was altered. With d'Orsay hunted by creditors and at the end both of his resources and his expectations, she had suddenly to secure their joint livelihood. While her own income lasted and while novels and Annuals remained productive, she could struggle along. But the task of making ends meet was gradually growing beyond her strength, and when, late in 1847, both jointure and book-making virtually failed her, the end came with horrid speed.

2

The story of d'Orsay, the shy cock, is in some ways the story of a d'Orsay almost sympathetic. He was still quite unrepentant, quite unaware of being in any way to blame for his own misfortunes; but he became gradually conscious of losing ground, and as prestige fell, pride rose.

His life was of course transformed. For six days a week between sunrise and sundown he must remain at home. After dark he could visit his clubs; but he did so in a chastened spirit and to find an atmosphere less cordial than before. On Sundays he would go riding with his few all-weather friends who remained — with Chesterfield or Duncombe or Lichfield or Stanley or Grantley Berkeley. In August, 1843, we hear of him on a picnic with Lady Blessington and some friends. "We had a most agreeable party," she wrote to Henry Bulwer, "at a rural spot near Harrow. 'Boz', Quin and Mr. Forster with Alfred enjoyed it like schoolboys." One can see them, laughing and active and for a few hours young again, while Lady Blessington, stout and quiescent, sits in the carriage or on a rug under a tree with the baskets of food and drink, and beams contentedly. The rest of the time he stayed indoors or walked the garden, and tried to think of ways of making money, and kept his chin up, and smiled.

His first idea was to exploit his skill in portraiture more thoroughly than he had done hitherto. For several years lithographic reproductions of drawings of prominent folk had been published singly by Mitchell of Bond Street; but an arrangement was now made for the issue of a large collection in portfolio form. Some time in the early forties an assemblage of over one hundred and thirty lithographed portraits was put on the market.[4] These portraits show a sensitive skill in likeness but, being almost all in dead profile, are monotonous in the mass and would, if no work of a different kind existed, label their creator as a gifted but limited amateur.

The Count also began sculpture, doing portrait busts of those who preferred this style of presentation. His sitters would knock at the great gates of Gore House and produce their credentials. After careful inspection, they would be piloted past two huge mastiffs to the studio door on the garden side. The artist was taking no risks of uninvited callers. Of his statuettes, the most renowned is that of the Duke of Wellington on horseback, which is said to have delighted its sitter more than any other of his numerous portraits. The Count also did a painting of the Duke, and one of the few portraits ever made of J. M. W. Turner.

Persons hostile to d'Orsay declared that his artistic productions (and particularly his statues) were not wholly or even mainly his own work. Vizetelly, in his memoirs, declared that T. H. Nicholson, an artist on the *Illustrated Times*, had a large share in several of them. "Nicholson modelled well in plaster," he says, "and no secret was made of Count d'Orsay's obligations to him in regard to his famous equestrian statuettes and miniature busts, the faces of which were modelled by Behnes before he became celebrated as a sculptor. The statuette of the Duke of Wellington on horseback was undoubtedly Nicholson's, and

[4] This figure is taken from a professedly complete list in Madden's book, but may well be incorrect. I have never been able to discover a copy of the portfolio (or volume) in its original shape, so cannot check the details or the actual method of presentation.

that famous bust of the Iron Duke which was to make the fortune of the lucky manufacturer who reproduced it in porcelain is said to have been his and Behnes' joint work." Other "collaborators" were suspected during the last years of the Count's life in Paris.

The truth or otherwise of these stories, so far as statuary is concerned, is impossible to establish. In regard to painting and drawing, however, one is inclined to treat them with scepticism, partly because of the susceptibility to interpolation (usually ill-natured) of the d'Orsay legend, but mainly on the evidence of the water colour reproduced in this volume, depicting Louis Napoleon, as President, returning from the Chambre des Députés. Even in monochrome the qualities of this brilliant drawing are manifest — a drawing of which Guys need not have been ashamed. This particular work was, it is true, produced during his last years, when his mind was in some respects no longer normal. But a man capable, even in partial derangement, of such a water colour as this, must always have been potentially a real artist; and one is encouraged to suggest that, even if he did seek help with his statues and portrait busts, the help was more likely to have been concerned with the preparation of the material than with the delicate work which gave to the results their final character.

Vigorous artistic activity was, however, more or less supplementary to a bigger ambition which now seized upon d'Orsay. He conceived the idea of securing a diplomatic post from the Government of Louis Philippe. The aspiration, in view of his known intimacy and sympathy with Louis Napoleon, seems peculiarly unreal; and one cannot be surprised that it was not fulfilled. Nevertheless for a while (as letters from him and Lady Blessington to Henry Bulwer show) he envisaged it most seriously, and with the bland assumption that others must take him at his own valuation which had always been one of his most amazing characteristics.

Henry Bulwer was British Minister in Paris from 1840 to 1843, and, as an intimate friend of Gore House, was naturally looked to as an ally. D'Orsay opened the matter with a long letter written on May 2, 1841, which is of great importance, not only for its matter but for the impenetrable vanity of its manner. It is virtually the only document extant giving d'Orsay's own version of his financial history, and at the same time registering the completeness of his self-satisfaction.

The original letter is in French and largely unpunctuated; but I have translated the extracts given and tried to supply the required punctuation.

May 2, 1841

When I first arrived in this country I hoped that my money affairs would soon be on a proper basis. My lawyers encouraged me to think this; but hope was always deferred, and I went on month after month borrowing money and expecting any moment to be able to pay it back. I began to play. I won, and was able to buy renewals right and left. But I did not really notice how far I was getting involved; everything was so mixed up with the fluctuations of my luck at hazard, that I seemed one moment to be paying our common enemy Crockford, the next paying some Jew money lender. My credit was immense, and people were glad to lend to me. All this time the lawyers did nothing to push my business forward. Each of the parties interested in the Irish properties pulled a different way. Years went by and nothing happened. I lost my luck at the tables, and prudently drew in my horns. I sold my house and my hunters. I cut down expenses right and left.

This procedure, which should have been considered as greatly to my credit, alarmed my Jewish money lenders and they became very insistent that I should pay them the principal of their claims. This to some extent I did by borrowing from other Jews, and thought to have achieved a certain balance. But all the Shylocks now want their pound of flesh at any price, and I have begun seriously to consider my position. . . .

Now my prestige here is very high. I do good on all hands. For ten years I have helped distressed French people of every class in this country and am proverbially and in a moral sense the real ambassador of France. It would be a catastrophe to destroy so fine a position for the sake of a crowd of usurers (and money lenders are the only folk who bother me; my tradespeople adore me because I have made their fortunes). Some of my friends and my lawyers advise me to go abroad, saying that in six months the Jews will be only too eager to accept any terms I like to dictate. But I reply that if I do this I shall be regarded by society as a welsher and a levanter. Other friends urge me to stay here at home, never show myself and so avoid arrest for debt. But suppose I were caught and locked up in the King's Bench? I should like that even less! . . .

Others again recommend my getting a job in the French Embassy, where I should be safe and have time to arrange my affairs. To this I reply that I do not stand well with the present Government, being regarded as a Bonapartist if not a legitimist [5] . . . and that even if I could get an appointment, were I, with my social position, to accept a minor place in the Embassy it would be obvious to the whole of Europe why I had done so.

But suppose, in view of all that I have done for France in this country, the King were asked to give me some sort of an appointment attached to the Embassy; and suppose, through you and Brougham, I were to explain my position, [then] I could avoid all the unpleasantness implicit in the business. Please think this over carefully and let me have your candid opinion.

Now Henry Bulwer, for all the languor and over-subtlety of his manner, had an extremely level head and was free from all illusions, including those of sentiment. D'Orsay's request put him in a difficult position, but he knew his own place and duty too well to become seriously involved with so dubious a piece of place-hunting as that suggested. Probably he made a show of great activity, though aware all the time that there was no prospect of success. Certainly d'Orsay himself pulled every wire within his reach, using his sister-in-law Lady Tankerville, such of Lady Blessington's political friends as were properly influential, and even paying direct court to the French Ambassador, St. Aulaire.

[5] "Legitimists" were the supporters of the Bourbons proper. When Charles X was driven from France by the revolution of 1830 and in due course succeeded by the Duke of Orleans, who became "Louis Philippe, King of the French", the royalists *pur sang* remained, some in embittered opposition, others in exile. The government of Louis Philippe was therefore as suspicious of pre-1830 royalism as of Bonapartism, and inasmuch as d'Orsay and his family had been in favor with Charles X as well as by tradition supporters of Napoleon, they were doubly distasteful to the existing régime.

But the scheme was hopeless from the first, and late in 1841 the post required by d'Orsay was definitely refused. Henry Bulwer, poor man, was cast for the rôle of culprit, and got his scolding in the form of a letter from Lady Blessington. On December 14, 1841, with the warm and pathetic indignation of a doting mother whose child has been denied his deserts, she wrote to him almost fiercely:

You seem to take for granted that Alfred has so mismanaged the negotiation that its want of success is to be attributed to him instead of to the bad faith and trickery of those with whom he has had to deal . . . That candid and amiable person St. Aulaire consulted a coterie of foolish women with all the *méchanceté* of Madame Lieven without her talent for intrigue; and listening to their malicious gossiping, engendered by spite at Alfred's not seeking their society, he concluded that the nomination would not be popular in London and so was afraid to ask for it.

This is the source of the atrocious falsehoods of Alfred's name being *rayé* by the Queen when a list of invitations to a ball was laid before her, and of her having refused to allow Alfred's presentation to her by Prince Ernest. Lady Jersey and Lady Harriet Baring were the persons whose opinions exercised so great an influence on St. Aulaire, which proves him to be nearly as silly an old woman as each of the ladies in question.

St. Aulaire, then, with the low cunning worthy of an agent de police but disgraceful in an ambassador, tells Alfred that he has heard of his embarrassments and requests that he will confide in him as in a father and tell him the whole truth. This, as it now appears, was a snare; and Alfred, too honourable to suspect such baseness, walked into it, and acknowledged that the appointment would enable him to make more advantageous terms with his creditors than he could effect without it.

If the gossiping act of the Foreign Office at Paris led all this to become the subject of a salon, the fault is not Alfred's, as he and I anxiously wished to keep the whole a profound secret. You are therefore wrong in adding to our annoyance at the humiliation to which Alfred has been subjected, by laying the blame of mismanagement on him instead of on the falseness and mystification of which he is the victim.

With regard to the feminine inventions relative to our Queen there

THE PRESIDENT COMING FROM THE CHAMBRE DES DÉPUTÉS

(1851)

After a water colour by d'Orsay.
By permission of the Print Room, British Museum

is not even a shadow of truth in them. Alfred never was presented at her Court and never would, although I, as well as all his other friends, urged it — his motive being that, never having left his name at any of the French Ambassadors of Louis Philippe (not even at Count Sebastiani, a connection of his, or at Marshal Soult, also nearly connected with his family) he could not ask to be presented at Court by the French Ambassador and did not think he ought to be presented by anyone else. Prince Ernest he never knew, consequently could not be presented by him; and the etiquette of not being engaged to meet the Queen unless previously presented at Court is too well known to admit of mistake . . . I enter into these details merely to prove to you the utter falsehoods which have been listened to against Alfred.

I think Alfred has been shamefully ill-used in the business, and if an *amende honorable* be not made to him by those in power they will do themselves no good by their hypocritical prudery in the affair. . . . If the appointment in London is still deemed impracticable, why should they not offer him the secretaryship at Madrid, which is vacant?

I have bored you and myself by entering into all these affairs; but as the Duchesse de Gramont wrote us that the lies about the Queen were brought up against Alfred, I thought it right you should know all on the subject.

Henry Bulwer's reply is printed by Madden.[6] He avows that in his *personal* view, the employment of d'Orsay by the French Embassy in London would have been an excellent thing. But he asks Lady Blessington to realise that the Count has many enemies both in London and Paris, that he is still suspected of complicity in Louis Napoleon's escapade to Boulogne, and further that his financial embarrassments are said to be the real reason for his application for a post involving diplomatic immunity. For these causes Henry Bulwer begs Lady Blessington not to be disappointed at the failure of the application — at any rate immediately. "I think d'Orsay wrong to have asked for London specially. . . . The French Ambassador did not wish for the appointment . . . and M. Guizot is at this moment afraid of anything that might excite discussion and opposition. I did not think he would obtain the situation he wished for in

[6] Vol. II, p. 484, *et seq.*

London, and I think it may be some time before he gets such a one as he ought to have and that would suit him. . . . Do not let him lose courage. Nobody succeeds in these things just at the moment he desires. . . . Alfred has all the qualities for success in anything, but he must give the same trouble and pains to the pursuit he now engages in that he has given to other pursuits."

Thus ended poor d'Orsay's hopes of enjoying the patronage of the Government of Louis Philippe.

It will have been noticed that in his long letter to Henry Bulwer, d'Orsay referred to his attempts to help distressed French people resident in England. Presumably during the thirties this charitable activity was purely personal; but early in 1842 it took a more official form. In February of that year was formed the French Benevolent Society, the Articles of Association stating that the body had been established on the proposal of Count d'Orsay and decreeing that d'Orsay be its first president.

It was specially laid down that no appeal for subscription should be made to Englishmen, who had sufficient poor of their own to succour, particularly during the cruel winter of 1841–42 which caused widespread distress. The French Benevolent Society should subsist by French support. Nevertheless a few English names appear in the first list of subscribers and the influence of d'Orsay is manifest in the donation of ten pounds each by Lords Chesterfield and Pembroke. The president of the association in his inaugural speech made a remark which merits ironical survival: "Every human being," he declared, "whoever he may be, whatever may have been his past life, is entitled to sleep under cover and to receive a morsel of bread. Of those who seek nothing further, no man has a right to ask questions." Some of those present must have smiled to hear this most splendid of down-and-outs thus bravely assert the right of every human being to maintenance. But d'Orsay was innocent even of whimsicality; and as he bowed gravely to the French Ambassador, whose presence on the platform had perhaps secured for him a temporary immunity from arrest, his presidential dignity was undisturbed, alike by personal embarrassment or by the memory of his so recent contretemps with St. Aulaire.

From the date of this inaugural meeting until to-day the French Benevolent Society has healthily progressed, and still continues its good work among French nationals who, for one reason or another, fall on evil days in England. Its first president, when the applause which greeted his speech had died away, returned to the seclusion of Gore House and the pondering of his private problem.

Having failed in his place-hunting, the Count determined to seek profit in other directions. First he turned his attention to speculation in stocks, then to the invention of a contrivance designed to prevent railway accidents. The former led to further appeals for assistance to the unfortunate Henry Bulwer, who was now ploughing an extremely difficult furrow as Minister in Madrid. In March, 1845, d'Orsay wrote to him for advance information about Spanish railway securities: "Whatsoever you tell me will be kept absolutely private. You are in a position to extricate me from my embarrassments, and as I am convinced that to do this would be one of the greatest pleasures you could have, I venture to ask you this service." The letter proceeds: "I have just made a statuette of the Duke of Wellington on horseback which is almost causing a revolution here. The Duke declares it is the finest thing he has ever seen and the only portrait by which he would wish to be known to posterity. He comes here continually to admire himself." Three months later d'Orsay was urging Henry Bulwer to join in a scheme for financing an entirely new railway in Portugal; and there is some reason to believe, from correspondence of this date between Edward Bulwer-Lytton and Henry, that to this speculation, at any rate, the Minister in Madrid lent a sympathetic ear.

As for the railway invention, it provided for a means of instantaneous communication between the guard of a train and the driver. Here is the outline of it, taken from a letter to John Forster:

June 18, 1845

I have thought for some time that it is very important in the interests of the safety of railway travellers that someone should be put on guard in the last coach of a train who should be able by means of a wire communicating with the engine to ring a bell if he sees anything out of order, then the train would stop immediately. . . . My idea is that there should be a raised seat at the back of the last carriage to each train, like the driver's on a hansom cab, and that a long cord should run along the roof of the carriages, which cord when it be pulled will strike a gong indicating that the train should stop.

A series of accidents which had recently taken place gave point to this scheme; but (as d'Orsay later wrote) "*ces sacrés directeurs de railroad ne veulent pas adopter mon idée par économie . . . Il faut les attaquer jusqu'à ce qu'ils pensent a la safety des passengers.*" Needless to say, and despite the fact that the Count persisted till 1848 in trying to get his scheme adopted, the invention was shelved and forgotten. And yet, to judge by the description of it just quoted and others given in letters printed in Madden's book,[7] it had in it the idea of the "communication cord" of to-day.

And so to the last excitements of d'Orsay's life while at Gore House — the revolution in Paris of February, 1848; the flight of Louis Philippe; and, in December, the proclamation as President of the Prince Louis Napoleon. Throughout the forties, the Count's Bonapartism had remained staunch and active. While Louis Napoleon was in prison at Ham, d'Orsay had kept the legend of his name and claims alive by letters to France, in England by word of mouth. When the Prince escaped and re-

[7] Vol. I, pp. 381–386.

appeared in London and at Gore House, d'Orsay was eager with plans and reports on the state of feeling on both sides of the Channel. Naturally, when revolution broke out and the heir to the traditions and throne of Napoleon hastened to Paris to fish in the troubled waters, his loyal supporter could hardly bear the degrading poverty which kept him imprisoned in Kensington. The year 1848 passed in a fever of excitement. Hardly a refugee from the rapidly succeeding administrations in Paris but came to Kensington, paced the garden with d'Orsay, told his tale and gave his opinion as to the chances of the Prince's party. And then in the last month of the year the miracle happened, and the man to whom d'Orsay had been faithful through years of obscurity and failure became President of the French Republic. Not surprisingly — indeed with justification — the Count looked for instant recompense.

But nothing happened. In the moment of bitter disappointment, the idealism of his Bonapartist faith came into conflict with his vanity, and produced a new and curiously two-natured d'Orsay. He is bitterly resentful of Napoleon's neglect; obsessed with his own importance, he is convinced that his ill treatment is the talk of London; but he will not damage the Prince's reputation in English society by divulging that no offer has been made, nor stoop, even at second hand, to ask largesse from one who should have thrust rewards upon him. To the world he will pretend that he is considering alternative appointments; privately he will try to shame Napoleon into fulfilment of his obvious duty. The result of this conflict of motives is the queer mixture of dignity and childish temper which marks his letters on the subject to his friend Bulwer.

Henry (now Sir Henry) Bulwer was back in Paris. He had been recalled from Madrid at the request of the Spanish Government, but was in high favour at home and already talked of as a candidate for Washington. To him, on December 21, d'Orsay wrote as follows:

Herewith a letter which please hand on to Napoleon. Write him a line with it or leave your card so that he will know your address. You will approve, I'm sure, of my having determined to ask nothing of him at all. I was the courtier of his days of misfortune, and my part ended when he began to be prosperous.

Again on December 30:

England is up in arms because it is said that I have been passed over, that he is ungrateful. It is useless for me to say that I want nothing now. No one believes me. . . . I have never spoken to him of my plans or wishes. I could not descend to that.

Again on January 5, 1849:

I have had a long letter from Paris from a reliable source which tells me all goes admirably badly. I am regarded as partly to blame, because it was due to me that *La Presse* and *Le Constitutionel* supported the Prince. . . . I want nothing. The only thing I would accept probably does not exist. I would agree to be Minister of Fine Arts, but not a sort of Director with a seat in the Cabinet, because the arts are vital in France and I am the man to champion them. But it would have to be an important ministry, with all the arts — including the theatre — subject to its rule. . . .

Once it were known that Napoleon had offered me nothing, there would be an outcry here and perhaps in France also. It is well known what I have done for him. One day I am told I am going to Petersburg; the next to Naples. But I would refuse all this kind of thing, because I have something on here worth all the Embassies in the world.

Everyone here, from the Duke of Wellington to the merest cabby, expects that something big will be done for me, although John Bull is not too glad to see the name of Napoleon revived. . . .

So do not ask for *anything* on my behalf. Just try to make him feel he ought to come to some sort of understanding with me, that at least I ought to have something to refuse.

Again, a week or two later:

I only ask you to prevent him forgetting that I have been of real use to him, first here and then in France.

And finally:

I want nothing and I beg you not to put me on any pedestal of difference. I repeat — d'Orsay has done too much for anything adequate in the way of recompense to be found easily.

It was his last letter from Gore House, for immediately afterward the bottom fell out of his world.

D'Orsay, indeed, had done too much. . . .

BOOK FOUR

THE PAGEANT CRUMBLES

CHAPTER I

Collapse

One Saturday afternoon early in April, 1849 (so runs a story one would like to believe), a youth from the pastry cook's called at the back door of Gore House with a tray of cakes and jellies for the evening's dinner. He was admitted to the kitchen, placed his tray on the table, and then, instead of going outside again, walked upstairs. Enquiring of a servant for d'Orsay's dressing room, he knocked at the door. The Count was dressing and demanded to know who was there. The young man turned the handle, walked into the room, and showed his badge of a sheriff's officer. The siege of Gore House was over; the enemy were in the citadel.

Serene as ever, d'Orsay asked the intruder to sit down while he finished his toilet. For nearly an hour and a half he concentrated on his tie, his polished shoes, his handkerchief, his scent, his hair. From the window of the dressing room he could see the sun sinking in the west. As it dropped out of sight, he bowed to his visitor and regretted that as it was now after sunset, the writ no longer ran. A servant conducted the sheriff's officer to the outer gates.

But the moment the man had gone, d'Orsay ran to find Lady Blessington. She was sitting motionless, staring into space. A slip of paper, held in one hand, lay on her knee. It announced that Howell and James, the great department store where fashion did its shopping, had put in an execution for a debt of some thousands of pounds. As is shown by a letter of John Forster's printed below, Howell and James had some little while before taken out an insurance policy on Lady Blessington's life as security for this very debt, which probably went back to the time when Gore House was being lavishly equipped for occupation. But the firm, sensing from gossip in commercial circles that a run on the establishment was imminent, decided that they would prefer their money at this moment rather than at a future and necessarily uncertain date. So, by something more than mere coincidence, d'Orsay and Lady Blessington received simultaneously their notice to quit.

Characteristically, she said almost nothing of her own trouble, but listened to Alfred's tale. Realising, now that her goods were to be distrained, that he was no longer safe even in Gore House, she began making plans for his immediate flight. Fortunately Sunday was ahead of him; if he left very early in the morning, he could be clear of England before Monday came.

He urged her to accompany him. But she shook her head. She was in no danger of prison, as he was. Besides, she wished to remain and meet her creditors; then to arrange for all her furniture and collections to be sold. She would follow in due course. At three o'clock the following morning, with his valet, one portmanteau, and a French umbrella with a jewelled handle, d'Orsay slipped out of Gore House and drove to the coast. By Sunday evening he was in France. Cupid, his wings clipped, but his spirit undismayed and his complacency unshattered, was at large again.

Meantime Lady Blessington faced with courage and method the problem of liquidating her London career. Several offers of financial help were immediately made to her by individual friends. But she refused them all. She secured her principal creditors' permission to offer the entire contents of Gore House for sale. Over and above the large debt to Howell and James she herself owed little enough, having regularly paid her way until the crowding difficulties of the last two years had overwhelmed her. But tradespeople of d'Orsay's (those who adored him for having made their fortunes) seeing that the attack had finally been launched, determined not to be left behind. She was confronted with debts of his amounting to as much again as her own, and (again on the authority of Forster's letter) must plan to raise by her sale some twelve thousand five hundred pounds.

Mr. Phillips, the well-known auctioneer of New Bond Street, assured her that the pictures, *objets d'art* and furnishings of her home should realise the sum she required, and a sale of the lease of the house should produce a modest surplus. While he was starting on his catalogue of her effects, she and her two nieces gave presents to the servants and helped them by letter and recommendation to new situations. To a few old friends she wrote her farewells: to Edward Bulwer-Lytton, to Forster, to Disraeli and to Landor; then packed a few purely personal belongings (except for her own portrait by Chalon and one or two other pictures, she withheld nothing from the sale) and in the middle of April, accompanied by the Misses Power, left England for the last time.

The sale at Gore House was announced for Monday, May 7, 1849, and for twelve subsequent days. Three days prior, on Friday, May 4, the doors were thrown open and the public streamed to Kensington to view the "costly and elegant effects of the Right Honourable the Countess of Blessington, retiring to the Continent." Complacent virtue, gratified jealousy and common curiosity were the chief impulses which drove thousands of Londoners to Gore House. Fine ladies, headed by Lady Jersey and Lady Hertford, loitered through the rooms, fingering, appraising, smiling a little contemptuously, joking one with another. Stolid middle-class families — the fathers pompously severe, the mothers concealing behind pursed and disapproving lips a grim eagerness to witness the downfall of the Scarlet Woman, the children pulling and squeaking — straggled over the house from attic to basement. Dealers of every kind whispered hoarsely in corners; debated the values of china, plate, books, pictures, linen, carpets and bedding; took their intervals of ease by sprawling over the sofas. Only here and there was an old friend, come to pay a final and sorrowful visit to the hospitable house where so many pleasant evenings had been spent.

> I visited Gore House for the last time on the 10th May [says Madden]. The auction was going on. Every room was thronged. The well-known library saloon, in which the conversaziones took place, was crowded — but not with guests. The armchair in which the lady of the mansion was wont to sit, was occupied by a stout coarse gentleman of the Jewish persuasion, engaged in examining a marble hand, extended on a book.
>
> People, as they passed through the room, poked the furniture, pulled about the precious objects of art and ornaments which lay on the table. And some made jests.
>
> It was the most signal ruin of an establishment I ever witnessed. Here was a total smash, a crash on a grand scale of ruin, a sweeping clearance of all the house's treasures.

Thackeray (who seemed to one of the servants still in the house the only person really affected by the tragic scene) wrote to Mrs. Brookfield:

> I have just come away from a dismal sight — Gore House full of snobs looking at the furniture. Foul Jews; odious bombazine women; brutes keeping their hats on in the kind old drawing-room — I longed to knock some of them off and say: Sir, be civil in a lady's room! Ah, it was a strange sad picture of Vanity Fair!

Other friends, according to a letter written to Lady Blessington by her French valet, came during the early days of the sale. We hear of Albert Smith and Doctor Quin. Doubtless Forster came; and perhaps Disraeli. Bulwer-Lytton bought her special set of Byron's works in three volumes, bound with her arms and with painted fore-edges, and ordered it to be sent to her in Paris with his compliments.

The sale went its course and realised rather more than the sum required. A number of the prices made are given by Madden. It is sufficient here to note that the lovely Lawrence portrait of Lady Blessington, now in the Wallace collection, cost Lord Hertford three hundred and thirty-six pounds. But the real interest would be to know whither went the countless minor but very individual items, any one of which would be treasured by such as would do posthumous honour to their kindly and gallant owner. Where is the collection of miscellaneous books, which included innumerable presentation copies from authors of the day? Where are the hundreds of originals of d'Orsay's drawings of his friends, the parcels of "proofs before letters"; the original steel plate of the portrait of Byron? Where are the dozen portraits of Lady Blessington by various artists and in various media? It should be possible, one day in a second-hand furniture shop, to light on a pair of hands in silver; on a single hand in alabaster; on the "square-backed indulging chair" from Lady Blessington's dressing room; on a pipe or a cup and saucer painted with her head and shoulders; on her own set of "The Book of Beauty"; on the Gothic pattern bird cage; on the "ancient ewer, shaped as a helmet." They must be somewhere, these pitiful and rather garish relics of the break-up at Gore House. Unless indeed, with the grim logic of fate, they are all broken and lost; unless, like the rest of that forlorn adventure in tolerance and hospitality, even the miscellaneous furnishings have vanished for ever.

The results of the sale made certain that every creditor would be paid, and various small charities, for which Lady Blessington had left instructions in the event of there being money to meet them, would be liquidated. Negotiations to sell the lease were in train, and it was expected that a surplus of about fifteen hundred pounds would await her instructions.

CHAPTER II

The Death of Lady Blessington

1

But no instructions came.

She and her nieces, on their arrival in Paris in mid-April, had gone to a hotel, whence she wrote to Henry Bulwer in England:

Hôtel de la Ville de Paris
Place de la Ville d'Éveque
April 27, 1849

I ought sooner to have thanked you for your kind note, but the truth is I have hardly had a moment to myself since I arrived at Paris, between receiving and paying visits, and house-hunting. I find that nineteen years' absence have not obliterated me from the recollections of my old friends here, and that marriages and inter-marriages have so greatly increased the members of their families that I have acquired several new friends, with many of whom I am much pleased.

I am too old to enter with much interest or spirit into the gaieties that offer to tempt me; but for my nieces, I am glad to avail myself of the kindness pressed on me on every side and they excite much attention and have what the French term it, great success.

The President has not forgotten old times, nor old friendship. He has been unceasing in his kindness ever since our arrival. We dine with him tomorrow and hold communication with him every day. His old attachment to Alfred revived with fresh force the moment they met. My other old friends the Duchesse de Gramont, the Legouis and Mademoiselle de Boissex have reclaimed me with open arms. *Enfin* everyone has been most amiable and Lord Normanby[1] most kind. Nevertheless I, who like quiet and repose, look back with regret to Gore House and shrink from the hustle of Paris. In short I have lived too long out of the gay world and in the rational one to enjoy soirées and fashionable parties . . . How like a dream the events of the last few weeks appear!

[1] Normanby had been appointed Ambassador to Paris in 1846.

This letter is mainly important for its references to Louis Napoleon. It seems difficult to believe that she would have written thus to a really intimate friend, if the President's welcome to herself and to d'Orsay had not been warm and genuine. This it might perfectly well have been, even though he could not immediately see his way clear to give the latter an official appointment. He seems, virtually at once, to have attached the Count to his person. According to Monckton Milnes, who was with d'Orsay in Paris at Easter, 1849 (*i.e.*, very shortly after his escape from Gore House), the newcomer was already "a sort of chamberlain to the President." Surely, a confidential appointment of this kind was ideal recognition of an old friend's loyalty, and at the same time a means of avoiding the storm of criticism which anything more obvious would have provoked?

Is it not possible that Louis Napoleon has been unreasonably blamed by certain contemporary writers and subsequent commentators for his ingratitude to d'Orsay? It must not be forgotten that his own position was still none too secure. He was far from being an all-powerful despot, who could fill public offices with his private friends and rely on his unshakeable strength to silence opposition. To have given a lucrative post forthwith to so equivocal a being as d'Orsay — a man who had lived out of France for twenty years and had only returned thither in flight from English justice — would have been a far more direct challenge to public opinion than the President yet dared to give.

But the showing of personal civility to old friends — and especially to Lady Blessington — was a different matter; and it is satisfactory to have from her own pen an assurance that the civility was prompt and unmistakable. Unfortunately this satisfaction has one blemish. If we are to believe her letter to Henry Bulwer, we can no longer accept as genuine the most famous of all her witticisms. It is said that shortly after her arrival in Paris she was driving in the street, and in a tangle of traffic the wheels of her carriage became locked with those of the President.

He turned and recognised her. Raising his hat, he greeted her politely: "*Vous restez longtemps à Paris,* Lady Blessington?" "*Je ne sais pas, monsieur,*" she replied. "*Et vous?*"

Inasmuch as this admirable anecdote cannot possibly be squared with her own story of the President's welcome, it must, one fears, be treasured solely for its own sake.

House-hunting ended with the renting of a pleasant flat of modest size in the Rue du Cirque, close to the Élysées, and it seems likely that this proximity to the home of the President was a direct result of his cordiality.

While the new flat was being made ready, Lady Blessington was busy renewing acquaintance with former friends. The Duc and Duchesse de Gramont were particularly kind to her, realising perhaps more than d'Orsay yet realised himself, what sacrifices she had made and what toils she had undergone on behalf of their relative. She herself, now that the break had been made — and although the thought of all her treasures being lost to her was a bitter one — was happier than she had been for two or three years. She was very tired, but the grinding anxiety which she had borne for so long had been at last removed. We learn for the first time from a letter written by d'Orsay to Henry Bulwer on June 1, 1849, that she had wished to give up her hopeless battle against debt and ostracism some while before she did, but that d'Orsay (for reasons of his own, of course) had persuaded her to hold on. This letter is so typical in its egoism, its insensitiveness to her sufferings, and its failure to understand that the parting from her house and belongings was, even though she desired it, a grievous wrench for her, that a portion may be quoted:

Paris, June 1

My dear Henry,

It was you who told me the portrait of the Duke of Wellington had been bought by the City of London. I had heard the buyer was Lord Normanton. As you say, it is a compliment to have one of my works in a place from which it will never depart — any more than Gog and Magog will leave Guildhall. Douro ought to be pleased. I am astonished he said nothing about it in his last letter.[2]

The Gore House sale really succeeded very well. Lady Blessington is pleased, though rather vexed at the number of really good things which went very cheap while less good ones got big prices. Being myself more or less of a Candide, I think all has been for the best, and that if we had stayed on at Gore House she would have got really ill, seeing me pecked at by my cormorant-creditors and my continual disappointments over Ireland, and with the refusal of the publishers to pay. She wanted to make an end of it a long while ago, but I persuaded her to hold on because I was so sure (as I still am) that I shall pull off something big.

Fate was to make this letter in a double sense the climax of d'Orsayism. Not only was it his masterpiece in callous levity, but it was the last time he was ever to write of Lady Blessington save as a tragic memory.

Four days after it was written and within twenty-four hours of moving into her new flat, Lady Blessington was dead. She was seized early in the morning with severe difficulty of breathing; her nieces, d'Orsay and the doctor were instantly at hand and thought to have relieved her by timely remedies; but although the spasms had passed, her heart could not rally and she sank rapidly into unconsciousness and died.

It has from time to time been suggested that Lady Blessington committed suicide. But the long letter from Mary Ann Power to Madden,[3] describing the last hours and the state of the poor lady's heart after autopsy, together with the general testimony to her greater ease of mind after leaving London, prove, surely, that death was natural. She had never lived a healthy life, being in youth too inclined for reading and talking to take sufficient air and exercise, and during later years too burdened with her household and her writing even to sleep well at nights. Between worry and overwork she was worn out; and when at last she

[2] The portrait is not in Guildhall. According to Madden, it was bought at the Gore House sale by Lord Hertford.

[3] Vol. I, pp. 215–217.

began to enjoy a time of blessed relaxation, it brought with it a reaction too strong to be resisted.

She was in her fifty-ninth year.

2

The news of Lady Blessington's death came as a great shock to her friends in London. It happened that Bulwer Lytton had left England in May for a year's residence abroad. He had been near to a breakdown at the end of 1848 as a result of ceaseless writing, two unsuccessful election campaigns and, most exhausting of all, the squalid wrangle with his wife round the deathbed of his unfortunate daughter Emily. It fell therefore to Forster to apprise him of the loss of his great friend, which was done in a long and important letter, supplying many details of matters differently described in Madden's book.

June 11, 1849

Poor Lady Blessington died last Monday — this day week — at about 10 o'c. in the morning.

She and d'Orsay and the girls had dined the previous night with the Duc de Guiche, after which they had walked home to Rue du Cirque II, Champs Élysées, which they had taken possession of that morning. It was the first night she had slept in the place she meant to be her home in Paris.

During all the previous week she had suffered from difficulty of breathing which attacked her in the mornings and obliged her to take refuge in a chair by the bedside in which she found she could breathe more freely. This, however, was supposed to be an attack of bronchitis and not the least danger was dreamt of. On the Sunday night she was more restless than usual — did not sleep at all — and as early as six o'clock on the Monday morning she appears to have got out of bed, called d'Orsay and had just strength enough remaining to reach the chair by her bed. They were all soon round her, of course, and everything was done that could be thought of. Danger was obvious from the first — the stopping of circulation, the difficulty of breathing, but not much apparent pain. She could not speak and her face gradually became black, so with her hands and feet. They did everything, but she sank and died about 10 o'c. in d'Orsay's arms.

Guthrie says it was disease of the heart, that he had known of its existence for some time and no doubt her late griefs and anxieties had tended to bring it suddenly to a head. For she had had many anxieties — the first the worst, most grievous of all, her too great reason to suppose that Louis Napoleon would do nothing for d'Orsay, that he felt his claims and hers already an intolerable burden to him, and that he was doing his best to throw them off.[4]

She had another anxiety in the want of immediate supplies of money — and here the case was one of much hardship. The sale of furniture, pictures etc. at Gore House realised £12,500 and for the lease £1,300 has been offered. Altogether the result of the sale will not be less than £14,000 and her entire debt is certainly considerably less than £13,000. Thus a clear £1,500 was to be reckoned on as hers after every liability was discharged. And with this in hand (she meant to have devoted £500 to furnishing the Rue du Cirque rooms) and her £1,800 a year, I believe she looked forward cheerfully enough, with what little additional she might make by literature. But those damned rascals of Jews would not send her the remittance she wanted — pleaded delays and so forth and vexed and irritated her beyond measure. You can suppose that the circumstances of her departure from England would make her more than usually sensitive on these points. The end of all was that Guthrie's letter, enclosing the half of a £500 note which at last he had forced the Jews to disgorge, arrived by the Monday's post when she was dead.

There is another sad thing. Howell and James insured her life some years ago for £3,500 (when their debt was of that amount) and had offered the policy to her agent for £800 and interest (the sum paid by them upon it), about half an hour before the intelligence of her death reached London. He declined to pay the interest, but was willing to have given the £800. The whole sum is now Howell and James' and every sixpence of their debt paid beside.

Whether she had any other insurance I greatly doubt, and have not the slightest idea of how her affairs are left with reference to d'Orsay and the girls. The latter are with d'Orsay's sister, who is most kind to them; but what they are to do, and especially what he is to do (at the worst they could but return to their father in New Brunswick) are very painful questions. I really think that to come over here and es-

[4] This statement does not tally with Lady Blessington's own description of the President's attitude. Either, therefore, she purposely misled Henry Bulwer, or Forster, who was writing at second-hand, was misinformed. The latter alternative seems the more probable.

tablish himself as an artist would be his best resource. But there is very little chance of his obtaining the necessary protection.

But d'Orsay was making no plans. On him the effect of the loss of the woman who had killed herself in his service was truly shattering. At last, and for the first time in his life, he understood what she had endured for him, how she had loved him. He seemed dazed and almost unconscious of his surroundings. His sister and her husband carried him off with the two Misses Power to their quiet country house at Chambourcy, near St. Germain. From there the elder niece wrote on July 12, 1849 to Madden:

Count d'Orsay would himself have answered your letter, but had not the nerve or the heart to do so. Although the subject occupies his mind night and day he cannot speak of it but to those who have been his fellow sufferers. Much as she was to us, we cannot but feel that to him she was all — the centre of his existence, round which his recollections, thoughts, hopes and plans turned.

On July 31, Forster wrote to Bulwer-Lytton:

Of d'Orsay I hear very little. He writes to no one, not even his most intimate former associates here, and I believe it to be quite the truth that poor Lady Blessington's death has been a frightful blow to him. They are all living at Chambourcy and d'Orsay's whole employment is to mow hay and devise a monument for Lady Blessington.

"The erection of the monument," writes Miss Power six days since, "which will we hope one day contain us all, and everything that relates to it, is now his only study and consolation. It is to stand among a group of chestnut trees some centuries old in a lovely and retired spot but a little way from the house where we now all live together with the Duc and Duchesse de Gramont, which we hope may continue to be our home."

Even as late as September, he was still wholly disconsolate. "You can form no idea," wrote the two Misses Power in concert to Henry Bulwer, "how utterly overwhelmed he was by the blow which had fallen on him and us. . . . He is far other than you knew him in those happy days so lately fled. His chief occupation is in superintending the building of the monument, the exterior of which is nearly completed. You remember his picture of Our Saviour, and how fond my aunt was of it? Strangely enough, the sum for which he has just sold it exactly covers the expense of the monument, to which purpose he applies it."

The mausoleum was rapidly completed and the body of Lady Blessington, which after embalming had been placed in the vaults of the Madeleine, was transferred to its final resting place. Landor composed an epitaph in Latin and Barry Cornwall one in English,[5] which were engraved on two tablets and affixed to the inner walls of the hollow pyramid which is the tomb.

D'Orsay's anguish, when accompanying Lady Blessington's body to the mausoleum he had so lovingly devised, was said to have been heart-rending. He passed from frenzy to stupor and then, seeming to realise all over again the sorrow which had overtaken him, would break out into lamentations as though the death had been but yesterday. Even three years later, when Madden visited him in Paris, all the old misery flooded back at the mention of Lady Blessington's death. "In losing her," he said, "I lost everything in this world. She was to me a mother, a dear dear mother, a true loving mother!"

These were words as true as d'Orsay ever spoke. In his last and loneliest period of his life his eyes were opened, and he saw himself at last for what he had always been — an utterly selfish child, whose caressing ways had weakened a mother's power to discipline, whose vanity and lack of principle had broken a mother's heart.

3

Thus ended the strange and poignant career of Sally Power, who became Marguerite, Countess of Blessington. Her life had plotted a curve from a miserable childhood in Ireland to a

[5] Landor's epitaph, both as he originally wrote it and in the altered form which, much to his indignation, it was finally engraved, is printed in "Last Fruits off an Old Tree" (London, 1853); Barry Cornwall's epitaph is printed in Madden, Vol. I, p. 218.

lonely death in Paris. It reached at its highest point a social prominence and a reputation for wealth and beauty than which few have been more brilliant. Its quiet close in a little village in the Île de France has a simple serenity very dignified, after the turmoil and gilding and desolate splendour which had marked its course. Landor, in addition to his Latin epitaph, composed a poem in his old friend's memory, beginning with the lilacs on the terrace of Gore House, ending with the chestnuts at Chambourcy:

White and dim purple breathed my favourite pair
Under thy terrace, hospitable heart,
Whom twenty summers more and more endeared;
Part on the Arno, part where every clime
Sent its most graceful sons to kiss thy hand,
To make the humble proud, the proud submiss,
Wiser the wisest, and the brave more brave.

. . . .

Thou sleepest, not forgotten nor unmourn'd
Beneath the chestnut shade by Saint Germain.

That was written eighty years ago. To-day a visitor to Lady Blessington's tomb finds himself confronted with a sort of palimpsest of past and present. So much is different, so much unchanged. Chambourcy is a tiny undistinguished village of the ordinary French provincial type, lying on a steep north-facing slope. There is a long tortuous street with houses in a dozen styles built right on to the road; there is a yellow and red brick post office in the worst manner of the early nineteen hundreds; there is a nondescript church, a *mairie*, and a small uneven place planted with dingy planes. Just outside the village, as you enter from St. Germain, stands the château where the de Gramonts lived, whither d'Orsay and Lady Blessington's nieces retired after her death. It is a tall boxlike house with rows of windows and ivy on the walls, strangely like a small English country house of the late eighteenth or early nineteenth century. It is withdrawn a little from the road and raised above it. A walled garden surrounds the house.

THE TOMBS OF LADY BLESSINGTON AND COUNT D'ORSAY AT CHAMBOURCY

After a photograph (1930)

On the hillside above the village lies the cemetery, at whose extreme southeastern corner projects the small plot of land bought by d'Orsay in perpetuity for the mausoleum he intended to design. This plot is not part of the cemetery and is not under the control of the curé. It faces over the cemetery to northward, with an immense view of the wide valley with its tilth and woods. There stands the tomb, a grey stone pyramid on a wide high base, with a little porched doorway closed with a grille. Outside there is no inscription or decoration of any kind. The "chestnut trees of large size and great age" have long since been cut down. In their place is a thick hedge, with a few modest trees rising from it to about the height of the pyramid.

It is queerly exciting to discover this reticent, distinguished monument, hidden away on the hillside above the forlorn straggle of Chambourcy — exciting and comforting. Visit the place on a day of heat; and ask yourself whether it would be easy to devise a better resting place for young Mrs. Farmer of Hampshire, for Lord Blessington's most gorgeous bride, for the mature beauty who drove in a green chariot under the green trees of Hyde Park, for the queen of Gore House and its shady garden, for the broken bankrupt of the Rue du Cirque. Here is a symbol of everything she had known — solitude, tricksy ornament, a self-forgetful dignity, a wide and peaceful landscape. She lies under dusty and faded marble, with her feet pointing toward the daylight which shines through the grilled door of the pyramid. A few yards from that door, and a little below it, are the trivial decorations, the artificial flowers, the elaborate and foolish wirework of the small bourgeois and peasant graves of Chambourcy. But she has only to raise her head, to look over and beyond the dusty cemetery, beyond the squalid village, beyond the great black motor road from Paris to Évreux, ashimmer in its own petrol-laden heat, to where for miles stretches the green and gracious valley of the Seine.

And by her side lies Alfred d'Orsay.

CHAPTER III

The Last of the Dandies

1

Not until the beginning of 1850 did d'Orsay set about reconstructing his life. It was a new experience to have to plan and fend for himself and, in his listless state, needed an effort. He rented a large studio in Paris, with a couple of rooms adjoining, moved thither his belongings from Chambourcy and made a show of working seriously at his painting and sculpture. But it was little enough even of a show; rather the spasmodic gesturing of a forlorn automaton. The present was far less alive to him than the past; yet the past and all it stood for, were dead. In April, 1850, he wrote to Forster:

> Indeed I live entirely in my memories and they are such a mixture of regrets and of pleasures that I often shrink from writing to those who would be most likely to understand me. Indeed, until today I have not even written to Edward Bulwer.

Later in the same letter, after saying what a melancholy and desperate pleasure it is to think of all in England, he adds:

> Never has a man suffered as I have suffered from my great loss. I wonder at those religious people who go in for regular religion in search of rapid consolation. They do not realise that one of the greatest of all religions is a real grief which cannot be forgotten.

His melancholy began to take ever stronger forms, and there can be no doubt that before long his mind became definitely unhinged. Lord Lamington describes his bedroom all hung with black curtains, a black coverlet on the bed. Everywhere were souvenirs of Lady Blessington and of Gore House.

A French visitor pictured the studio as in the nature of a curiosity shop of catholic tastes. There were paintings, drawings, statuettes, glass, china, old weapons, all "arranged with such sureness of taste that one might imagine oneself in the Palais Dusommerard" — which building is now the Musée de Cluny.

Only Thackeray seems to have had the wit to realise that the unfortunate man was mad, and his account of a visit paid to him in the summer of 1850 is gruesome in its vivid perception:

> Today I went to see d'Orsay, who has made a bust of Lamartine, who is mad with vanity. He has written some verses on his bust — verses so fatuous and crazy I never saw.[1] Well, d'Orsay says they are the finest verses that ever were written, and d'Orsay believes in his mad rubbish of a statue which he didn't make; believes in it in the mad way that madmen do — that it is divine and that he made it. Only as you look in his eyes, you see that he doesn't quite believe; and when pressed, hesitates and turns away with a howl of rage.
>
> D'Orsay has fitted himself up a charming atelier, with arms and trophies, pictures and looking glasses, the tomb of Blessington, the sword and star of Napoleon, a crucifix over his bed. And here he dwells without any doubts or remorses, admiring himself in the most horrible pictures which he has painted, and the statues which he gets done for him.[2]

"Without any doubts or remorses" — such was the impression taken away by Thackeray from that macabre visit. It may have been a true one at the moment. But permanently free from the miseries of memory and remorse, the wretched

[1] They are printed in Madden, Vol. I, pp. 338–359, but there described as "not the least admirable of the celebrated poet."

[2] Thackeray is so positive that the bust of Lamartine was not d'Orsay's work and so contemptuous of the poem written in praise of it, that it is only fair to record an equally positive opinion on the other side from one brought up in the Gramont family tradition. Elizabeth de Gramont, great granddaughter of d'Orsay's sister, Ida, describes in the first volume of her memoirs (see Appendix VIII), the house at Chambourcy as it used to be with its wealth of d'Orsay relics, now, alas, scattered and untraceable. There were busts by him on the corners of the building, leaden plaques affixed to the walls; inside were books, more statues and drawings. "A place of honour," she says, "was reserved for the bust of Lamartine, a fine work which showed d'Orsay to have been inspired with genuine flame by the personality of the poet. The two men understood one another, and Lamartine returned thanks for his bust in immortal verse."

man was not. Probably from day to day his moods changed — moods no longer under safe control. Abraham Hayward's letters picture him dining in company here and there, and talking rationally, if not merrily. To Houssaye, who saw him at Lamartine's, he was a fascinating man "with a smiling air which comes from and speaks to the heart." At other time he was full as ever of political talk and political schemes. He had advised the President to do this; he had persuaded the President to do that. . . . It is reported that once again he made application for a diplomatic post — this time for the actual Embassy in London. But when one of his friends was appointed, he uttered no word of bitterness or disappointment; merely smiled.

Yet the intervals between these dinings and debates — intervals spent behind the black curtains of his solitary home — thrust him back into misery; and though he kept his head high among his own people, English visitors were apt to bring with them memories which pierced his guard and wounded him afresh. "I saw Count d'Orsay in Paris," wrote an English authoress to Bulwer-Lytton. "He was very sad and dejected, and his strong attachment to Lady Blessington is now more striking than ever."

So it went on, the broken spirit swaying from cheerfulness to desolation, the only attitude left, the attitude of pride. Now and again, at his painting, the genius of madness would possess him, and he would produce a drawing such as that of Napoleon riding in pageantry through Paris. But no contemporary would have seen in work of the kind anything but pretentious incompetence; and d'Orsay would be left mumbling angrily in his chair before the easel, a man who had outlived his time but yet was in advance of it.

Late in 1851 Louis Napoleon made his *coup d'état;* and the "courtier of the days of misfortune" went about, speaking his mind with a rashness only possible to one who has lost hope. To Hayward he wrote letters of the most reckless criticism of the new policy, and bitterly attacked the clique who surrounded the President. His arrivism had vanished with sanity; he no longer thought, even of himself.

And with this abandonment of calculation and intrigue came, with the fantastic irony characteristic of his whole history, the recognition that all his life he had striven in vain to win.

The year 1852 found him troubled with a disease of the spine, which grew slowly worse. He was often in great pain, but bore his suffering with serenity and patience. In the early summer Madden visited him. "The wreck only of the beau d'Orsay was there," he says. "He was able to sit up and walk about his room, though with difficulty and evidently with pain." At this moment he received from Napoleon his official appointment to the post of Director of Fine Arts. He was able to use his new powers on one or two occasions and with real intelligence; he was also able to read savage attacks on his appointment from more than one jealous and disappointed rival. Then his sickness rose and overwhelmed him. On August 4, 1852, at the age of fifty-one, and in his way "magnificent, but without warmth and full of melancholy", he died.

They buried him at Chambourcy by the side of Lady Blessington, under the plain stone pyramid of the mausoleum which he had himself created. On the wall above his tomb was fixed a tablet bearing this inscription:

A LA MEMOIRE
DE
GILLION GASPARD GABRIEL
ALFRED DE GRIMOD D'ORSAY
COMTE DU SAINT EMPIRE
etc. etc. etc.

Cher à deux peuples
Eminent par la grâce dans la jeunesse
Illustrée par l'art dans la maturité
Bienveillant et bienfaisant a tous les ages
Il aima la gloire, il admira le génie,
Il fût devoué au malheur

SA SŒUR
ET SES AMIS LE REGRETTENT DANS LE
TEMPS QUE DIEU LE
RECOIVE DANS L'ETERNITE

2

Thus the curtain fell on the last of the dandies.

It rose again, almost exactly half a century later, with the production in October, 1902, at His Majesty's Theatre of a play by Clyde Fitch. The play was called "The Last of the Dandies", and the part of d'Orsay was taken by Herbert Beerbohm Tree. The impressive anecdote which follows was told by Tree to his friend Charles Boyd, and by Boyd to an intimate friend of my own. There seems no reason to doubt its truth.

During the run of "The Last of the Dandies", at the close of an afternoon performance, Tree was informed that an old lady would like to speak to him.

"What sort of an old lady?"

She was small, they said, would not give her name, and was shabbily dressed in some kind of uniform. Tree gave instructions for her to be brought up.

The little old woman looked very poor, but spoke in an educated voice. She explained that she had read in a paper about the play in which Mr. Tree was acting, that it was about Count d'Orsay and that in the play he dies.

"From what I read," she said, "the death scene is not correct."

Tree was suddenly interested.

"Go on," he said.

"Count d'Orsay," the visitor continued in her tired and gentle voice, "became during the last months of his life very fond of waltz music, and one of [there was a moment's hesitation] his nieces would play to him when he was exhausted or in pain. One August evening he was sitting in his chair, listening to the piano. 'Play it faster,' he said suddenly. And again, 'Play it faster; play it faster!'

"THE LAST OF THE DANDIES"

Poster used to advertise Clyde Fitch's play produced by H. Beerbohm Tree at His Majesty's Theatre, London, 1902

"When the tune was finished, she turned her head. The Count was motionless and a little sunken in his chair. He was dead."

Tree was deeply moved.

"But how — how do you know this?"

"It was I who was playing the piano," the little old woman replied.

Her name was not mentioned in the story as told to me, but it can only have been Power. She told Tree that she was an inmate of a charitable institution in Fulham; and it is said that he did what he could to make her last years comfortable.

Thus across the gulf of two generations the wind of chance wafted back to London a faint rococo memory of Alfred d'Orsay. Into the surge of a new century and to the very threshold of the last carnival of the pre-war world, wandered this ghostly reveller from a previous carnival — playboy, pierrot, parasite and artist, who had died fifty years earlier (was it at Chambourcy or in his Paris studio?) to the tune of Chopin's waltz in C-sharp minor or perhaps of Strauss' "Lorelei", played faster . . . and faster still. . . .

THE END

APPENDIX I

Landor's Version of the Affair Blessington-Jenkins

In the course of a brief article by Landor entitled "Lady Blessington", and printed in the *Athenæum,* February 17, 1855, occurs the following:

> Enough has been said vitupatory about the mistress of Gore House. I disbelieve in the tales of her last friendship [*i.e.,* that she was ever d'Orsay's mistress]: an earlier one affords more cause for admiration than for censure. She had been attached to a very handsome man, whose habit of gaming ended, as it often does end, and always should, in utter ruin and expatriation. She resolved to follow him. At that time she resided at Brighton. Lord Blessington was also there and heard of her distress. He had seen enough of her to love her ardently; but instead of making any proposal to her, he wrote a request to know whether "a thousand pounds or two" could bring back her friend in safety. She answered as only a generous heart can answer one equally generous, and wrote immediately to the person concerned. He replied that he was ruined beyond redemption and never could return to England nor stand between her and her future. Lord Blessington, on receiving this intelligence, called on her.
>
> The exile received from her one hundred pounds quarterly until his death.

As stated in a footnote to Chapter II, Part One, of this book, I am unable from any other source to explain, to dispute or to confirm this contribution of Landor's toward the history of Lady Blessington's early life. The incident described is nowhere else even referred to.

The strongest probability is that the "very handsome man" was Jenkins; we know from the "Blessington Papers" (p. 169), that he was imprudent and extravagant. In such a case Landor's declaration can be welcomed as supplying additional and helpful details of Blessington's first gesture of friendship toward the woman he was to marry. Also, if circumstances were indeed as here described and the poor young woman had been left behind in a bankrupt's flight, the Earl's understanding with Mrs. Farmer and his payment of money to Jenkins for expenses incurred during her residence in Hampshire become more reasonably comprehensible. If, on the other hand, the fugitive was not Jenkins but some one altogether different, Landor's story must await the gloss of a biographer better informed than I.

APPENDIX II

Lord Blessington's Will

(Transcribed verbatim from the copy in Somerset House, and correcting in several important particulars the faulty text printed as an Appendix to Madden's first volume.)

This is the last will and testament of me, Charles John, Earl of Blessington, of that part of the United Kingdom called Ireland. I give to Luke Norman, Esquire, for and during the time he shall continue agent of my estates, in the county and city of Dublin, and in the county of Tyrone, twelve hundred pounds per annum, in lieu of receivers' fees. I appoint Alfred d'Orsay, Court [*sic*] of (——), in France, Luke Norman, Esquire, and Alexander Worthington, Esquire, my executors; and I give unto each of them one thousand pounds. I give to Isabella Binny, Michael McDonough, and John Bullock, one hundred pounds each. I give and devise my real and personal estates to said Alfred d'Orsay, Luke Norman, and Alexander Worthington, for the following purposes. First for the payment of two thousand pounds, British, per annum (inclusive of one thousand pounds settled on her at the time of my marriage), to my wife. Margaritte, or Margaret, Countess of Blessington; and I give to her all her own jewels, requesting that she may divide my late wife's jewels between my two daughters at the time of her decease. I give to Robert Power and Mary Ann Power one thousand pounds each. I give to my daughter, Harriet Anne Jane Frances, commonly called Lady Harriet, born at my house at Seymour Place, London, on or about the 3rd day of August, 1812, all my estates in the county and city of Dublin, subject to the following charges, provided she intermarries with my friend, and intended son-in-law, Alfred d'Orsay. If the said Harriet Anne do not marry the said Alfred d'Orsay I bequeath her the sum of ten thousand pounds only. I give to my daughter, Emily Rosalie Hamilton, generally called Lady Mary Gardiner, born in Manchester Square, on the 24th June, 1811, whom I now acknowledge and adopt as my daughter, the sum of twenty thousand pounds. In case the said Alfred d'Orsay intermarries with the said Emily, otherwise Mary Gardiner, I bequeath to her my estates in the county and city of Dublin. The annuity of two thousand pounds per annum British to be paid to my beloved wife out of the said estates. I give to my son, Charles John, who I [desire] may take the name of Stuart Gardiner, born in Portman Square on the 3rd day of February, 1810, all my estates in the county of Tyrone, subject to the following charges: also the reversion of my Dublin estates in case of failure of male issue of said daughters. In case of male issue lawfully begotten, I leave these estates to the second son of Alfred d'Orsay and my daughter; or if only one son to him; in case of failure of male issue, to go to the male issue of my other daughter. My estates are to be subject, in the first instance, to the payment of my debts. I give to my wife the lease of my house in London, at the expiration of which the furniture, books, etc., etc., are to be removed to the intended residence at Mountjoy Forest; and I direct that the said house be built according to the plan now laid down, and do empower my said executors to borrow money for the said purpose. I give to my wife all my carriages, paraphernalia and plate. I give to my son, Charles John, my plate, wardrobe, [swords], etc. etc. etc. I appoint Alfred d'Orsay guardian of my son, Charles John, until he arrive at the age of twenty-five years, the settlement of twelve thousand pounds to be null and void on his obtaining the Tyrone estates. I appoint my beloved wife guardian of my daughter, Harriet Anne; and I appoint my sister Harriet, guardian of my daughter, commonly called Lady Mary. I give to Isabella McDougal, of Perth, one hundred pounds per annum for her life, it being bequeathed her by my first wife, Mary Campbell, Viscountess Mountjoy. I give to the National Gallery, intended to be formed in London under royal protection, my picture of the "Three Graces" by Sir Joshua Reynolds, with a desire that "the gift of Charles John, E[arl] of B[lessington]", may be affixed to the said picture, as an encouragement to others to contribute to the said collection. I give to my sister, Harriet Gardiner, five hundred [pounds] per annum for her natural life. I revoke all other wills, by me made, and declare this to be my last will and testament; In witness whereof, I have to this my last will, contained in five sheets of paper, set to the first four my hand, and to this, the fifth and last, my hand and seal, this 31st day of August, 1823.

Blessington [seal]

[The witnesses included C. J. Mathews.]

APPENDIX III

Hand List of Lady Blessington's Books

"The Magic Lantern: or Sketches of Scenes in the Metropolis"
1 vol. Post 8vo. Longman. 1822.

"Sketches and Fragments", by the author of "The Magic Lantern."
1 vol. Post 8vo. Longman. 1822.

"Journal of a Tour through the Netherlands to Paris in 1821", by the author of "Sketches and Fragments", etc., etc., etc.
1 vol. 16mo. Longman. 1822.

"The Repealers"
3 vols. Post 8vo. Bentley. 1833.
2nd edition. "Grace Cassidy or The Repealers." 3 vols. Bentley. 1834.

"Conversations of Lord Byron with the Countess of Blessington"
With a frontispiece portrait of Byron after Count d'Orsay.
1 vol. 8vo. Bentley. 1834.
New edition. With a memoir and portraits. Post 8vo. Bentley. 1893.

"The Two Friends"
3 vols. Post 8vo. Saunders & Otley. 1835.

"The Confessions of an Elderly Gentleman"
With six illustrations after E. T. Parris.
1 vol. Post 8vo. Longman. 1836.

"The Victims of Society"
3 vols. Post 8vo. Saunders & Otley. 1837.

"The Confessions of an Elderly Lady"
With eight illustrations after E. T. Parris.
1 vol. Post 8vo. Longman. 1838.

"Desultory Thoughts and Reflections"
1 vol. 8vo. Longman. 1839.

"The Governess"
With a frontispiece after E. T. Parris.
2 vols. Post 8vo. Longman. 1839.

"The Idler in Italy"
With a portrait after Landseer.
2 vols. 8vo. Colburn. 1839.
2nd edition. 3 vols. Post 8vo. Vols. I and II. Colburn. 1839.
Vol. III (new material). Colburn. 1840.
"The Belle of a Season"
Illustrated by A. E. Chalon.
1 vol. 4to. Longman. 1840. (published December, 1839)
"The Idler in France"
2 vols. 8vo. Colburn. 1841.
"The Lottery of Life"
3 vols. Post 8vo. Colburn. 1842.
"Meredith"
3 vols. Post 8vo. Longman. 1843.
"Strathern or Life at Home and Abroad"
With, as frontispiece to Vol. I, the Landseer portrait already published in "The Idler in Italy."
4 vols. Post 8vo. Colburn. 1845.
"The Memoirs of a Femme de Chambre"
3 vols. Post 8vo. Bentley. 1846.
"Marmaduke Herbert or The Fatal Error: A Novel founded on Fact"
3 vols. Post 8vo. Bentley. 1847.
"Country Quarters": With a Memoir by Miss Power and a frontispiece portrait after Count d'Orsay.
3 vols. Post 8vo. Shoberl. 1850.

"EDITED" BY LADY BLESSINGTON

"Lionel Deerhurst or the Days of the Regency"
[by Mrs. Barbara Hemphill]
3 vols. Post 8vo. Bentley. 1846.

For Lady Blessington's contributions to the Annuals see Mr. Andrew Boyle's "Index to the Annuals" (forthcoming as a supplementary title in the Bibliographia Series. London, Constable; New York, R. R. Bowker Co.).

Amateurs of curiosa may wish to note the following parody of Lady Blessington's annualising activity:

"The Shilling Book of Beauty"
edited and illustrated by Cuthbert Bede
1 vol. J. Blackwood. 1856.

The contributors include Mrs. Bore, Sir E. L. B. L. B. Little, Rt. Hon. B. Bendizzy, Alfred Tennison, Thackaway, N. Warker Pillis, the Earl of Snarlisle and Lady Slip-Slop (who, one fears, represents Lady Blessington).

APPENDIX IV

Key to "The Repealers"

Duchess of Heaviland	Duchess of Northumberland
Marchioness of Bowood	Marchioness of Lansdowne
Countess of Grandison	Countess of Grantham
Lord Albany	Lord Alvanly
Lady Elsinore	Lady Tullamoore
Lady Kidney	Lady Sidney
Duke of Lismore	Duke of Devonshire
Mrs. Grantly	Mrs. Norton
Countess of Guernsey	Countess of Jersey
Lord Key	Earl Grey
Marchioness of Stuartville	Marchioness of Londonderry
Lord Montagu	Lord Rokeby
Duchess of Lenox	Duchess of Richmond
Marchioness of Burton	Marchioness of Conyngham
Marquis and Marchioness of Mona	Marquis and Marchioness of Anglesey
Lady Augusta Garing	Lady Augusta Baring
Marchioness of Glanricarde	Marchioness of Clanricarde
Lady Emmeline Hart Burtley	Lady E. S. Wortley
Lady Yesterfield	Lady Chesterfield
Mrs. Branson	The Hon. Mrs. Anson
Lady Lacre	Lady Dacre
Lady Norrely	Lady Morley
Mrs. Manley	Mrs. Stanley
Sir Robert Neil	Sir Robert Peel
Mrs. Butler Ferguson	Mrs. Cutler Ferguson
Mr. Errice	Mr. Edward Ellice
Mr. Thiel	Mr. Shiel
Lord Rafton	Lord Sefton
Lady Castlemount	Lady Charlemont
Lord Leath	Lord Meath
Duke and Duchess of Cartoun	Duke and Duchess of Leinster

APPENDIX V

Some Contemporary Opinions of Lady Blessington

Here is a selection of judgments — hostile and friendly — passed on Lady Blessington, her household and her personal appearance by contemporaries, most of whom actually knew her.

In the conflict of opinion which she provoked among her contemporaries there remains something both interesting and significant. Some of them resented her social attitude, distrusted her wit and lack of formality; or genuinely believed her a menace to society. Others relished her beauty, her lack of snobbery, her admiration for mental achievement and her scorn of mere rank. In their very contradictoriness the reader of to-day may find a clue to the conventions, at once baffling and elementary, of the England of ninety years ago.

I. The Enemy

1. *Greville's Diary for February, 1839.*

Lady Blessington's existence is a curiosity, and her house and society have at least the merit of being singular, though the latter is not so agreeable as from its composition it ought to be. . . . Her house is furnished with a luxury and splendour not to be surpassed; her dinners are frequent and good; and d'Orsay does the honours with a frankness and cordiality which are very successful; but all this does not make society, in the real meaning of the term. There is a vast deal of coming and going, of eating and drinking, and a corresponding amount of noise, but little or no conversation, discussion, easy quiet interchange of ideas and opinions, no regular social foundation of men of intellectual or literary calibre ensuring a perennial flow of conversation, and which, if it existed, would derive strength and assistance from the light superstructure of occasional visitors, with the much or the little they might individually contribute. The reason of this is that the woman herself, who must give the tone to her own society, and influence its character, is ignorant, vulgar, and commonplace. Nothing can be more dull and uninteresting than her conversation, which is never enriched by a ray of genius or imagination.

2. *Cyrus Redding in "Fifty Years' Recollections."*

Lady Blessington, shrewd, clever, not among the best of mankind, and tolerably hackneyed in what were not exactly the virtues of any age, began a speculation in a literary way, in order to turn her "fair" fame to account, near the end of her fortune's feast. She invited herself, and deputed others to invite, literary men, from Lord Brougham to penny-a-liners, who had naturally no objection to dine with a fine woman, if not quite *en regle,* and somewhat gone in years, who wished to play Aspasia, though history informs us the lapses of the Grecian lady were simple and uncompounded. A friend was deputed to ask me, but I declined, not that I censured any man for accepting the lady's disinterested invitations, for men might do so, and not injure caste; but I knew her gross early history, and disrelished her on that account. No lady, who regarded her own reputation, on the other hand, could possibly visit her; that was a very different affair.

She was a fine woman; she had understood too well how to captivate the other sex. She had won hearts, never having had a heart to return. No one could be more bland and polished, when she pleased. She knew from no short practice, when it was politic to be amiable, and yet no one could be less amiable when her temper was roused; her language then being well-suited to the circumstances of the provocation, both in style and epithet.

3. In 1842, Mrs. M. A. Hughes, the old friend of Harrison Ainsworth and grandmother of the author of "Tom Brown's Schooldays", wrote to Mrs. Southey:

Lady Blessington has grown old, coarse and unattractive — she is fighting against wrinkles and a scorbutic complexion and a very unwieldy person; and her contemptible paramour is also growing too old to be the glass of fashion and is overwhelmed with debt. What an old age theirs must be!

This was sent in reply to a letter from Mrs. Southey referring to "the much injured Countess d'Orsay" and her "indignant abhorrence of those whose youthful victim she was"; also deploring the "clever fascinating works of Sir L. Bulwer . . . the most mischievous writer of his class — the most insidiously misleading."

4. Mrs. Mathews (mother of Charles Mathews) wrote to Madden when he was compiling his book about Lady Blessington:

I really thought well of my poor friend and believe I can *afford* to *own* my friendship for her.

This remark may be contrasted with letters written by Mrs. Mathews to Lady Blessington while the latter was alive ("Blessington Papers", pp. 179 *et seq.*).

5. This contribution to the Blessington-d'Orsay legend comes from a chap-book "History of Lizzie Howard" printed *sous le manteau* by some Holywell Street bookseller about 1866:

At the Tuileries Lizzie Howard was once more introduced to Count Alfred d'Orsay and to Lady Blessington, who had been true to the Prince in his adversity and had followed him in his change of fortune. Two such accomplished personages as the Count and the smart novelist were not precisely adapted to the taste of Lizzie Howard, and they, on their part, detested the presence of the strumpet. But there was no alternative. Nevertheless, it should not be forgotten that, except in natural and acquired tastes, the once notorious Sally Power, Countess of Blessington, had little cause to pride herself since her liaison with the Count and *faux pas* with others of the *haut ton,* for which scandal gave her credit, had made her an outcast from what is called "society" in London, and she was therefore glad to fly from that capital to form a régime in one where anarchy prevailed for a time. The Count was penniless, and the Countess in exactly the same position. They were perforce therefore obliged to make a virtue of necessity and accept the advances of the low-born cobbler's daughter, whose dictum was law after she became Empress Regnant.

The *coup d'état* was accomplished and Louis was crowned Emperor. The Empress elect was made Countess de Beauregarde and provided with an ample allowance. . . . Licentiousness was the order of the day, and the grosser the form in which it appeared, the more acceptable did it become to the Countess de Beauregarde and her clique.

With such a task as the Emperor had before him, few opportunities offered for his being present at the orgies nightly enacted in the salons of his superb palace. The honours of the Empire were consequently dispensed by the Countess de Beauregarde under the superintendence of Lady Blessington, Count d'Orsay and the Duke of Brunswick.

In case the relevant dates escape the reader's memory, he may be reminded that Lady Blessington died in June, 1849; that Louis Napoleon's *coup-d'état* was made in December, 1851; that d'Orsay died in August, 1852; and that Louis Napoleon was not crowned Emperor until three months after — on November of 1852.

II. Opinions either Judicious or Definitely Favourable

1. *Mrs. S. C. Hall, in a letter to Madden.* [probably 1853]

I have no means of knowing whether what the world said of this most beautiful woman was true or false, but I am sure *God* intended her to be good, and there was a deep-seated good intent in whatever she did that came under my observation. She never lost an opportunity of doing a gracious act or saying a gracious word!

Her sympathies were quick and cordial, and independent of worldliness; her taste in art and literature womanly and refined. I say "womanly," because she had a perfectly feminine appreciation of whatever was delicate and beautiful. There was great satisfaction in writing for her whatever she required, labours became pleasures from the importance she attached to every little attention paid to requests, which as an editor she had a right to command.

Her manners were singularly simple and graceful; it was to me an intense delight to look upon beauty, which, though I never saw it in its full bloom, was charming in its autumn time, and the Irish accent, and soft, sweet Irish laugh, used to make my heart beat with the pleasures of memory. I always left her with a sense of enjoyment, and a perfect disbelief in everything I heard to her discredit. Her conversation was not witty nor wise, but it was in good tune and good taste, mingled with a good deal of humour, which escaped everything bordering on vulgarity, by a miracle.

A tale of distress, or a touching anecdote, would at once suffuse her clear intelligent eyes with tears, and her beautiful mouth would break into smiles and dimples at even the echo of wit or jest. The influence she exercised over her circle was unbounded, and it became a pleasure of the most exquisite kind to give her pleasure.

2. *Gronow in his Reminiscences.*

Those who, like myself, are old enough to recollect the beautiful Lady Blessington in her brightest days, can remember that she always wore a peculiar costume, chosen with artistic taste to suit exactly her style of beauty. The cap she was in the habit of wearing has been drawn in Chalon's portrait of her, well known from the print in the *Keepsake* [actually *The Book of Beauty*], and in all the shop windows of the day. It was a "mob-cap" behind, drawn in a straight line over the forehead, where, after a slight fulness on each temple, giving it a little the appearance of wings, it was drawn down close over the cheeks, and fastened under the chin. Nothing could have been more cunningly devised to show off the fine brow and beautifully shaped oval face of the deviser, or to conceal the too great width of the cheeks, and a premature development of double chin. Lady Blessington had also a style of dress suitable to her figure, which was full, but then not "of o'er-grown bulk." She always wore white in the morning, a thick muslin dress, embroidered in front and lined with some bright colour, and a large silk bonnet and cloak to match.

3. *William Archer Shee in "My Contemporaries: 1830–1870."*

"Lady Blessington is conspicuous for her dress, which is always in excellent taste, and, though it may be sometimes more elaborate than is necessary in a circle generally composed exclusively of men, it is always adapted to set off the attractions, and soften the exuberance, of a figure where the only defect is the *embonpoint*, the effect of which, however, she knows how to mitigate with much skill.

"Lady Blessington has the art of collecting around her all that is best worth knowing in the *male* society of London. She has the peculiar and most unusual talent of keeping the conversation in a numerous circle *general*, and of preventing her guests from dividing into little selfish *pelotons*. With a tact unsurpassed, she contrives to draw out even the most modest tyro from his shell of reserve, and, by appearing to take an interest in his opinion, gives him the courage to express it. All her visitors seem, by some hidden influence, to find their level, yet they leave her house satisfied with themselves."

4. *William Harrison Ainsworth,* in a letter to a friend, November, 1836: "that jolly old girl, Lady Blessington."

5. *H. F. Chorley, as quoted in Hewlett's Memoirs.*

I went with Willis to the studio of Mr. Rothwell, who was engaged on a half-length portrait of Lady Blessington, which he never, I believe, completed, and was introduced to her. She said a few kind words in that winning and gracious manner which no woman's welcome can have ever surpassed; and from that moment till the day of her death in Paris, I experienced only a long course of kind constructions and good offices.

She was a steady friend, through good report and evil report, for those to whom she professed friendship. Such faults as she had belonged to her position, to her past history, and to the disloyalty of many who paid court to her by paying court to her faults, and who then carried into the outer world depreciating reports of the wit, the banter, the sarcasm, and the epigram, which but for their urgings and incitements would have been always kindly, however mirthful.

She must have had originally the most sunny of sunny natures. As it was, I have never seen anything like her vivacity and sweet cheerfulness during the early years when I knew her. She had a singular power of entertaining herself by her own stories; the keenness of an Irishwoman in relishing fun and repartee, strange turns of language, and bright touches of character. A fairer, kinder, more universal recipient of everything that came within the possibilities of her mind, I have never known. I think the only genuine author whose merits she was averse to was Hood; and yet she knew Rabelais, and delighted in "Elia." It was her real disposition to dwell on beauties rather than faults. Critical she could be, and as judiciously critical as any woman I have ever known, but she never seemed to be so willingly. When a poem was read to her, or a book given to her, she could always touch on the best passage, the bright point; and rarely missed the purpose of the work, if purpose it had.

Her taste in everything was towards the gay, the superb, the luxurious; but, on the whole, excellently good. Her eye was as quick as lightning; her resources were many and original. It will not be forgotten how, twenty years ago, she astounded the Opera-goers by appearing in her box with a plain transparent cap, which the world in its ignorance called a Quaker's cap. . . .

So, too, her houses in Seamore Place and at Kensington Gore were full of fancies which have since passed into fashions, and which seemed all to belong and to agree with herself. Had she been the selfish Sybaritic woman whom many who hated her, without knowing her, delighted to represent her, she might have indulged these joyous and costly humours with impunity; but she was affectionately, inconsiderately liberal — liberal to those of her own flesh and blood who had misrepresented and maligned her, and who grasped at whatever of bounty she yielded them, with scarcely a show of cordiality in return, and who spread the old, envious, depreciating tales before the service had well been done an hour!

6. *Mrs. Newton Crosland in her Memoirs.*

Through all the years I knew her she never varied her style of head-dress. What hair was visible was of a chestnut hue, braided down the cheeks, while straight across the forehead, in what I can only describe as the lady-abbess fashion, was a piece of rich lace or blonde, but the same material was brought down one side of the face and drawn tight as if supporting the chin, and invisibly fastened on the other side. The lace set her face as if in a frame, and hid many tell-tale lines of advancing years. No doubt Lady Blessington studied dress, as every woman to a certain degree should do; but she never attempted to conceal her age, talking freely of the long ago and of Byron, whom of course she called *Birron*. She was about fifty when I first knew her, and very stout, a circumstance which she spoke of and lamented; but she had the remains of great beauty, though her nose was slightly "tip-tilted." She had abundant command of language, speaking, in my opinion, more eloquently than she wrote, and in tones where now and then the delicate flavour of the Dublin accent could be detected — that accent which gives emphasis and expression to kind words, and is wholly different from what is called brogue. She told a good story capitally, and was quite the best *raconteuse* I ever met.

7. *Anne Cooper (Lady Blessington's maid) in a letter to Madden (1853).*

Lady B. was naturally very cheerful, droll, and particularly amusing, this was natural to her, but so overwhelmed with cares and expenses, and the calls for assistance from everyone of her family. Madame de St. Marsault depended wholly and solely on her, [as did her] father as long as he lived. Mr. Power's eldest son, the second was at Charter House, all extra expenses; the eldest to be fitted out for India after an expensive education; two nieces' clothing; Mrs. Fairlie's family; for years a great anxiety not to be in debt, trying to curtail all expenses in her own establishment, labouring night and day for money, worried and vexed not being able to pay when bills were sent; and no money no sleep at night; wishing to give up Gore House, have a sale and pay off for two years before she left England.

The famine in Ireland rendered her income more irregular, her payments became more difficult; at last Howell and James put an execution in the house, the cause of our departure from England. She did a great many charities; for instance, she gave to poor literary people, poor musicians, something yearly to old servants, to Miss Landon's mother, to Mrs. Mathews, in fact too many to mention and add to all other miseries the most shameful ingratitude. . . .

My opinion is that no woman ever was loaded with such professions of friendship and attachment from so great a number of hypocritical friends; no woman was ever more abused.

8. *William Jerdan in his Autobiography.*

I visited her constantly in St. James's Square, Mayfair, and Gore House; and the more I saw and knew of her, the more I loved her kind and generous nature, her disposition to be good to all, and her faithful energy to serve her friends. Full of fine tastes, intelligence, and animation, she was indeed a loveable woman; and, by a wide circle, she was regarded as the centre of a highly intellectual and brilliant society.

9. *J. C. Jeaffreson in "Novels and Novelists."*

Those who watched and were fascinated by her graces, tried in vain to analyze them, and say in what her witchery consisted. Her dazzling clear complexion, dark hair, and rich dark eye-brows and lashes, delicate features ever radiant with the warm light of her mirthful nature, small mouth and thin pink lips curling with playful irony, small white hands, tiny feet, and incomparable shape, were the theme of universal admiration, not less than her frank, generous, cordial manner. Irish in heartiness, French in its piquancy, and English in its delicacy and refinement — and her rich, soft voice, which alike in laughter and in speech enlivened its hearers with a sense of new-found happiness.

But what most elicited enthusiastic praise, was the perfect harmony of her entire appearance in rest and in action. The emotion of the moment was as manifest in her step, her form, her slightest alteration of attitude, as in her countenance. She was young and triumphant, gentle, and of a constitution naturally mirthful; these were her halcyon days, every moment brought with it a fresh joy, and the delight she experienced, manifested in the strangely subtle language of her beauty, was itself the quality with which, beyond all her other charms, she swayed the affections and imaginations of her astonished and almost incredulous admirers.

10. *Leigh Hunt in "Blue Stocking Revels."*

"Lady Blessington!" cried the glad usher aloud,
As she swam through the doorway, like moon from a cloud;
I know not which most her face beamed with — fine creature!
Enjoyment, or judgment, or wit, or good nature.
Perhaps you have known what it is to feel longings
To pat silken shoulders at routs, and such throngings; —
Well, think what it is at a vision like that!
A Grace after dinner! a Venus grown fat!
Some "elderly gentleman" risk'd an objection;
But this only made us all swear her "perfection."
His arms the host threw round the liberal bodice,
And kiss'd her, exactly as god might do goddess.

11. *Bulwer Lytton, in an autograph note endorsing such letters of hers as he kept.*

Lady Blessington was essentially sympathetic and admired with enthusiasm. She had all the Irish cordiality of manner and a peculiar grace of her own. She was benevolent, kindly and generous to a rare degree.

She was confessedly of a cold temperament, though most affectionate to her friends and most true to them. She was middle-aged when I first knew her and much of her early beauty was then gone. But she had a singularly sweet and gracious face, and a wonderful symmetry of form until she grew too stout.

12. *[Lady Wilde] in the Dublin University Magazine, March 1855.*

That she was happy appears nowhere, either in her letters or diaries; yet hers was a life diffusing happiness. Her kindness was instinct, yet ardent as though it had been passion; and above all women of her time she fascinated, and fascination is a moral grace, for it has its source in the soul. . . .

She did not write absolute trash — on the contrary she sometimes uttered very shrewd commonsense opinions. But there was such a total want of elevation of feeling or depth of thought in her works that it was impossible to read them with profit or remember them with interest. She had neither Lady Morgan's wit nor Mrs. Norton's agonising pathos; and if compared with the lady authoresses her contemporaries, must in all things be named lowest in the list.

The great fault of her character seemed to be an incapacity for profound thought on any subject. She lived on passionately from day to day — excitement the very vital breath of her existence; never caring or thinking whither it was all tending but purposing, some day or other when she had time, to think seriously about religion — and thus it was till the end came. There is therefore no tragedy in her life; no deep earnestness and therefore no despair.

13. *The Crim Con Gazette, May 4, 1839.*

Whatever may be the foibles of the Countess of Blessington, great merit is due to her for not obtruding them on the notice of the public. . . . In the bosom of elegant retirement or in the display of noble hospitality have the days of this lady been chiefly spent. . . .

Few if any persons have been subjected to so many libels. Her ladyship had however met the slanderers with so much spirit and (dare we use the word?) manliness, that her calumniators have generally received the worst of it. A degraded wretch connected with a low and scurrilous Sunday print a short time since waited on her, and producing a MS. sketch of her life had the audacity to demand one hundred pounds for its suppression. Her ladyship politely told the gentleman that she could not give one hundred pounds for its suppression, but she would undertake to pay two hundred pounds, if he would print it and bring a copy in person on the following Sunday morning. It is scarcely necessary to say that the scoundrel took the hint and made his bow.

This extract is included for the sake of its obscure and disreputable source. The *Crim Con Gazette* was a gutter-weekly of the most unscrupulous kind, but it chose to treat Lady Blessington as a "sportsman" after its own heart. The result may be regarded as a compliment or a super-insult, according to the prejudices of the reader.

APPENDIX VI

Books Primarily Concerned with Lady Blessington and Count D'Orsay

"The Literary Life and Correspondence of the Countess of Blessington"

By R. R. Madden. 3 vols. Newby. London. Second edition. 1855.

The three volumes of this work are indispensable to any study of the life of Lady Blessington. Doctor Madden had all the documents and information available at the time, and undoubtedly set out to do the very best he could for a woman of whom he was genuinely fond. Unfortunately, the discretion necessary at the time he wrote and, even more disastrously, his own genius for disarrangement and prolixity, turned what should have been a treasure house of original material into a heart-breaking jumble of repetitions, irrelevances, inaccuracies and self-contradictions. Consequently, while every friend of Lady Blessington must be grateful to Madden for his chivalry and good will, no one who attempts to use his book can help but deplore the chaotic arrangement, the faults of copying, the digressions, and the frequent errors in plain statement of fact which disfigure it. "Never," as Landor wrote to his sister, "was book so negligently printed", or (he might have added) so erratically and confusingly put together.

"Un Roi de la Mode: Le Comte D'Orsay"

By G de Contades. Paris. 1890.

The extreme rarity of this book heightens the anticipation of him who seeks for it. Unfortunately, when it has been found, it proves of little importance. No doubt at the time it was written it provided the French reader with a useful summary of the admitted facts of d'Orsay's life; but it contains almost nothing of value peculiar to itself and can be allowed to disappear unwept.

"The Blessington Papers"

From the Collection of Autograph Letters and Historical Documents formed by Alfred Morrison (Second Series. 1882–1893). Printed for private circulation. 1895.

For the incompetence with which this work was produced no possible excuse can exist. Here was a portion of a magnificent collection of autograph letters, belonging to a wealthy amateur and, at his expense, printed for private issue. If ever there was an occasion for intelligent and informative editing, here was one. Yet what happened? No explanation is given of the source of the papers (they must to a large degree represent the documentary material on which Madden's book was based; but to what degree? And have other letters been added?). There is neither contents list nor index; the running headlines give no indication of the writer of the letter printed on each page, nor are there even shoulder-heads to help the reader through documents often several pages long.

It seems that every book devoted to poor Lady Blessington is cursed by obscurity of arrangement. But, given its opportunities, this volume of "Blessington Papers" is the most infuriating and unhelpful of the lot. It is full of valuable original material; but unless the reader is prepared to do an editor's work for himself he will find that material virtually unusable.

"The Most Gorgeous Lady Blessington"

By J. Fitzgerald Molloy. London. Downey & Co. 1897.

This is a very much better book than it looks. Externally, and as a volume in a series of "Biographical and Historical Studies" which includes works of a suspiciously "picturesque" kind, it suggests a piece of faintly scandalous bookmaking of an all too familiar type. But in fact, Molloy took the trouble to study his subject in other places than the purely obvious, and wrote his story with skill and a certain grace. Unfortunately, either he or his publishers were determined to give the book the appearance of an *histoire galante* rather than of a work of research. There is no index; there are neither footnotes nor bibliography; the very headlines to the pages repeat the title of the book throughout, without even giving the chapter titles. In consequence it is almost impossible to find anything a second time, unless at a first reading one has made a private index. The pity is the greater, because although the work borrows from Madden and elsewhere a number of assumptions now, one hopes, disproved or amended, it contains many details of interest and, within its limits, comparatively few inaccuracies.

"D'Orsay or The Complete Dandy"

By W. Teignmouth Shore. 1 vol. 1911.

As Molloy's book on Lady Blessington is ill served by its appearance, so is this life of d'Orsay flattered. An exterior of dignity and a number of interesting illustrations are in fact mere appendages to a piece of writing both haphazard and facetious. The author takes the pseudo-worldly line of assuming the worst about both d'Orsay and Lady Blessington, and then being roguish. He provides a perfunctory index but no references.

"Un Cupidon Déchaîné: le Véritable Comte d'Orsay"

By P. L. Flers. Paris-Chambéry. 1928.

There is an engaging impudence about this lively attempt to debunk the d'Orsay legend. M. Flers is very hostile to his subject, and occasionally suggestive in his quick-witted ill-nature. But where his book can be checked, it is inaccurate, and where it cannot, inevitably suspect.

* * *

The several works of critical or social retrospect in which the story of Lady Blessington is incidentally told, are not here recorded. All with which I am familiar represent remanipulation of material already printed, and are of no importance to students.

This list may, however, close with reference to two books of direct relevance to the problem Blessington-d'Orsay, though of a different kind from those above catalogued.

"D'Horsay or the Follies of the Day"

By a Man of Fashion [John Mills]. 1 vol. 1844. (New edition with an Introduction, etc. by Joseph Grego and plates in colour. 1902.)

"Phillips' Catalogue of the Gore House Sale", 1849

APPENDIX VII

GENERAL LIST OF BOOKS AND PERIODICALS CONSULTED [1]

ARCHER SHEE, William: "My Contemporaries." 1893.

BARBEY D'AUREVILLY: "Du Dandysme et de Georges Brummel." Paris. 1861. Published in English (1) with an introduction by Douglas Ainslie. London. 1897; (2) with an introduction by D. B. Wyndham Lewis. London. 1928.

BAUDELAIRE: "Le Peintre de la Vie Moderne (L'Art Romantique)." Paris. 1868.

BEAVAN, Arthur H.: "James and Horace Smith." 1899.

BECKFORD, William: "The Vision and Liber Veritatis." Edited by Guy Chapman. 1930.

BERKELEY, Grantley: "My Life and Recollections." 4 vols. 1865.

BULWER-LYTTON, Edward: "Life of Edward, first Lord Lytton." By his grandson, the Earl of Lytton. 2 vols. 1913.

"Edward and Rosina, 1803–1836." By Michael Sadleir. 1931.

BULWER-LYTTON, Rosina: Unpublished Letters to A. E. Chalon. 1914.

CASTEL, Count Horace du Vieil: Memoirs. 2 vols. 1888.

CHATEAUBRIAND: Memoirs. Translated by A. Texeira de Mattos. 6 vols. 1902.

CHORLEY, H. F.: "Autobiography, Letters and Diary." Edited by Hewlett. 2 vols. 1873.

"The Authors of England: a Series of Medallion Portraits of Modern Literary Characters." With illustrative notices. 1838. 1 vol. 1838.

COBDEN: Life, by Morley. New Ed. 1883.

COLE, G. D. H.: "Robert Owen." 1925.

CROSLAND, Mrs. Newton: "Landmarks of a Literary Life." 1893.

DICKENS: Life by Forster. Edited by J. W. T. Ley. 1 vol. 1928. Letters. (1833–1870) 1893.

DISRAELI: Life by Monypenny and Buckle. 6 vols. 1910–1920.

DINO, Duchesse de: Memoirs. 3 vols. 1909–1910.

[1] The editions cited are those actually used; place of publication London unless otherwise stated.

DUNCOMBE, Thomas Slingsby: Life and Correspondence. By T. H. Duncombe. 2 vols. 1868.
ELLIS, S. M.: "William Harrison Ainsworth and his Friends." 2 vols. 1911.
GALT, John: Autobiography. 2 vols. 1833.
GRAMONT, E. de: "Mémoires: au temps des Equipages." Paris. 1928.
GREVILLE'S "Journal of the Reign of Queen Victoria, 1837–1852." 3 vols. 1885.
GRONOW: Reminiscences. New Edition. 2 vols. 1900.
GUEDALLA, Philip: "The Second Empire." 1922.
"The Duke." 1932.
HALL, S. C.: "Retrospect of a Long Life." 2 vols. 1883.
"A Book of Memories." 1871.
HAYDON, Benjamin Robert: Life. 3 vols. 1853.
HAYWARD, Abraham: Correspondence. Edited by H. E. Carlisle. 2 vols. 1886.
JEAFFRESON, John Cordy: "Novels and Novelists from Elizabeth to Victoria." 2 vols. 1858.
JEKYLL: "Correspondence of Joseph Jekyll with Lady Gertrude Sloane Stanley." 1894.
JERDAN, William: Autobiography. 4 vols. 1852.
LAMINGTON, Lord: "In the Days of the Dandies." Edinburgh. 1890.
LANDOR, Walter Savage: Life by Forster. 2 vols. 1864.
Letters, edited by Stephen Wheeler. 1899.
"Landor-Blessington Papers" in "Literary Anecdotes of Nineteenth Century", by W. Robertson Nicoll and T. J. Wise. 2 vols. 1895.
LENNOX, Lord William Pitt: "Fifty Years Biographical Reminiscences." 2 vols. 1863.
"Fashion Then and Now." 2 vols. 1878.
LESLIE, C. R.: "Autobiographical Recollections." 2 vols. 1860.
MARCELLUS, Count: "La Politique de la Restauration en 1822 et 1823." Paris. 1853.
MATHEWS, C. J.: Life, edited by Charles Dickens (Jr.). 2 vols. 1879.
MAUROIS, André: "Byron." 2 vols. Paris. 1930.
MAYNE, Ethel Colburn: "Byron." 2 vols. 1912.
MILNES, Richard Monckton (Lord Houghton): "Life, Letters and Friendships." By T. Wemyss Reid. 2 vols. 1891.
MOORE, Thomas: Memoirs, Journal and Correspondence. 8 vols. 1853–1856.
NAPIER, Macvey: MS. in British Museum.

NICOLSON, Harold: "Byron: The Last Journey." 1924.
PATMORE, P. G.: "My Friends and Acquaintances." 3 vols. 1854.
REDDING, Cyrus: "Fifty Years' Recollections." 3 vols. 2d edition. 1858.
ROBINSON, Henry Crabb: Diary, Reminiscences, etc. 3 vols. 1869.
SALA, G. A.: "Life and Adventures." 2 vols. 1895.
THACKERAY, W. M.: A Collection of Letters (1847–1855). 1887.
"Thackeray: a Personality." By Malcolm Elwin. 1932.
THOMSON, Mrs.: "Recollections of Literary Characters." 2 vols. 1854.
VIZETELLY, Henry: "Glances Back through Seventy Years." 2 vols. 1893.
WILLIS, N. P.: "Pencillings by the Way."
(Serial issue in *New York Mirror;* American book issue. 1835; English book issue. 3 vols. 1835.)
"People I have Met." 1850.
WILSON, D. A.: "Carlyle on Cromwell and Others." 1925.
"New Letters and Memorials of Jane Welsh Carlyle." 2 vols. 1903.
YATES, Edmund: Recollections and Experiences. 2 vols. 1884.

In addition to the above books, a large number of contemporary novels and periodicals have been consulted for information relevant to Lady Blessington's life and times.

APPENDIX VIII

Acknowledgments

For important unpublished material and family information, either printed verbatim or introduced into the argument of this book, I am indebted to the Earl of Lytton; Madame la Duchesse de Clermont-Tonnerre (E. de Gramont); M. le Duc de Gramont; Professor R. Warwick Bond; Colonel Edward Bulwer; the Reverend A. F. Whyte; Mr. Richard Bentley; M. le Comte A. de Suzannet; Mr. W. Roberts; M. André L. Simon; Messrs. Maggs Brothers and Messrs. G. Michelmore & Co. Advice on matters of technical detail has been given by Mr. Godfrey Mellor, Mr. Beresford Chancellor, Mr. J. P. Sewell and Mr. T. J. Patterson. Generous permission to quote from his book "Byron: the Last Journey" was granted by Hon. Harold Nicolson. Mr. Philip Hofer supplied me with photostats from the New York Public Library, and Mr. O. Kyllmann contributed a vital anecdote. I should like to express to all of these my grateful appreciation of their help.

Finally, I have most warmly to thank Miss Helen Waddell and my father, Sir Michael Sadleir, for reading the book in typescript, also Mr. R. Ellis Roberts and Mr. Malcolm Elwin for reading it in proof, all of whom suggested alterations which have greatly improved it.

M. S.

INDEX